THIS IS MY TRUTH

THIS IS MY TRUTH
ANEURIN BEVAN IN *TRIBUNE*

Edited by Nye Davies

UNIVERSITY OF WALES PRESS
2023

© Nye Davies, Introduction, 2023

All rights reserved. No part of this book may be reproduced in any material form (including photocopying or storing it in any medium by electronic means and whether or not transiently or incidentally to some other use of this publication) without the written permission of the copyright owner except in accordance with the provisions of the Copyright, Designs and Patents Act 1988. Applications for the copyright owner's written permission to reproduce any part of this publication should be addressed to The University of Wales Press, University Registry, King Edward VII Avenue, Cardiff CF10 3NS

www.uwp.co.uk

British Library Cataloguing-in-Publication Data

A catalogue record for this book is available from the British Library.

ISBN 978-1-78683-967-1
e-ISBN 978-1-78683-968-8

The rights of authorship of this work have been asserted in accordance with sections 77 and 79 of the Copyright, Designs and Patents Act 1988.

The University of Wales Press gratefully acknowledges the funding support of HEFCW and Cardiff University in publication of this book.

Typeset by Geethik Technologies
Printed by CPI Antony Rowe, Melksham, United Kingdom

CONTENTS

Acknowledgements	ix
Introduction	1
Bevan and the search for truth	3
Bevan the writer	10
Bevan's truth	11
Chapter 1 Capitalism, Power and Politics	19
People Versus Property – 11 February 1938	19
Class War in Commons Committee 'A' – 25 March 1938	23
Highwaymen in The Upper House – 8 July 1938	27
Make the government act! – 17 March 1939	31
Blind Men are Leading Us! – 11 October 1940	35
The Tories' Prisoner – 18 October 1940	39
Next Steps to a New Society – 25 October 1940	43
Hope and new strength – 2 May 1941	48
The T.U.C.'s Two Voices – 13 October 1944	52
The Fatuity of Coalition – 13 June 1952	59
Can Parliament do it? – 26 November 1954	62
Automation: The Socialist Answer – 8 July 1955	64
Tory gamblers pour £1,500 million down the drain – 7 November 1958	68
Bevan on Parliament – 5 June 1959	72

Chapter 2 Labour and the Unions 75
  Wanted – A New Drive For Wages – 22 July 1938 75
  A job for the trade unions – 23 August 1940 79
  M.P.s' tongues must be loosed – 21 March 1941 82
  To any Labour Delegate – 11 June 1943 86
  Coalition of the Left – 18 June 1943 92
  Trade Unions and the Labour Party – 23 July 1943 98
  Rubber stamp M.P.'s – 20 August 1943 103
  All set for a new thrust forward – 26 September 1952 107
  Why we lost West Derby – 3 December 1954 111
  Aneurin Bevan gives his verdict – 3 June 1955 113
  The Struggle for Socialism: Why I am standing for treasurer – 7 October 1955 117
  Being very, very practical – 24 February 1956 123
  How to avoid shipwreck – 11 December 1959 126

Chapter 3 Ideas, Values and Society 131
  A swastika nailed to England's mast – 24 June 1938 131
  This is How Fascism is Born – 1 July 1938 135
  Freedom is not enough – 26 July 1940 138
  Meaning of the Alliance – 18 July 1941 141
  Wales – 20 October 1944 145
  The Parties' Line-up in Parliament – 1 December 1944 147
  July 5 and the Socialist Advance – 2 July 1948 153
  The People's Coming of Age – 3 February 1950 157
  Do not dismiss our ideas of freedom – 3 September 1954 163
  Freedom and Socialism – 5 November 1954 167
  Why Winston Churchill has been gagged – 20 May 1955 169
  Russia must take her share of the blame – 25 November 1955 173
  This famous victory – 3 February 1956 176
  At last the Socialist International wakes up! – 12 July 1957 180
  Spectre over Europe – 19 July 1957 184
  Why Russia wins the space race – 11 October 1957 188
  Communism or suicide? That's not the real choice – 14 March 1958 192
  Private enterprise v. public ownership: The moon and the £ – 9 January 1959 196

Chapter 4 War 201
  Inside Teruel – 21 January 1938 201
  The blackest page in Britain's history – 3 March 1939 206
  Are you a traitor? – answer now – 24 May 1940 209
  The way to win through – 31 May 1940 213
  We and the Germans – 25 June 1943 218
  What Eden cannot do – 14 April 1944 223
  We asked for it – 18 September 1953 229
  Aneurin Bevan attacks radioactive nonsense – 15 July 1955 233
  The disarmament breakdown – 11 May 1956 236
  Destroy the bombs before they destroy us! – 24 May 1957 240
  The clash of the giants – 23 August 1957 243
  Platitudes won't save mankind – 13 December 1957 247
  Arms and the slump – 31 January 1958 251

Chapter 5 International Relations 255
  Stop that nonsense now! – 20 December 1940 255
  Why is Duff Cooper so bad? – 4 April 1941 259
  Complacency will not win the war – 5 September 1941 263
  Here is a real plan to put the war machine in
  reverse – 7 August 1953 267
  Empire and the Tories – 18 December 1953 272
  America must be told: 'you go it alone' – 16 April 1954 275
  The second Cold War – 23 December 1955 279
  It must be world control for all the commercial
  waterways – 3 August 1956 282
  Give the United Nations a real job to do – 5 October 1956 286
  Crisis time for United Nations – 1 February 1957 290
  Warning to the wreckers – 28 June 1957 294
  Back to free markets – and the jungle – 30 August 1957 298
  We must save India – or lose democracy's
  hope – 5 September 1958 302
  Independence – then hard work: how to maintain
  the frontiers of liberty – 21 November 1958 306

Bibliography 311

Index 315

ACKNOWLEDGEMENTS

I would like to thank my PhD supervisors, Richard Wyn Jones and Peri Roberts for their support and their encouragement to write this book. I would also like to thank Daniel Williams and David Moon for their advice and guidance while I was preparing the collection. I am also very appreciative of the constant support and guidance provided on all aspects of the project by everyone at the University of Wales Press. I would particularly like to thank Adam Burns, Dafydd Jones, Georgia Winstone, Llion Wigley and Elin Williams.

I am very grateful for the help provided by Andrew Rosthorn in sourcing copies of and to Bhaskar Sunkara for his permission to use the articles in the collection. I would like to thank the staff at the British Library, the National Library of Wales and the South Wales Miners Library for their help when I was collecting and exploring these articles.

A special thanks must go to James Phillips whose feedback, advice and enthusiasm towards the project were an enormous help during the process of putting together this collection. I would also like to thank Rob Jones for organising weekly virtual writing retreats, which provided me with the opportunity to dedicate time to the book, and to everyone on those retreats who gave me encouragement throughout.

Three people above all deserve special mention: my parents and my partner Verity. Being in the position to write about the subjects I enjoy and to do what I do would not have been possible without the constant love and support of my parents and I thank them for everything. Verity's encouragement and patience have been invaluable. From reading through drafts, to putting up with my constant ramblings about everything Bevan-related, her support has been immense. Thank you so much.

INTRODUCTION

Aneurin Bevan has earned a substantial legacy in British politics. For members of the Labour Party and people across Britain, he has become a hero figure as a result of his role in establishing the National Health Service (NHS).[1] From Tony Blair to Jeremy Corbyn,[2] references to his politics are littered throughout the speeches of Labour politicians; it is rare to find a speech on health, for instance, that does not mention Bevan. In fact, this is a tendency that goes beyond the realm of party politics. Bevan is often invoked by politicians outside his own party, even including former Conservative Health Secretaries.[3] His memory is marked by a statue in Cardiff as well as the Aneurin Bevan Memorial Stones north of his hometown of Tredegar. Both monuments stand as reminders of the high regard in he is held. Over 125 years since his birth, Bevan is still revered as a inspirational politician.

It is not only his actions that receive significant attention, but also his words. Dai Smith notes the importance of speech as an expression of Bevan's politics and the aspirations of his people:

> Public speech, as interpreted and practised by Bevan, was an indictment of the suffocating wisdom of established superiority in its settled forms, whether in the mode of a sweeping Churchillian oration or a humble Baldwin homily. His rhetoric, not on one note but rich in its tonality of meaning and expressiveness, was designed to offer available forms of representative leadership. How else in a democracy should socialists offer themselves in a

representative capacity to the people? ... The question of his power of speech becomes central to our view of this man. Bevan understood that it was language alone which allowed his listeners to comprehend reality as something which could be fashioned in its plasticity not just endured in its materiality.[4]

Bevan is hailed as a great orator. As a result, his pronouncements are frequently repeated, and his communication skills have become the subject of analysis.[5] Quotes, placards, posters and various merchandise have been adorned with Bevan's words, including lines that he likely never said, such as 'We will Tredegarise you', or 'The NHS will last as long as there are folk to fight for it'.[6] Genuine or fictitious, whether they are being repeated at anniversary celebrations for the NHS or to challenge political opponents, Bevan's words have become timeless and transmitted across generations.

Despite the admiration and respect reserved for Bevan, his legacy has often-times been reduced to snappy quotes and one-liners that can fit onto a tea towel or a Twitter banner. Furthermore, he is a figure championed by opposing characters, which often leads to his words being abused, misused or taken out of context.[7] It is not surprising to find, therefore, that people from different sides of the Labour Party have claimed Bevan's legacy when engaging in ideological, as well as personal, battles. He can be all things to all people: a radical and idealistic politician to some, and to others, a pragmatic institution builder.

Perhaps it is not surprising that Bevan is so often reduced to snappy lines: apart from his 1944 tract *Why Not Trust the Tories?*[8] and his 1952 book *In Place of Fear*,[9] a bibliography of Bevan's writing is not readily available. Consequently, there may be an over-reliance on key quotes, rather than a deeper engagement with his disparate works. Regardless of the reason, the reduction of Bevan into soundbite form simplifies the politics of a politician who had a significant impact and continues to invoke passion in society's popular memory. A politician who, this author argues, can provide lessons for contemporary politics.

Often overlooked in favour of Bevan's most famous speeches, there exist hundreds of articles in the pages of *Tribune*. Bevan wrote almost weekly for the socialist political magazine from 1937 until his death in 1960, amassing a collection of over 300 articles.[10] Unfortunately, these articles are not so readily accessible beyond the archives. While several limited examples have been reproduced in various forms, sometimes in their entirety or quoted in biographies and books, Bevan's contributions to the magazine have never before been brought together and disseminated more widely.[11]

This is My Truth represents the first dedicated curation of Bevan's contributions in *Tribune*. Many articles could have been selected to give us an insight into Bevan's political outlook; narrowing them down has therefore been a difficult task. Nevertheless, the current collection seeks to identify the most relevant and important articles by focusing on key themes, specifically those that appear most often in Bevan's work and shed light on his political philosophy. This introduction will outline these key themes in detail following an exploration into significant moments in Bevan's career in order to contextualise and demonstrate the development of his writing and of his ideas. The story of Bevan's life has been told many times,[12] but through this introduction we can gain an understanding of the events that shaped him, his influences and those subjects that he sought to analyse and understand.

BEVAN AND THE SEARCH FOR TRUTH

Born in Tredegar in 1897, Bevan left school at the age of thirteen and began working underground at Ty-Trist Colliery. Even as a youngster, Bevan became heavily involved in politics and gained significant popularity (and notoriety) within local trade union politics. In 1916, aged just nineteen, he became chairman of his miners' lodge and would also go on to become a local delegate of the South Wales Miners' Federation (SWMF) to the Labour Party Conference in 1917.[13] During this period, Bevan became associated with a number of local figures in the labour movement and the Plebs' League, which provided him with an education in Marxism. Individuals such as Sidney Jones, Walter Conway and Noah Ablett helped to provide Bevan with the intellectual tools to understand his environment. It was from these individuals, and attending education classes run by them, that Bevan was introduced to politics not just as a practical activity but also as a philosophy, a theory of work and a way of life.

It was not only the politics of the town and its activists that inspired the young Bevan. His family was also a major influence. For instance, Bevan's father, David Bevan, helped to shape him and his politics. A Welsh-speaker, David was a member of the Welsh cultural organisation Cymmrodorion and won prizes at local eisteddfodau. He was also a bookworm and 'delightedly he discovered that he had one son who would accompany him there'.[14] Although David did not pass on the Welsh language to his son, he inspired in him a love of reading, as well as his individualism.[15]

Bevan was an autodidact and soon won a scholarship to the Central Labour College (CLC) in London. Founded by former students of Ruskin College, the CLC was established in protest to increased control by Oxford University, as well as the resultant lack of Marxism being taught. The driving force behind the protest and the college was Noah Ablett, who sought to establish an institution that provided independent working-class education. Although there is dispute over the value Bevan placed on this period,[16] it nevertheless allowed him the opportunity to explore new ideas, debate with like-minded individuals, and to develop his writing and analytical skills.

It was while studying at the college that Bevan's first significant piece of writing was published in 1921: a review of the *Communist Manifesto*.[17] The review was published in *Plebs* magazine, organised by the Plebs' League, an educational organisation and political group formed to promote Marxist ideals.[18] At just twenty-three years of age, the article demonstrates remarkable maturity in Bevan's writing as well as his ability to comprehend, challenge and consume political ideas. The review also contains themes that would feature heavily in Bevan's writing throughout his life, including his analysis of class, capitalism and, more specifically, the relationship between public and private property. Bevan wrote that the 'treating of the development of the modern capitalist class and its counterpart the proletariat' in the *Communist Manifesto* is the 'best and most convincing exposition of the Marxian point of view'.[19] While Bevan's relationship to Marxism is a source of debate,[20] the themes he analysed in this review are identifiable in the articles collected in this book.

Bevan returned to Tredegar from London to find that there was no employment in the town, his father was sick and that the coal owners 'had the miners by the throat'.[21] On his return, he was unemployed for three years – apart from a six-week period as a labourer – and received unemployment benefit. However, despite poor economic conditions sapping the energy of the workers and the unemployed in the town, Bevan was determined to fight. He spent much of the 1920s in Tredegar organising, agitating and carrying out the roles of local and then county councillor. He was heavily involved in the local trade union movement, even being sent as a representative to conferences of the Miners' Federation of Great Britain (MFGB), and was chair of the Council of Action during the General Strike in 1926.[22] Consequently, he developed a formidable local profile. While this period did not produce a significant body of written work, the struggle for his class played an important role in shaping his ideas and his views on political strategy. The meetings of the Tredegar Urban District Council and the Monmouthshire County Council provided early signs of Bevan's oratory and his skills of argumentation, which would be deployed on a national scale in Parliament. In the words of S. O. Davies, a contemporary in the SWMF and later in Parliament, Bevan's experiences of unemployment and the class struggle in Tredegar during this period instilled in him his 'torrential vituperation, his deadly ridicule and acid wit'.[23] They also shaped his politics.

After his election as MP for Ebbw Vale in 1929, Bevan almost immediately began to make a name for himself, both for his continuing agitation outside the House of Commons, and for his contributions within it. He was not afraid to take on the giants of the House, notably using his maiden speech to attack former Prime Minister David Lloyd George and future Prime Minister Winston Churchill, the latter whose 'chameleon-like character in politics', Bevan concluded, 'is founded upon a temperamental disability. He fills all the roles with such exceeding facility that his lack of political stability is at once explained'.[24] A year later in 1930, Bevan's fellow Welshman David Lloyd George was the target of a memorable Bevan offensive.[25] In voting against a bill that attempted to ensure lower working hours for coalminers while at the same time protecting their pay, Bevan argued that Lloyd George's actions were 'characteristic of Liberal hypocrisy to pay lip service' to the consequences, which, Bevan predicted, would be lower wages for the miners, more hours and, as a result, more accidents. He declared that what they had been listening to during the debate was simply 'a desire on the part of the right hon. Gentleman the Member for Carnarvon Boroughs to use his Parliamentary position for the purpose of trying to put new life into the decaying corpse of Liberalism'. Bevan concluded with a withering attack on the former Prime Minister:

> We say that you cannot get from the already dry veins of the miners new blood to revivify the industry. Their veins are

shrunken white, and we are asking you to be, for once, decent to the miners – not to pay lip service, not to say that you are very sorry for them, not to say that you are very sorry that these accidents occur, not to say that you are very sorry for the low level of wages and for the conditions of famine which have existed in the mining districts since the War, and then to use all your Parliamentary skill, all your rhetoric, in an act of pure demagogy to expose the mining community of this country to another few years of misery.[26]

David Lloyd George was clearly disturbed by the scathing speech, being left 'visibly shaken as though by the ghost of his own radical youth'.[27] He replied that he was 'sorry to have fallen foul of a young countryman of mine … I have listened without interruption to a very bitter personal attack'. Despite being a newcomer in Parliament, Bevan was already making a name for himself, and was not intimidated by his new surroundings.

It was not just in the House that Bevan was articulating his ideas. He soon started demonstrating his writing skills by transferring these ideas onto the page. In 1932, he contributed a passage to *The Coming Struggle for Power* by John Strachey, later a minister in Clement Attlee's post-war government, but at the time a left-wing critic of the Labour leadership.[28] Bevan was not named in the book, only identified as a 'most gifted and young' supporter of the workers.[29] His contribution appeared during a period of unrest within the Labour Party after the formation of the National Government. Already, just three years into his career as an MP, Bevan was witnessing, and partaking in, the recurrent internal battles that have plagued the party. His passage is another early demonstration of his developing ideas, which included his critique of gradualism within the Labour Party, critical as he was of its failure to offer radical solutions to the growing economic and political crisis. Whether in speeches at Labour Party Conference, speeches in the House of Commons, or rallying calls at a public protest, Bevan was not afraid to challenge the orthodoxies of his own party. This theme would permeate his career.

It was five years later in 1937 that Bevan's writing career took off with the establishment of *Tribune*. The magazine, funded by Sir Stafford Cripps and George Strauss, included William Mellor as editor and Ellen Wilkinson, Harold Laski and Noel Brailsford (alongside Bevan) on its controlling board.[30] It was initially established as a mouthpiece to voice frustration with the Labour Party leadership amidst its rigidity in the face of a growing international crisis.[31] In 1947, Bevan recalled the founding of *Tribune* as a response by socialists who were:

> tormented as we were by the tragic closing phases of the Spanish Republican Government. It seemed to us that Socialists of the Left needed a weekly instrument of communion, or communication, call it what you will, otherwise we might languish to impotency from lack of self-confidence and continuing inspiration.[32]

The magazine would go on to become an important voice for the left both within the party and throughout Britain. It would also become a crucial outlet for Bevan. He regarded his work for *Tribune* 'as the Socialist activity of which I am most proud. Its service to the Movement has amply repaid all that we gave to its birth and growth'.

The magazine was launched at an ominous time in global as well as domestic history, demonstrated by Bevan's articles responding to the rise of Fascism in Europe, the Spanish Civil War, the onset of the Second World War Two and other events that took hold in Britain and throughout the world. Indeed, this period had a significant influence on the development of Bevan's outlook. However, the magazine was not only useful for commenting on the worsening international situation. Bevan also used *Tribune* as a conduit through which to publish his ideas on several issues ranging from unemployment to nationalisation and Labour Party politics, through to the decline of the British Empire. Initially, Bevan wrote under the pseudonym M.P. for several months and mainly focused on parliamentary debates. It was not long, however, until he started writing articles under his own name, continuing to write almost weekly for the magazine. He used these articles not only to provide commentary on the events of the day, but also to articulate his ideas and his view of the world, to challenge the Labour Party and its leadership and to theorise on the role of politics in shaping people's lives.

In 1942, with the assistance of Jon Kimche and Evelyn Anderson, Bevan became the magazine's editor. He was thus able to guide the editorial direction of the magazine during a crucial moment in history. As the articles in the present collection demonstrate, Bevan was keen to promote the interests of liberty and democracy during the war. Thus, the magazine gave him ample space to formulate and contemplate ideas for post-war society. The war did not prevent Bevan from considering these important issues, far from it in fact. The conflict strengthened his belief in a radical transformation of society and he used the pages of *Tribune* to set out how he felt this could be achieved.

After Labour's triumphant election victory in 1945, Bevan was appointed Minister of Health and Housing in Clement Attlee's new cabinet. It was a bold decision to appoint the 'squalid nuisance' of wartime (as Churchill had described him) into such an important position, particularly considering Bevan's willingness to challenge the leadership and party edicts. Nevertheless, Attlee's faith was rewarded when Bevan established the National Health Service, which cemented his enduring legacy as a minister with the required 'tenacity, the drive, the commitment to the NHS and the skills to see it into existence',[33] and for which people remember and revere him today. Bevan captured the importance of the NHS when he argued that 'no Government that attempts to destroy the Health Service can hope to command the support of the British people'.[34] While his role as a Minister prevented him from contributing much to *Tribune* during this period, he did provide a few words celebrating its ten-year anniversary in 1947, declaring its function as 'to carry on Socialist education and propaganda until political and economic power is equally matched'.[35] A year later, on the eve of the launch of the NHS, Bevan gave an interview where he declared the service as a beacon for the rest of the world and as a first step on the road to socialism.[36]

It was also during his time in government that Bevan started to come into closer contact with political opponents, the resultant tensions having significant consequences for both Bevan's future and the immediate future of the Labour Party. Oftentimes both ideological and personal, Bevan had many disagreements with colleagues such as Leader of the House Herbert Morrison and Chancellor Hugh Gaitskell, who was accused of comparing Bevan to Hitler – 'They are demagogues of exactly the same sort'[37] – and whom Bevan described as 'nothing, nothing, nothing!'[38] and a 'desiccated calculating-machine'.[39] The simmering animosities between Bevan and his colleagues were only the beginning of ideological and personal disputes that would be documented in the pages of *Tribune*.

Bevan returned as a regular contributor to the magazine in 1951 after his resignation from government. He was Minister of Labour at the time and resigned over the implementation of charges to teeth and spectacles to fund Britain's defence budget during its involvement in the Korean War. Again, while this incident has been written about extensively, it is important to note that the event reignited the aforementioned battles that the Labour Party is so prone to, this time between the Bevanites and the Gaitskellites/Revisionists. *Tribune* became the mouthpiece of the Bevanite position,[40] and was even accused of being the magazine of 'a party within a party', although its members vehemently denied this.[41] Nevertheless, its contributors, Bevan included, did not shy away from criticising the leaders of their own party.

It should also be noted that this battle did not completely occupy Bevan's mind during the 1950s. Quite often, Labour histories or reflections on this period can get lost in the personal over the political and the ideational. Bevan did not use *Tribune* simply as an outlet to attack the Labour leadership (Gaitskell in particular after he was elected as Labour leader in 1955): rather, he continued to sketch out his ideas, his political philosophy and his vision for society through analysing the world around him. He continued to outline his arguments for nationalisation, the need to extend democracy in society and his belief that property relations needed to be significantly altered. In the field of international relations, Bevan continued to write extensively on the emerging problems of power politics. This led him to analyse subjects such as the role of the United Nations, global poverty and the decline of empire. Further, the Cold War led Bevan to critique the major ideological battle taking place in the world between communism and capitalism, as well as allowing him to state his case and his vision for democratic socialism.

While Bevan published his ideas on these issues early in the 1950s in *In Place of Fear*, he developed them in the pages of *Tribune* throughout the decade. Bevan's appointment as Shadow Foreign Secretary in 1956 and his subsequent election to Deputy Leader of the party in 1959 did not prevent his continued writing in *Tribune*. Further, these roles did not silence his views, despite accusations of having betrayed the left through his denouncement of unilateral disarmament at Labour Conference in 1957[42] and suggestions of an accommodation with Gaitskell.[43] He may have upset many of his supporters as a result of his outburst at that conference, but Bevan nevertheless continued to express his opinions in *Tribune* right up until his death in 1960.

BEVAN THE WRITER

Bevan's speeches have become famous for showcasing his sharp wit, powerful oratory[44] and his ability to understand an opponent's argument, target its strongest and most logical points, but then dissect them one by one.[45] His contributions in the House of Commons are easily searchable[46] and several speeches exist on YouTube and in other formats online. Yet, arguably, apart from *In Place of Fear*, his writing has not generated the same level of popularity. This is unfortunate, as, when it comes to understanding Bevan's ideas most completely, his writing was as insightful and informative as his speeches. *In Place of Fear* is highly quotable, yet, as noted above, his writing did not begin or end there.

What was significant about the way Bevan wrote, particularly in *Tribune*, was that his articles combined two important elements. First, the articles in this collection reveal Bevan's journalistic writing as he reported on events from around the world, Westminster and the political machinations of the day. This led him to go into significant detail about debates in Parliament, to interrogate legislation and the arguments of his opponents, and to unpick and analyse them just as he did in his speeches. Yet, Bevan was not only a journalist: his writings also expressed his political philosophy. While dissecting and analysing an event or a certain topic, Bevan would relate the discussions to wider concerns. He regularly referred to the primary importance of principles, priorities and those specific values that guided his writing. Even John Campbell, Bevan's most critical biographer, praised his adeptness for combining commentary with philosophy in *Tribune*:

> Bevan is not normally thought of as much of a writer; but these weekly articles reveal a surprisingly good journalist. Though strictly political, their variety expresses the richness of his mind, always able to focus a general argument on a telling detail or extrapolate an historical theory from a trivial episode.[47]

Examples of this style are numerous in the present collection. For instance, on 1 July 1938, Bevan wrote an article criticising the government's foreign policy ('This is How Fascism is Born', Chapter 3), particularly its failure to condemn and be stirred by Italy's sinking of British ships trading with the Spanish Republic.[48] After detailing the negative effect of the government's policies, Bevan delved into the ways in which the British ruling class attempts to maintain its grip on power. Echoing an almost Gramscian understanding of the role of hegemony, Bevan argued that the:

> ruling class succeeds by appearing to identify its class interests with the general interest ... They are able to represent their sectional interests in terms of the national symbols, and the emotional and traditional associations with which these latter are seeped are an immense source of strength to the ruling class.

Far from just writing an article that criticised the government, Bevan located its failures within a wider theoretical point about the nature of class conflict in British society. A further example, from 1957 ('Platitudes won't save mankind', Chapter 4), saw Bevan analysing an upcoming meeting of NATO. He discussed the build-up of arms and its effects, in addition to the power politics being inflicted upon the world. However, he did not stop there. He proceeded to relate power politics to wider questions of sovereignty, world integration and the nature of force in international affairs, providing more than just an analysis of the facts. These are only two examples of many, with this feature of Bevan's writing on display in the present collection.

BEVAN'S TRUTH

A consideration of Bevan's *Tribune* articles is therefore vital in understanding the details of his politics and his ideas. This collection gives readers the opportunity to do just that. Due to this book's aim of presenting Bevan in his own words, I have endeavoured not to put too much of a 'lens' on the collected articles, but rather to present them on their own terms.[49] This is to give readers the opportunity to form their own judgements. Similarly, the selection of these articles does not necessarily equate to an agreement with Bevan's views. Nevertheless, the organisation of the book inevitably entails some degree of editorialising as the chapters are divided by key themes, identified as being central to Bevan's worldview. It is hoped that organising them in this way will not sway the reader to view Bevan in a particular direction, but rather assist and guide them through the collection so they can make their own conclusions on Bevan's written word. In fact, the necessary editorialising of Bevan's work usefully proves beneficial in elucidating key elements of his political thought. In reproducing the articles, editorial intervention has been made to correct any spelling and grammatical errors in Bevan's writing.

The collection is divided into five chapters: Bevan's writings on capitalism, parliament, politics and the state; the Labour Party and the trade union movement; ideas, values and society; war; and international relations. They encompass Bevan's views on how the working class could achieve power, the role of the Labour Party in doing so, the world at war, ambitions for peace and his vision for a new society based on the principles underpinning his conception of democratic socialism. Rather than organise the book chronologically, the collection homes in on these key themes, while organising each chapter chronologically to see these themes develop over time throughout Bevan's life. In doing so, the thought, the philosophies and the ideas of Bevan himself can take centre stage.

Chapter 1, 'Capitalism, Power and Politics' provides the foundation for understanding many of Bevan's ideas. It focuses on his analysis of capitalist society and the role of politics in establishing democratic socialist principles: essentially, the importance of economic and political power. The articles reveal his understanding of class conflict and his outrage at the pernicious effects of the poverty and exploitation he fought against throughout his life. Further, it focuses on the importance of democracy and the centrality of Parliament and the state in Bevan's writing as avenues to rectify the ills of society. This inevitably overlaps with the subsequent chapter on the Labour Party, but its specific focus is to understand the role Bevan attributed to democratic politics in achieving change. These core themes permeate and shape the articles collected in the following chapters.

Chapter 2, 'Labour and the Unions' collects Bevan's writings on the Labour Party and the trade unions. Rather than simply consisting of articles that discuss the role of party politics, this chapter also includes articles where Bevan grapples with the internal machinations of the party, the battle of ideas and personalities within it, and the role that Bevan envisioned the party playing in implementing democratic socialism. Further, the chapter includes articles Bevan wrote on the nature of trade unionism in Britain, particularly its intrinsic relationship to the Labour Party. Bevan's career, particularly throughout the 1950s, has often been defined in conjunction with his role as part of the Bevanite movement within the party. These articles therefore provide a fascinating insight into Bevan's perception of these disputes at all levels in the party and the wider labour movement.

This is particularly important when we consider the prominence of similar arguments and debates in contemporary Labour Party discourse. As noted at the beginning of this introduction, internal disputes continue to define the Labour Party today, and Bevan is often invoked by different sides in the debate to support their own positions. Therefore, understanding Bevan's views not only helps us to appreciate his own politics, but also to understand the nature of the Labour Party itself.

Chapter 3, 'Ideas, Values and Society' collates Bevan's thoughts on the role of ideas and values in politics and society. As noted above, Bevan's politics were developed amid deepening international tensions, and he wrote extensively on the ideological debates between Communist states, such as China and the Soviet Union, and supporters of capitalism and western democracy. These articles tell us much about how Bevan saw the world developing and reveal his vision for society and his hopes for the future. Bevan often repeated the phrase that 'the language of priorities is the religion of socialism'[50]: the articles in this chapter identify those priorities.

The final two chapters in this collection focus their attention on the international level. They comprise Bevan's writings on the nature of conflict in Chapter 4, 'War' and the world and international affairs in Chapter 5, 'International Relations'. Throughout his career, Bevan was deeply concerned with what was happening on the international stage. His sights were not solely set on domestic issues; he recognised the significance of unfolding events in other countries and their role in defining politics and political debate beyond borders. *Tribune* itself was a product of this understanding, established during the rise of fascism and while the wheels of war were beginning to turn. Therefore, Bevan's politics were shaped by the darkening international situation. As noted above, Bevan was also Shadow Foreign Secretary from 1956 to 1959, and continued to write for *Tribune* while carrying out this role. Chapter 4 demonstrates the link Bevan made between war, democracy and socialism, while Chapter 5 continues this theme, showcasing Bevan's perspectives on international relations, empire and his vision for an international organisation that would bring competing countries together.

***

One may ask the question: why Bevan? Why is it important to consider the ideas of a politician from decades ago? One of the reasons has already been discussed – Bevan lives on in Britain's collective memory. The NHS is still considered as one of the most important British national institutions, and Bevan's name is synonymous with it. However, this does not answer the question of why we need to explore the rest of Bevan's output, or why now. Despite his writing being over eighty years old in some cases, domestic debates over the role of parliament, the relationship between representatives and society, the ideology of the Labour Party, and the role of the state in the economy, particularly in light of close to forty years of market deregulation and neoliberalism, are still as relevant as ever. Further, many of the international issues Bevan grappled with – power politics, ideological disputes, the build-up of arms, imperialism – are still prevalent in the world today. Some of Bevan's language is of his time and may be offensive to modern readers. While we should not simply dismiss these features, the present collection provides an opportunity to re-engage with Bevan's writings and his political philosophy. It will allow us to reevaluate and perhaps even learn lessons from a figure who had more to say about society and the world than snappy one-liners give him credit for.

This collection, therefore, gives Bevan a platform to state his case. While it represents just a snapshot of Bevan's writings throughout his career, and while there is much more to uncover, until recently there have been relatively few opportunities to read Bevan in his own words. Providing the opportunity to do so is critical: as noted at the beginning of this introduction, Bevan's words have been used, abused and misused in equal measure by politicians across the political spectrum. Further, Bevan still has much to say to us in contemporary society, as attested to by the continued reverence for him. This collection, therefore, is an opportunity to read Bevan's truth.

NOTES

1 BBC, *Bevan is ultimate Welsh hero* (2004), *http://news.bbc.co.uk/1/hi/wales/3523363.stm* (accessed 20 December 2021); A. Sparrow, 'Who is Labour's greatest hero?', *The Guardian* (2008), *https://www.theguardian.com/politics/blog/2008/sep/22/labour.labourconference1* (accessed 20 December 2021).

2 T. Blair, 'Foreword', in G. Goodman (ed.), *The State of the Nation: The Political Legacy of Aneurin Bevan* (London: Victor Gollancz, 1997), pp. 11–13;

J. Corbyn, *We must include everybody and exclude nobody. They were Nye Bevan's values, they are Labour's values. #NHS70* (Twitter, 2018), https://twitter.com/jeremycorbyn/status/1014026451299942406 (accessed 20 December 2021).
3   N. Davies, 'Why does Jeremy Hunt keep comparing himself to Aneurin Bevan?', *Left Foot Forward* (2016), https://leftfootforward.org/2016/07/why-does-jeremy-hunt-keep-comparing-himself-to-aneurin-bevan/ (accessed 20 December 2021).
4   Dai Smith, *Aneurin Bevan and the World of South Wales* (Cardiff: University of Wales Press, 1993), pp. 184–5.
5   A. S. Crines and K. Laybourn, 'The oratory of Aneurin Bevan', in A. S. Crines and R. Hayton (eds), *Labour orators from Bevan to Miliband* (Manchester: Manchester University Press, 2015), pp. 14–30.
6   M. Belam, 'Jeremy Corbyn's Nye Bevan quote is pure fiction', *The Guardian* (2017), https://www.theguardian.com/politics/2017/may/17/jeremy-corbyn-tweets-fake-nye-bevan-quote-on-fighting-for-the-nhs (accessed 20 December 2021).
7   N. Davies, 'Liberty, Bevan and Welsh Labour', *Thinking Wales* (2017), https://blogs.cardiff.ac.uk/thinking-wales/liberty-bevan-and-welsh-labour/ (accessed 20 December 2021).
8   Written under the pseudonym 'Celticus': Aneurin Bevan, *Why Not Trust the Tories?* (London: Victor Gollancz, 1944).
9   Aneurin Bevan, *In Place of Fear* (London: William Heinemann, 1952).
10 This does not include editorials written during his time as editor between 1942 and 1945.
11 A few were collated in a 1958 collection of *Tribune* articles: Elizabeth Thomas (ed.), *Tribune 21* (London: MacGibbon and Kee, 1958).
12 Several of these books are referenced throughout the introduction. See also: Clare Beckett and Francis Beckett, *Bevan* (London: Haus Publishing, 2004); Vincent Brome, *Aneurin Bevan: A Biography* (London: Longmans, Green and Co., 1953); S. E. Demont, 'Tredegar and Aneurin Bevan: A Society and its Political Articulation 1890–1929' (unpublished PhD thesis, University of Wales, 1990); Mark M. Krug, *Aneurin Bevan: Cautious Rebel* (New York: Thomas Yoseloff, 1961); Jennie Lee, *My Life with Nye* (Middlesex: Penguin, 1981); K. O. Morgan, 'Nye Bevan', in R. L. Louis (ed.), *Resurgent Adventures with Britannia: Personalities, Politics and Culture in Britain* (London: I. B. Tauris, 2011), pp. 181–95.
13 Nicklaus Thomas-Symonds, *Nye: The Political Life of Aneurin Bevan* (London: I. B. Tauris, 2015), pp. 25–6.

14 Michael Foot, *Aneurin Bevan: 1897–1945* (London: Granada Publishing, 1975), p. 15.
15 Foot, *Aneurin Bevan: 1897–1945*, p. 71.
16 See W. W. Craik, *The Central Labour College: A chapter in the history of adult working-class education 1909–29* (London: Lawrence and Wishart, 1964) and Foot, *Aneurin Bevan 1897–1945*, pp. 38–45.
17 A. Bevan, 'Socialist Classics: The Communist Manifesto', *The Plebs*, 13/1 (1921), 19–21.
18 Thomas-Symonds, *Nye: The Political Life of Aneurin Bevan*, p. 22.
19 Bevan, 'Socialist Classics: The Communist Manifesto', p. 20.
20 See N. Davies, 'Top Marx: Bevan and the importance of Karl', *Thinking Wales* (2017), https://blogs.cardiff.ac.uk/thinking-wales/top-marx-bevan-and-the-importance-of-karl/ (accessed 20 December 2021).
21 Foot, *Aneurin Bevan: 1897–1945*, p. 40.
22 Foot, *Aneurin Bevan: 1897–1945*, p. 72.
23 S. O. Davies cited in Robert Griffiths, *S. O. Davies: A Socialist Faith* (Llandysul, Dyfed: Gomer Press, 1983), p. 51.
24 HC Deb., 16 July 1929, vol. 230, col. 339.
25 Foot, *Aneurin Bevan: 1897–1945*, pp. 116–19.
26 HC Deb., 27 February 1930, vol. 235, col. 2468.
27 John Campbell, *Nye Bevan and the Mirage of British Socialism* (London: Weidenfeld and Nicolson, 1987), p. 37.
28 Strachey was one of the founders of Oswald Moseley's New Party in 1931, although he left it a few months after its founding due to the party's turn towards fascism. See Foot, *Aneurin Bevan: 1897–1945*, p. 152.
29 John Strachey, *The Coming Struggle for Power* (London: Victor Gollancz, 1932), p. 318.
30 Foot, *Aneurin Bevan: 1897–1945*, p. 246.
31 Foot, *Aneurin Bevan: 1897–1945*, p. 244.
32 A. Bevan, 'Ten years – Tribune, 1937–1947', *Tribune* (31 January 1947), p. 7.
33 Thomas-Symonds, *Nye: The Political Life of Aneurin Bevan*, p. 148.
34 Bevan, *In Place of Fear*, p. 92.
35 Bevan, 'Ten years – Tribune, 1937–1947', p. 7.
36 A. Bevan, 'July 5th and the Socialist Advance', *Tribune* (2 July 1948), p. 7.
37 From the diaries of Richard Crossman, cited in Michael Foot, *Aneurin Bevan: 1945–1960* (London: Granada Publishing, 1975), p. 471.
38 Foot, *Aneurin Bevan: 1945–1960*, p. 292.

39 Thomas-Symonds, *Nye: The Political Life of Aneurin Bevan*, p. 216.
40 Although identifying a collective Bevanite position is difficult due to the lack of ideological coherence within the group. See Geoffrey Foote, *The Labour Party's Political Thought* (London: Croom Helm, 1986), ch. 12.
41 Harold Wilson, *Memoirs: The Making of a Prime Minister 1916–64* (London: Weidenfeld and Nicolson, 1986), p. 138.
42 Foot, *Aneurin Bevan: 1945–1960*, pp. 571–5.
43 T. Nairn, 'The nature of the Labour Party – 2', *New Left Review*, 1/28 (1964), 33–62.
44 Thomas-Symonds, *Nye: The Political Life of Aneurin Bevan*, pp. 15–16.
45 Foot, *Aneurin Bevan: 1897–1945*, pp. 260–2.
46 Hansard: *https://hansard.parliament.uk/*.
47 Campbell, *Nye Bevan and the Mirage of British Socialism*, p. 74.
48 Foot, *Aneurin Bevan: 1897–1945*, pp. 276–7.
49 I will be publishing a book with University of Wales Press entitled *The Political Thought of Aneurin Bevan* in the near future that will analyse these writings, and others, in detail.
50 A. Bevan, 'Rationed – or "free"?', *Tribune* (29 October 1954), pp. 1–2.

1
CAPITALISM, POWER AND POLITICS
People Versus Property –
11 February 1938

THE LAST WEEK in the House of Commons gave us a number of interesting sidelights on the workings of capitalist democracy.

Students of constitutional theory at our Universities would get more knowledge from a study of last week's Hansard than by the most diligent reading of abstract studies by University professors. They would learn, for example, what happens when the 'Will of the People' comes into conflict with the will of property.

The issue of People Versus Property was staged in terms of classic simplicity. Property won so easily; the democratic defences against it were shown to be so frail, that Sir Arthur Salter was moved to utter a warning against legislation which, as he said, '… builds up a kind of bastard Socialism which will have none of the advantages of private enterprise and none of the advantages of true Socialism.'

CONFLICT OF INTEREST

Politics are concerned almost entirely with a conflict of interest. The conflict usually occurs between a sectional interest and the general interest of the community.

When, as sometimes happens, conflicts arise between two sets of sectional interests, then, unless an important public interest is involved, the conflict is taken to the courts and settled there.

But when the conflict is between the sectional and the general interest, in a capitalist democracy, Parliament is invoked. As a rule, the sectional interest is powerful, cohesive, and is enabled to be socially and politically articulate by the possession of money. Where these advantages are not possessed by the sectional interest, conflict rarely arises, because the interest concerned cannot exert sufficient pressure.

ROLE OF TORIES

Now many people regard Parliament as a sort of Court of Arbitration, which hears the case and gives the verdict. That is a mistaken view. Parliament, properly considered, is a means by which the resources of the people are mobilised for the conflicts with the sectional interests which are always taking place.

If Parliament were universally understood in this light, the role of the Tories would be clear. Parliament is not the last Court of Appeal in the struggle between the sectional and the general interest or between Property and the People, which is endemic in capitalist society. It is itself one of the weapons of the general interest – the People.

The function of the Tory is to immobilise it, to weaken it, to render it useless, to defend the general interest.

The more effectively Parliament asserts the general against the sectional interest the more bitter grows the conflict between the People and Property, until the climax is reached, when either Parliament destroys the sectional interest, which is Socialism, or the sectional interest destroys Parliament, which is Fascism.

WITHOUT A STRUGGLE

When no conflicts are heard of, it is not because they are not taking place. It is rather because the sectional interests are winning without a struggle.

This is the situation usually described by Tory statesmen, like Earl Baldwin, as a sane or stable democracy. This is the state of affairs which normally exists when the Tories are in power; unless, of course, the workers by industrial struggle use another of the weapons in the arsenal of the general interest.

Political peace in a capitalist democracy is therefore a time in which the forces of the sectional interests, of Property in short, are universally triumphant.

That is the position at present, and it is this position that the events of the last week in Parliament served to illustrate. The sectional interest in this instance were the coal owners. It would be impossible to mention a sectional interest with less popular support than the coal owners.

Their die-hard defence of their property rights has not only created appalling economic anarchy in their own industry and indescribable misery among the mining population, but it has also threatened the stability of the capitalist state itself, as in 1926.

Here is a case in which one might think that even under the National Government the general interest would have a chance of success. If we thought so, last week disillusioned us.

SIR ARTHUR SAYS

Let me again quote Sir Arthur Salter, not because he has been conspicuous in the debates on the Coal Bill, but because his remarks bear on the point I am making.

He said: '... In the 1936 Bill the Government had, of course, taken into account the legitimate interest of the coal owners. They produced their Bill, which they thought was a right Bill, but at once they ran away from it and promised concessions. Then they delayed over a year, and produced a Bill obviously giving more concessions than had been promised.

'Now within a few hours of discussion in the Committee stage of this Bill we have the prospect of a further substantial concession ...

'An essential requirement of the new kind of order that we are building up is that any Government in power, and Parliament which supports that Government, should really be able to govern. A Government which gives these powers and attempts to impose its supervision should really be a Government which represents the people as a whole and is not captured successively by each industry which is the subject of the particular Bill before Parliament.'

REPROACH IS CLEAR

The language could not be milder, but the reproach is clear. That Sir Arthur Salter is surprised is of course due to his inability to understand the Tory attitude to parliamentary democracy. A Tory Government cannot be expected to stand up to a vested interest because it is itself a weapon of the vested interest.

The attitude of the Government to the coal owners contrasted sharply with their attitude when attempts were made to protect the miners and the local authorities in South Wales, Durham, and the other mining areas.

To the owners the Government conceded all they asked. To the miners they would concede nothing. Under their proposals they admitted that men would be thrown out of work, with no prospect of other employment; but they refused either compensation or alternative sources of employment.

They admitted that whole villages would be rendered derelict and social services ruined, but they refused all succour. To the coal owners the Government were as sensitive as an exposed nerve; to the miners they were blind, deaf and dumb.

GAG IN THE MOUTH

In the conflict between the sectional interests of coal owning and the general interests of the miners, not all the eloquence of the miners' members and the formidable armament of the Sir Stafford Cripps forensic skill and legal learning availed against the organised power of coal property.

And this for the simple reason that a Parliament dominated by Tories is a Parliament dominated by property, and such a Parliament, so far from mobilising the forces of the people, disperses those forces and renders them impotent. For a Tory majority puts a megaphone in the mouth of Property and a gag in the mouth of the People.

Class War in Commons Committee 'A' – 25 March 1938

This article has to be written before the Prime Minister makes his speech on the Government's foreign policy. Therefore it cannot deal with the main parliamentary event of the week.

This is not without its advantages, because it gives me an opportunity for directing attention to certain aspects of domestic legislation which are in danger of being obscured by the gravity of the international situation.

A great deal of the important work of Parliament is done in Committees, whose works gets little notice in the general press. In these Committees various Bills are discussed in detail and Members spend many hours of laborious and difficult effort in them.

Committee A is considering at present a Bill dealing with the de-control of different classes of cottage property. It is worth while paying attention to this Bill as we shall hear more of it in the years immediately ahead.

LANDLORDS' GAME

During the war, landlords took advantage of the shortage of houses, which was consequent upon the cessation of house building, to raise rents to heights which soon became such a scandal that public disorder was likely to result.

Consequently in 1920 an Act was passed which limited rents to forty per cent above the 1914 net rent for all houses which were built before the war.

Within the scope of this article it is not possible for me to explain the various provisions of the different Acts which have been passed since then. I must limit myself to the general principles.

Rents as a general rule obey the same laws as other things which are the subject of sale and purchase in the open market. Where the need for houses is greater than the supply rents tend to increase. Where the supply exceeds the demand rents tend to fall.

The most effective form of controlling rents is the supply of a number of houses in each locality in the excess of the number needed. These would serve to lever the rents downwards.

This situation has not existed since the war and does not look as though it will ever exist again.

In these circumstances the demand for houses is permanently in excess of the supply. The landlord is put in an exceptionally favourable position, and in the absence of some form of protection of the tenant by the State racketeering of the worst kind would result.

PROPERTY V. PEOPLE

The Rents Acts gave this protection and ever since they were passed the landlords through their Tory friends in Parliament have tried to get the Acts, either repealed altogether, or amended in favour of the landlord. It is another perfect example of Property versus the People and as usual the Tories are to be found on the side of Property.

They have already succeeded to an alarming extent, as workers in all parts of the country are learning to their cost.

Since 1931 the Tories have been in control of Parliament and the figures show how well they have served the interests of the landlords. In 1931 seventy eight out of every hundred houses were protected against increases in rent. In 1937 only 57 out of every hundred were protected. The figures for Scotland are 77 and 60 respectively.

These are working-class houses. The position of what might be called middle-class houses is even worse. They are 60 and 32 for England and 74 and 50 for Scotland.

Taking the two classes together more than half the houses built before the war have now passed from under control and in respect of these houses rents have already been raised to an extent which constitutes a grievous burden on the family budget.

25/- A WEEK

Tom Johnson showed that houses which were rented at 6/- in 1914 are now rented at 25/- per week. Other members of the Committee gave similar evidence.

Readers of the *Tribune* will know of cases even worse than this, and if they will send in to me instances of this sort which have come to their knowledge it will be treated in confidence and will be of help to the Labour Members of the Committee.

The shortage of working-class houses is still so bad that even Sir Kingsley Wood dare not recommend the repeal of the Acts dealing with them. The Bill therefore proposes to continue control until 1942. Labour Members tried to make control permanent but were defeated.

The Bill does, however, propose to decontrol all houses in the following classes. In London and Scotland all houses above thirty five pounds. In England and Wales above twenty pounds.

Subject to certain modifications all houses in these categories will cease to be protected by the Rent Restriction Acts, and the Landlords will be free to charge whatever rents they will be able to force the unfortunate tenants to pay.

The excuse offered for this is that building in these classes has reached the point where the shortage of houses is, or is about to come to an end. This is really not the case as members from all Parties were able to prove. It was a Tory member who unconsciously gave the real answer to his own side.

The Labour Members moved an amendment making it possible for a tenant to appeal to the County Courts against what he thought was an unreasonable rent demanded by the landlord. Sir F. Freemantle, the Tory Member for St. Albans, opposed this on the ground that landlords were suffering hardships as well as tenants.

Now what is the hardship from which the landlords of a controlled house suffers? Obviously, it is that control prevents him from charging more rent than the existing Act allows. But he could not do this if the supply of houses was sufficient and the tenant could go elsewhere.

WHAT TORIES WANT

The Government cannot have it both ways. It cannot on the one hand, argue that the supply of houses balances the demand, and that therefore no increase need be feared, and on the other hand, claim that the landlord is suffering the hardship of not being able to charge more rent because the house is controlled. The one argument cancels the other.

The truth of course is that the Tories are more concerned about the value of higher rents to the landlords than they are about the just treatment of the tenant.

The Amendment of the Labour Party, would, if carried, go some way to protect the tenant, by giving him the right of appeal to the Judge of the County Court. But this, up to the present, the Tories are resisting, because it would interfere with the landlords' opportunity to exploit to the full the prevailing shortage of houses.

We shall see what will happen when the Committee meets again next week. There are some who still think that there is no class war in politics. Such a view would not survive one sitting of Committee A.

Highwaymen in The Upper House – 8 July 1938

It is curious how these days almost all political events of any importance appear to raise the same fundamental principle. It is a portent of revolutionary change that no political issue can arise without bringing into question the very assumptions upon which the Constitution rests.

The immunity of the apparatus of the State from the influence of the day-to-day political struggle has always been the basis of the Reformist school of Socialist thinkers, who have advocated the 'capture of the State,' as though it is something that stands above the battle, unaffected by the changing fortunes of the various contestants in the political arena.

WHAT IS THE STATE?

In normal times everything seems to favour this view. We have but to achieve a majority in Parliament, so the argument goes, in order to have at our disposal the whole machinery of the capitalist State, to use against our enemies as they have used it against us.

From this standpoint the State looks very much like a gun which can be made to point in any direction at the will of the one who, at the moment, is in command of it.

If the Courts are biased against the workers, if the police serve property, if the Civil Service is saturated by Conservative thought, if the armed forces of the Crown are Officered by neo-fascists, if the Crown itself fertilises, by insidious channels, all the reactionary growths in society; all this, we are assured, will be transformed when the supreme centre of power the House of Commons is in the hands of the representatives of the workers.

The will of the people, we are told, must prevail, indeed is now prevailing, but it is a Tory will and we have only to convert it into a Socialist will, and the same instruments which favour the Tories will favour us.

It is a comforting thought and certain facts seem to justify it. When the Labour Party was in office in 1924 and 1931, they were served by the officials, so Labour-Ministers inform us, with the same fidelity with which these same officials had served alternate Liberal and Tory Administrations.

So much has this become the current coinage of Socialist thought in Britain today that it is considered unwise to cast even a shadow of doubt upon it. Nevertheless, doubt it we must, because I believe that this point of view is a dangerous delusion.

The machinery of the State and the assumption of the supremacy of the 'will of the people,' upon which it rests, are not immune from the issues of the economic and political struggles of the day.

On the contrary, they are involved in them and, as the struggle grows keener, crevices appear in the formerly solid façade of the State structure, until it breaks and finally melts away in the heat generated by contending social forces. That this has not been clearer before is due to the fact that as yet no deep fears have been aroused in the hearts of our opponents. Though the Sandys case is a warning.

One of the ways in which the cleavage in the structure of the British capitalist State may show itself is in the antagonism between the House of Lords and the Commons, which is latent in the relations between the two institutions.

FUNDAMENTAL CHALLENGE

As we have seen the fundamental assumption upon which certain people approach the possibility of a steady and even Socialist progress is that the will of the people is supreme in the British Constitution.

The very existence of the House of Lords challenges this principle. It shares power with the House of Commons and no Bill which does not involve taxation may become law without its consent. It is true that the Parliament Act can be invoked against it, but no serious political student regards the Parliament Act as a real restraint upon the Lords' power.

Unlike most Second Chambers in other countries, the House of Lords is not an elected assembly. Its Members sit in it by right of birth, so it is immune from pressure of the popular will.

In the view of many people, this very immunity is its chief virtue. We are told by these superior people that the fact that they are not compelled to soil themselves with the dust of the political arena at election times enables their Lordships to take a more balanced, a more dispassionate, a less emotional view of the welfare of the State.

They are supposed to enshrine the qualities of the aristocratic principle. By this phrase we are intended to understand that the House of Lords is above the vulgar self-interest which sways the Commons.

Not having to win votes they need not fear to lose them, and can, therefore, promote and support causes that are intrinsically good, but may not be able to command popular support.

Even if there were any merit in this contention, and there is not, it is no justification for the Lords, because, as they cannot make laws themselves, the Members of the House of Commons must still take whatever electoral risks are involved in the legislative proposals of the Lords.

SHEER RACKETEERING

This week in Parliament has afforded us an opportunity of judging the claims of the Lords to political purity. The Commons have been discussing the Amendments to the Coal Bill, which their Lordships had carried.

For sheer political racketeering nothing has been seen like it for years. Many of the Members of the Lords are, of course, royalty owners and so they have a direct interest in the amount of compensation which is proposed to be paid under the Bill for the purchase of their royalty rights.

Did this vulgar self-interest deter them from discussing the compensation clauses of the Bill? It did not. Not only did they discuss them, but they carried amendments which were designed to better themselves. They behaved more like highwaymen than legislators.

RAPACITY'S DISGUISE

Night after night they fought the Bill. The House of Lords was more animated than it has been for years. Peers turned up to vote themselves money who had never attended before, and if they have not met with more substantial success it is because the Tory Members of Parliament dare not agree with them and so expose themselves to the censure of their constituents.

In other words the principle of election in the Commons protects the people from pillage by the aristocratic Lords. The rapacity of property must always disguise itself before it can win the support of the people.

When the disguise wears thin, or the eyes of the people are too wide open to be deceived any longer, then the authoritarian principle, which is latent in the British Constitution and enshrined in the Lords, will be invoked to set aside the people's will as expressed in the vote.

Thus the Constitution itself becomes an issue in the struggle for the control of the Constitution.

Make the government act! –
17 March 1939

The duty of an Opposition is to fight for power, and in doing so, to create a public opinion to which the Government of the day is driven to make concessions.

If the Government finds it too difficult, or too repugnant, to make the concessions demanded by current public opinion then it must make way for the Opposition. Thus there is a sense in which the Opposition is directly responsible for legislation. Indeed, most of the social legislation of the last half century was achieved in this way.

A robust trades union movement, allied to a growing Labour Party, pressed hard on the Tory and Liberal governments of the time, and forced them to realise that they could keep power only by concessions to the public opinion which had been educated by the agitations of the Opposition. The extension of the social services since the war, particularly illustrates this progress of a healthy democracy.

The political defenders of property interests fought a series of stubborn rear-guard actions against demands for better unemployment, health, pensions, and housing services. In industry, the trade unions accomplished great improvements in limitations of hours, better wages and working conditions, trades boards, etc. The pace was agonisingly slow, but on the whole, it was continuous and reflected the growing political consciousness of the people under the direct inspiration of an Opposition which knew its business and was doing it.

*

In these conditions of normal political development an Opposition might never actually achieve power, and yet, be responsible for most of the major legislative achievements of the time.

The political representatives of property were always engaged in nicely balanced calculations as to how far they dare resist the pressure of public opinion and as to how little they need give in order to buy it off. This delicate and complicated task is the art of ruling-class government in a political democracy. The British ruling class have always won the admiration of their fellows throughout the world by the skill with which they do it.

They were helped, of course, by their fortunate economic position. They were able to make concessions which their counterparts in other countries often found impossible.

Tension increases and danger arises when the pressure of democratic opinion is regarded as unendurable by the propertied interests. It is at this point that they begin to entertain doubts about the wisdom and soundness of democratic institutions, and the virtues of an aristocratic tradition glow with romantic attractiveness.

If the leaders of democratic opinion become frightened in this situation and modify their demands, their retreat is soon turned into a rout. The historical process is reversed. Instead of the people improving their position at the expense of property, property takes the offensive and improves its position at the expense of the people and of the democratic tradition.

A crisis of this sort is always inherent in a capitalist democracy. Unless its possibility is understood and courageously faced by the leaders of democratic opinion they will lead their people to a succession of crises from which they will inevitably retreat with disastrous results for democracy, both material and, what is ultimately much worse, psychological.

It seems to me that we have reached such a situation in Great Britain. And it arises in the very difficult and dangerous field of foreign affairs. There is no doubt that the foreign policy of the National Government does not command the support of the majority of the British people.

The failure of the National Service campaign is the principal evidence of this. The agitation of the Labour Party has created a public opinion about foreign policy which the National Government has outraged. The people express this by a refusal to enlist in the service of the Government. The natural thing to do is for the Labour Party to give expression to this state of mind, by demanding either, a foreign policy more in keeping with the wishes of the people, or by a change of government which would mean the same thing.

In domestic affairs, the Government needs our votes to keep in power. To get them, the Government makes concessions. IN THE FIELD OF FOREIGN AFFAIRS THE GOVERNMENT NEEDS OUR BODIES. TO GET THEM, THE GOVERNMENT SHOULD BE DRIVEN TO MAKE CONCESSIONS IN FOREIGN POLICY.

At this point the leaders of the Labour Party run away. Instead of saying to the Government: 'the people don't agree with your policy and won't fight for it; change your policy or get out,' they urge the people to enlist, and thus outrage the very feelings the Labour Party has helped to create.

Turn again to the analogy of domestic affairs and apply the same logic. Suppose the people said to the Government: 'It is quite true that we want more pensions and better health services, and you refuse to give them. Nevertheless, we won't withhold our votes from you.' What would be the result? No social progress of any kind.

*

Turn back again to foreign affairs. The people are asked to say something like this: 'It is true that you have outraged every principle in which we believe. You have destroyed the last vestige of collective security. You have promoted the triumph of Fascism in Europe, and in the Orient. You actively assisted in the destruction of Czechoslovakia, and tied the hands of our Spanish comrades behind their backs whilst they were done to death by their Fascist enemies. You have openly encouraged Germany to attack the Soviet Union and you have consistently refused to bring the Soviet Union into a Peace Alliance with France and ourselves. You are now preparing for a war which will be fought only for the sordid defence of British Imperialism and of the British and French colonial empires. I may even be asked to fight for Fascism against my own friends. Nevertheless, I propose to join up immediately.'

Is not that exactly what the National Council of Labour is asking the British working class to say and do?

They attempt to excuse it by arguing that whatever Government is in power, Britain will have to be fully armed. The first answer to the National Council is that by behaving in this way you are ensuring that this Government will remain in power. The second answer is that no Government could remain in power for five minutes after the people signified their refusal to fight for it.

The third answer is, that by urging people to join up before they have secured any concessions in foreign policy you are asking them to strip themselves of any influence over the Government. Indeed, in the name of democracy you are asking them to throw away the only instrument by which democracy is implemented.

The last argument of the National Council of Labour is that a wide response to the appeal for recruits is the only way of avoiding conscription. Well, there is an element of truth in that. If you walk into prison, of course, you don't have to be dragged there. It will still be prison just the same. The logic of the National Council is impeccable. If you don't claim your rights, then of course, you won't have to fight for them.

THE ADVICE OF THE NATIONAL COUNCIL TO THE WORKERS OF BRITAIN IS SUMMED UP IN THE OMINOUS SENTENCE OF THE POLICEMAN WHEN ARRESTING SOMEONE: 'GO QUIETLY.'

Blind Men are Leading Us! – 11 October 1940

I must confess to a feeling of profound disappointment. I had been led to hope from statements in certain quarters that the Government were about to make a declaration of war aims. When I went to the House of Commons on Tuesday last it was with a sense of lively anticipation. It seemed to me impossible for the Prime Minister to make another speech without giving some coherent plan and intention to the war effort of Great Britain. I did not expect it to satisfy me, but that was not important. One thing would have been accomplished. We should no longer have to spend our time and energy insisting upon the need for war aims to be announced, but would be able to get our teeth into the much more exciting and important job of interpreting, explaining and amending a set of definite proposals.

A BLINDNESS SO COMPLETE ...

When the Prime Minister reached the end of his speech without even a hint that the Government is as much as thinking of war aims, my heart sank. It seemed to me evidence of a blindness so complete that I cannot see how such men can lead us to victory. Certainly I cannot understand what the Labour Party leaders are thinking about. For all the awareness they show of the mood of the workers of this country they might as well be on another planet. We expect Tories to show no enthusiasm for a new future. They would not be Tories if they were not on the whole satisfied with what we have been getting. But we look for an entirely different state of mind from Socialists.

THE CHANCE FOR SOCIALISTS

Quite apart from the overwhelming importance of the right kind of war aims for the waging of victorious war, a nation-wide discussion of our proposals would be of the greatest possible educative value. It is not often that the people can be brought to the state of awareness in which they are at present. War opens the most heavy-lidded eyes and makes the pulse of the sluggish beat faster. It is at this moment, when the stimulating emergencies of war have assembled an awakened and expectant audience, that the enlightened statesman should seize his chance to make the people his eager collaborators in the building of a new social order. Certainly Socialists should seize it.

***

What criminal folly it would be to neglect this opportunity and allow millions to slip back into that debility of political neutrality which is the despair of intelligent citizens! Not only has the war brought masses to an unprecedented political consciousness, but it has induced in them what I can only describe as a buoyant and optimistic attitude of mind. They have been brought to see that the vicissitudes they suffer are not implicit in an immutable pattern of life, but are the direct consequences of a particular kind of social organisation, and, therefore, capable of being dealt with by social action.

This is a state of mind that I call deeply optimistic. It no longer goes on its knees before disaster nor turns helplessly to the doubtful solace of resignation. It sees that poverty, ill-health, economic insecurity, unemployment, and war are socially preventable evils. It believes in the secular origin of man's fate, and that, when you come to think of it, is the biggest revolution that has occurred for thousands of years.

THIS IS THE DIFFERENCE

I do not claim that this state of mind has come to maturity in every man and woman, but I do claim it is the colour and mood of our generation. It is the distinctive difference between our time and any other, and no political creed that fails to take it into account is worth bothering about. The 18th and 19th centuries were concerned principally about personal, the relationship of men, and the American Civil War was its classical expression.

ECONOMIC ANARCHY

The 20th century is pre-occupied by the relationship between men and forms of social organisation; and when the history of our times comes to be written it will be seen as a sustained and often bloody effort to bring the organisation of society under conscious control and in accordance with a settled plan. Even Fascism will be seen as a phase in the development of collectivism, because on its best side it is an attempt to carve out from the rest of the world a piece of social organisation in which men can feel secure even though it might be the security of a gaol. Modern man is properly impatient of an economic anarchy which assails him with a multitude of evils and he will turn to anything which offers an escape.

The supreme test for democratic institutions is whether they can bring about a planned economy whilst at the same time preserving the decent personal liberties which were the best products of the Liberal Revolution. This is the very heart of the modern problem and it must form the centre of any statement of war aims if they are to command the support of the people.

***

It follows from this that the area of private property must be drastically restricted, because power over property is the instrument of economic planning. It will not be possible to make plans for a reconstructed Europe which will be any other than plain nonsense unless those plans provide for the public ownership of most of the essential services of society. To talk of a new social order in any other sense is merely a play with words. Probably that is one of the reasons why the Cabinet are so reluctant to frame our war aims.

War aims which leave out of account international economic planning would amount to nothing more than a peroration, and it will not be possible for Britain to frame intelligent proposals for other countries unless she is prepared to so adjust her own industries that they can be fitted into the international pattern.

CONDITION FOR DEFEAT

If the Tory members of the Government carry their defence of private property rights to the extent of refusing the public ownership of the industries I mentioned last week, then we shall lose the war. It will not be possible to prevail on the people of Britain to bear the agonies of continued warfare unless we are able to present them with a solution of their problems of a nature to command their affections. And this cannot be done if the rights of property remain supreme.

Many people will feel that if what I have said is true, then our case is hopeless. They are convinced that there is no hope of overcoming the resistance of vested interests sufficiently to compose rational proposals.

THE CASE OF THE DIEHARD

I believe they are unduly gloomy. The vast majority of the people of Britain are prepared to go a very long way towards the establishment of a decent society. The self-confidence of the most die-hard Tory has been undermined within recent years. There was a time when he rejoiced at the emergence of Fascism in Italy and Germany because it seemed to him that at last he was given something to frighten the Socialists with, and if the worse came to the worse, something to turn to if the workers proved too clamant. So thought Thyssen of Germany when he financed Hitler to destroy the German workers' organisations.

***

But Fascism does not wear so attractive a face to our property owners as formerly it did. War is a heavy price to pay for resisting Socialist demands, and a Fascist totalitarian economy is nothing like so pleasant as it looked when it was some distance away. Many who before the war were deeply opposed to any radical change now see that we cannot go back to the old world. What they want to be satisfied about is that it is possible to reconcile the necessities of economic planning with the preservation of individual liberty. Can the state be given power over our work without the same power swallowing the whole of our life?

That is the question millions are asking. I believe it can be done and next week I hope to show how.

The Tories' Prisoner –
18 October 1940

This week I must leave the discussion of war aims to consider another question which has arisen in the course of the past few days. Mr. Churchill has accepted the leadership of the Tory Party. Some time ago I wrote in the *Tribune* a warning that this might occur and gave reasons why I thought Mr. Churchill would succumb to the temptation. He must realise by now that his decision has not strengthened his position in the nation's esteem. Everyone knew he was a member of the Tory Party and it is his right, as it certainly is a proper ambition in normal times, to aspire to the leadership of the Party of which he is a member. But these are not normal times and Mr. Churchill's position was unique.

His appointment as Prime Minister was forced upon the Tory majority in the House of Commons as a consequence, not of his Party position, but in spite of it. He was the choice of the nation and his unpopularity in his own party, so far from being a weakness, was a source of strength, not only to himself, but to the nation as a whole. Party politics do not command much affection in Britain just now, and certainly the reputation of the Tory Party had never fallen so low. It was associated with policies which have brought disaster upon the nation, and the treatment the Tory Party machine had inflicted upon Mr. Churchill and his friends had resulted in as much obloquy for the Tory machine as it had in universal acclaim for Mr. Churchill.

WHEN THE TORIES SULKED

For months after Mr. Churchill assumed the Premiership the congeries of Tories grouped round the Tory Party, caucus sulked and muttered under their breath, not daring to speak openly the resentment they felt at seeing a man of whom they disapproved thrusting their own leader from 10 Downing Street, despite the fact that they enjoyed an overwhelming majority in Parliament. Time after time, when he entered the House of Commons, the new Prime Minister was greeted with a loud silence from the packed Tory benches. His warmest reception came from the Labour and Liberal Members. I doubt if a parallel situation had ever existed in the history of the British Parliament.

Students of politics watched the drama with keen interest. Seen against the huge canvas of the Battle for Britain, which was about to begin, it appeared of little moment to many. Actually it always seemed to me to be of only less importance than the outcome of Hitler's attack upon this country. For the politics of this country were in a more fluid condition than they had been for a century. It is now clear that Mr. Churchill's advisers were all the time guiding and advising him in the direction of the leadership of the Tory Party. Partly by the political calculations involved in listening to this advice, and partly because of his generous and romantic disposition, Mr. Churchill was induced on several occasions to make passionate defences of the Men of Munich whom he had retained in office despite the obvious and often expressed desire of the people. To have thrown over men like Lord Halifax, Sir Kingsley Wood and Mr. Neville Chamberlain would have meant a break with the Tory Party machine, and a complete re-grouping of Party alignments in the House of Commons. It would, indeed, have been almost an heroic step to take. Mr. Churchill was not bold enough to take it. Or perhaps it would be less cynical to say that the outcome of the Battle for Britain commanded all his energies and gifts of experimentation.

THE MEN OF MUNICH

Whatever was the cause, he kept in office men whose policies had been discredited, whose very names were execrated, whose retention in high places depressed the spirit of the country and caused dismay among our friends throughout the world, and who had nothing to fall back on except their power with the Tory Central Office.

After a time the Tory bosses breathed again. The crisis was over. The unfolding epic of war distracted the attention of the people from the demand for the punishment of the guilty. These thought gratefully of the Dunkirk days when nothing was left between them and the anger of an outraged populace except the mantle of protection the nation's hero had thrown over their wilting shoulders. By one of those graceful and emollient acts for which the British governing class is justly famed, Mr. Chamberlain was slipped inconspicuously from the political scene, and Mr. Churchill was unanimously elected leader of the Tory Party which for years had been seeking his political extinction.

Whatever else may be said about the whole transaction, there can be no doubt concerning the gain to the Tory Party. With consummate guile it has made a Tory asset of Mr. Churchill's national reputation. With this inestimable advantage it can manoeuvre itself into a position of impregnable strength. So long as Mr. Churchill retains the national ascendancy he won as a non-party man, any attack against the Tory Party will be made to appear as an attack on the nation's leader and through him on the nation itself. Once more the Tory caucus drapes itself in the national flag. Once more the skull-and-cross-bones of private brigandage conceals itself in the decent garments of patriotic effort. Once more private pelf is joined in unholy union with the public weal. Once more the Battle for Britain and the Battle for Profits are inextricably mingled, to the hurt of the one and the enlargement of the other.

WHO SHALL COMMAND?

There are one or two otherwise astute publicists who see in the transaction an advantage to the nation in the present crisis. Mr. A. J. Cummings in the *News Chronicle* welcomes it because he thinks it will strengthen Mr. Churchill in his command of the Tory members who form the majority in the House of Commons. It was not in order that he might command them that the Tory Bosses made Mr. Churchill their leader. It was that they might command him. Politics is not a conflict between personalities. It is a conflict between power groups.

Mr. Churchill may, and probably will, make changes in the personal direction of the Tory Party machine. He may elevate his friends who have been faithful to him in the years of his exile and cast out those who conspired against him. These are the incidental superficialities of such changes, and they affect nothing but the personal fortunes of those involved. Nothing is necessarily altered by them in the alignments of social forces as expressed through political parties. *The Tory Party is the politically organised body of the most powerful vested interests in the British Empire.* No personality, even one so dominating as Mr. Churchill, can alter that essential fact. And there is no evidence that Mr. Churchill wants to alter it. What his leadership will do is to provide those vested interests with the precious political capital of his colourful personality and international stature. His behaviour since he has assumed office has reassured them that they can trust him, and we can more safely rely upon their judgment of what benefits them than we can upon the genial credulity of Mr. Cummings.

When a Tory candidate is selected by the Tory Central Office to stand for a seat he will receive the benedictory message of Mr. Churchill as the Party Leader. Every local Tory Party in the country will bask in the reflected glory of his reputation. He will pump new life into a dying cause, and the vigour of the national war effort will tend to flow more and more into narrow party channels.

NEW ROLE FOR LABOUR

The relations of the Labour Party and Mr. Churchill are bound to be worsened by the change. It will be necessary in future to watch Mr. Churchill from two aspects: as a national leader in an unprecedented situation, and as the spokesman of the Tory Party. And it will not be easy to do so. The Press, the radio and almost all other organs of public opinion are very much under the direct control and influence of the Government these days. This is always a dangerous state of affairs. It is no answer to me to say that this was the position of the last war, because it was just not so. Mr. Lloyd George had to practically break the Liberal Party to form the Coalition which won the war; and when it was over he found himself having to set up what amounted to an interim cross-party arrangement to fight the post-war election. This will not be possible against so strong and traditional a body as the Labour Party. The Party leaders will be compelled to keep their eyes on the future prospects of their parties from now on. All this is bound to detract from the immense effort which will be needed to win through to victory.

It is ten thousand pities that Mr. Churchill should have chosen to take a step which must agitate dormant suspicions and awaken to life rivalries which are best forgotten when the enemy's knife is at our throat. It is a million pities that he should have chosen to give new vigour to elements in our national life which must be progressively weakened if we are to gather sufficient strength to win through.

Next Steps to a New Society – 25 October 1940

In the two previous articles on War Aims I tried to make a number of main points.

1. A declaration of War Aims by Great Britain is urgently needed, (a) in order, by means of them, to win over the active support of the populations under Nazi domination, and (b) so that the people of Britain itself should be inspired to bear the ordeals that lie between us and victory.
2. Such is the cynicism left over from the flamboyant and unfulfilled promises of the last war that steps must be taken here and now to carry out, as far as may be practicable, such items of our plans for a new social order as lies within our immediate power.
3. These plans must envisage an end of the economic anarchy which existed before the war, and consequently the instruments of economic planning must be at the disposal of the nation. These instruments are the principal industries and services, the land, and of course the banks, and – as I was reminded by a correspondent in the *Tribune* last week – the health services.
4. There is a widespread conviction that we are bound to see fundamental changes emerging from this war, and there is a disposition to welcome them in hitherto stubborn quarters. Some are reconciled to them, others are eager for them.
5. Nevertheless, there does exist a universal fear that to entrust the ownership and direction of vital industries to the state might result in the totalitarian excesses of the Fascist States, the submergence of the individual by swollen bureaucracies, and the extinction of precious personal freedoms.
6. Any proposal which hopes to commend itself to the people of this country must therefore assuage this fear.

***

Most Socialist proposals have failed to do this because they have boggled at facing the changes in the political constitution which must follow from fundamental changes in the economic organisation of society. Consequently, they have contented themselves with demands for the nationalisation of certain industries and the promotion of public utilities like the London Passenger Transport Board, which merely have the effect of consolidating vested interests and converting the absentee shareholder into the securely entrenched bondholder. These public utilities and 'nationalised' industries obey the logic of the same kind of archaic balance sheet as private industry and therefore defeat the first important aim of socialism, which is to increase the consumption of certain agreed products.

A planned economy in this machine age cannot succeed if it limits itself to 'tidying up' the disorders of private economic adventure. It must seek that enlarged and predictable mass consumption which alone can keep the giant machines in full employment. And, of course, it is now hackneyed to say that this cannot be done if the purpose and motive of the enterprise is private profit. To ensure the profit, the price of the product is kept at a point which denies consumption to large numbers of people. If production for *use* is substituted for production for profit, then the price is fixed at the level which will secure whatever rate of consumption is considered desirable in the interests of the whole community.

We must therefore visualise a certain number of industries and services where the margin of profit ceases to exist. These are the ones which must come under the direct control of the State. We must therefore have in mind three main streams of economic life:

(i) Industries the products of which are distributed. That is to say, they have no price because they are provided free. What these shall be is a matter for discussion.
(ii) Industries the products of which are sold at an artificially fixed price in order to secure the agreed standard of consumption. Some of the industries in this second category will be publicly owned, and some of them will remain in a sort of quasi-private relationship, subject to some form of public direction, like milk production for instance.
(iii) The third class will remain the domain of private economic adventure, the motive will be profit, and the arbiter will be competitive selling.

Society will then be provided with a measure of progress – the extent to which products pass from the third to the second and thence to the

first category. The conscious application of this idea will give the economic life of the nation a sort of concrete raft, a kind of economic backbone, fixed and stable, around which the activities of privately owned industry will group themselves, supplying the infinite diversification of products which the caprice of private choice may determine, without at any time threatening economic chaos.

The reader will have noted that all that I have said so far is only an extension of trends which exist now and have been imposed upon us by the necessities of war time conditions. The important thing is that they should be recognised as permanent features of our lives, that they should be extended during the war so that when peace comes we shall not only have the means of dealing with the post-war readjustment, but we shall have built up a vested interest in public ownership which will withstand the efforts of those who will want us to return to all the discords of economic anarchy.

***

It is at this point that the important question arises – what changes in the political constitution of the nation will be made necessary by this economic ground-plan, bearing in mind all the time our main fear of the rise of totalitarian tyranny?

Our conclusion we must make at once. Parliament, as it is at present, cannot possibly hope to direct and control such a system in detail. If it tries to do so it will break down and from the breakdown will come demands for the limitation of democratic rights in the service of economic stability. What is needed are constitutional alterations which will leave with the elected representatives of the people all power over general citizen rights, leaving to another body the day to day administration of the economic plan, whose main outlines also Parliament would determine. The proposal I make is provisional, and I make it in order to focus discussion on what I consider to be the central problem of our time. In the space available I can only sketch its outlines. I realise I shall be open to misunderstanding, but I must risk that.

I suggest five main organs of the state, as follows:

1) Parliament, supreme over all, elected on the basis of proportional representation. The past eight years have shown us the dangers of an obese

majority. The lifetime of Parliament should be for a fixed period, and it should consist of one Chamber. That is to say, the House of Lords should be abolished. Parliament would reserve to itself all legislation and control over education, the police, the penal institutions, the radio, the press, and the armed forces, etc. Parliament would also lay down the main provisions of the plan for the nationalised industries which would be entrusted to a:

2) Supreme Economic Council, consisting of a small number of highly trained executives. All the appropriate existing departments of state would be handed over to that body, with the removal of the present immunities from dismissal which enervates them. The Economic Council would promote the greatest measure of industrial democracy consistent with the retention of ultimate authority by the Council.
3) A permanent Planning Commission appointed by the Government and charged with the task of preparing the next plan.
4) A National Costing or auditing department charged with the task of checking and reporting upon the administration of the industries responsible to the Supreme Economic Council.
5) A Judiciary with all the immunities and protection appropriate to such a body.

No Member of Parliament would be allowed to question the day to day administration of the Economic Council. Only by a special resolution, moved in the House and carried by a majority, could the persons or behaviour of the members of the Economic Council be indicted in Parliament. It would open the door to unlimited nepotism if Members of Parliament were allowed to harass the economic executives by daily questions and criticism.

The Trade Unions would remain free and voluntary bodies. To make the Trade Unions extensions of the Government would be to exaggerate the vices into which some of them have fallen and to divert them from their proper function as watch-dogs of the welfare of their members. The Government, of course, would represent the majority in Parliament, and the fact that the House of Commons would sit for a fixed period should bring the Government itself more under the direct control of the representatives of the people than has been the case in recent years. The stability introduced into the economic system by the Economic Council and the economic plan itself would cushion the country from the consequences of the frequent changes of Government which proved such an evil in France.

There is nothing in these proposals which could not be fitted into a system of international co-operation. They correspond to the essential needs of all nations which have experienced any degree of machine production. What we propose for ourselves should also satisfy the yearnings of the oppressed peoples of other lands.

As I have said, I put forward these proposals in order to excite discussion. The only merit I claim for them is that they are based on an appreciation of the functional needs of the kind of society it is desirable to create. One last word. I do hope that readers will not assume that what I have not had space to say I therefore necessarily disagree with.

Hope and new strength – 2 May 1941

Next weekend the organised British workers will celebrate May Day. In thousands of meetings all over the country the workers will dedicate themselves once more to the principles of international socialism.

To many this will appear either a stale fairy story or a piece of cynicism, and certainly there is nothing in the immediate international situation to create hope, much less buoyancy. Nevertheless I regard this as a superficial view, for if we penetrate beneath the appearance and see the reality there is more cause for hope and optimism than for pessimism and despair. If our souls sicken, it is because we always had a romantic view of what the struggle for international socialism would be.

It would appear that international socialism has received a fatal setback, for nowhere now on the Continent of Europe does a free, organised working-class movement exist. From the sunny shores of the Mediterranean, north to the Arctic, men live under the shadow of a tyranny as black as any in the records of mankind. All the institutions that free men built up by a century and a half of struggle have been overthrown in a short ten years. Only in Great Britain and America, and in Australia and New Zealand, do the institutions of Western democracy survive; and even here they are called upon to engage in a struggle for mere survival.

***

Up to now our enemies have proved themselves invincible in every major engagement, for it is slowly, oh so slowly, that the forces of freedom gather themselves for this supreme battle – slowly and reluctantly, because men have not yet discerned the essential pattern of events.

By the subtle use of mass suggestion the enemies of the people have made it appear that democracy is an ancient and senile creed, and that it is now being swept away by the vigour of renovating ideas. That is not only a lie but it is the reverse of the truth.

For democracy is a new arrival on the stage of history. It is only a short time since ordinary men and women have enjoyed even the par-

tial right to shape the policies that govern their countries. It was only with the beginning of the 20th century that ordinary folk emerged from the darkness of despotism into the light of freedom, and began to consciously shape the governments of the world. And yet in that short time mankind has made more progress in the sciences, in the arts, in literature, than was made in the ten thousand years that preceded it.

So far from democracy having failed mankind, it lifted man higher and quicker than any other lever which has suggested itself to the brain of man. What we are now witnessing is an attempt on the part of ancient despotism to thrust ordinary people back into the shadows.

IDEALS IN TYRANNY

If the war is going badly for us it is not because of any inherent deficiency in democratic ideals, but because those ideals have not yet released themselves from the stranglehold of partial tyrannies. It is now possible to discern three stages in the present war. The first was represented by the retreat from liberty under the leadership of Mr. Neville Chamberlain and his opposite numbers in France. This retreat had reached the brink of irretrievable disaster when the democratic forces rallied themselves last year under the leadership of Mr. Winston Churchill. The time has now arrived for the people to insist upon the third stage, and the third stage is the positive adoption of methods and of measures that accord with the essential spirit of democracy.

**

So far, therefore, from our May Day meetings being held in gloom and despondency, there is every occasion for buoyancy and new vigour. If every resource open to us, if every method and device which could suggest itself to us had been tried and failed, then indeed there would be occasion to despair. But we know that they have not been, for not yet have the resources of Socialist inspiration been tried anywhere. What we are witnessing is not the defeat of democracy but the natural failure of Tories to wield the democratic weapon. Our principal industries like mining, like transport, like steel, like ship-building, all limp ineffectually under the opposing motives of patriotism and profit. It will be known to the workers who gather at these May Day meetings that in countless industries the output of essential war materials is retarded because the motives of profit sabotage production.

The deep and inexhaustible reservoirs of moral strength that lie in the common people are un-tapped because the principles of social equality which are the foundation stone of Socialism, are not applied even at this critical time. The inequalities arising from a system of limited rationing, face us every day with the spectacle of wealth being able to cushion itself against the hardship of war. On the streets of our principal cities streams of motor cars carrying well-to-do people about, mock the heroism of our merchant seamen, carrying petrol to our shores. Millions of acres of idle land kept barren by the palsy of private ownership, make harsher the trials of siege.

OPEN THE THROTTLE

If we lost the war it would be because the essentially anti-democratic Toryism of Great Britain sits on the democratic throttle. The fact is that the British people have not yet been mobilised for war in the deep spiritual sense of that term. Therefore, every May Day meeting in Great Britain should say to the British Labour Party: 'Press on. We refuse to allow the light of democracy to be extinguished from the world because we are too timid to insist upon our own principles being tried.'

A great leader of social democracy in Germany in the last century, Ferdinand Lassalle, said: 'You cannot be clever in big things,' and the offensive which the democratic forces must launch against the Nazis cannot be engineered by the intrigues of political compromise. True, it would be absurd to suggest that in the midst of a war of this kind it is possible for British Labour to thrust aside its ancient political enemies and take full charge. But what British Labour can do is to say that the inspirations of the British governing class have exhausted themselves, and by their exhaustion have brought our hopes and the hopes of humanity into the direst peril. They must therefore be prepared to accept the compulsion of events and cooperate in the infusion of fresh ideas, fresh impulses and wider conceptions of human liberty.

So, to the thousands who gather at our May Day meetings throughout the country, I say this: 'Do not despair; do not be cast down, for if we will it the war will soon take on the form and the appearance which bears the authentic stamp of history: A war for the status and dignity of ordinary men and women against the forces that threaten to engulf them once more, in the enslavement and ignominy of ancient tyranny.'

The T.U.C.'s Two Voices – 13 October 1944

'A controlled economic system is a modern necessity in advanced industrial communities. The choice before us is not between control or no control, but in principle, between control by public authority responsible to the community, or control by private groups and persons owning a final authority to themselves alone and, in detail, between degrees and types of control.'

In these words the General Council of the Trades Union Congress defines the main problem dealt with in its interim report on Post-War Reconstruction. No Socialist will disagree with the definition so far as it goes. Where Socialists will join issue is in the assumption that effective public control can be exercised over industries left in private ownership.

There can be no question of the importance of the document, not only for the trade unions themselves but also for the Labour Party, having regard to the dominant position of the unions in the Party. It can, therefore, be taken for granted that whatever policy the unions decide upon they will seek to make it the official policy of the Labour Party. Nor is there any ground of complaint against the General Council making up its mind on these questions. It is their undoubted right to do so.

Sir Walter Citrine insisted some time ago that the Trades Union Congress claimed the right to make pronouncements on any aspect of public policy. In asserting this independence he admitted an equal status for the Labour Party. Unfortunately the Labour Party is not a body independent of the trade unions. On the contrary it is largely the political instrument of the trade unions. Because of this relationship an examination of the mind of the unions on the future organisation of British industry is necessary, not only for its own merits but on account of its bearing on the policy of Labour as a whole.

NATIONALISATION OF BASIC INDUSTRIES

The Report illustrates the extent to which Socialist ideas have won ascendancy within the unions, and the extent to which they have failed. In coal and power, transport and steel the victory is complete. The Report advocates the immediate nationalisation of these basic industries, and what it says about them is wholly admirable.

'For those industries,' the Report says, 'for which nationalisation is proposed, therefore, a Public Corporation would be established by Act of Parliament to take over all the undertakings in the particular industry or group of related industries. In relation to corporations of this type, it is essential that responsibility to the public shall be maintained by the appointment of the members of its governing body by a Minister responsible to Parliament, and they should, therefore, be selected on the basis of their competence and ability to manage the industry efficiently in the public interest. It is further essential that their organisation shall make proper provision for the representation and participation of workpeople, and to this end statutory provision should be made for the interests of workpeople to be represented on the Governing Board.'

Socialist thought is again evident in the proposed relationship between the unions and the management of these public concerns. The Report insists that the unions should not seek direct representation on the Management Boards. The function of the union is to promote the welfare of the workers, and this may not always be consistent with the obligations of management. At the workshop level the participation of the worker in the administration of the industry is an essential condition of industrial democracy, and a direct contribution to increased efficiency and smooth working. But his trade union must maintain its independence of the machinery of management or it will fail to represent him in its capacity of defender of his interests as a wage earner, as distinct from his function as a technical operative.

In all these questions the Report is objective and clear-minded. Where the decision is made to pass the industry over to public ownership, the line of demarcation between the public and sectional interest is obvious, and provision can be made for both. In other words, where Socialist theory is applied, Socialist practice is coherent, and the accumulated experience of the trade unions' leaders is seen working at its best. This is particularly evident in the section dealing with compensation for nationalised industries.

'We are of the opinion,' it says, 'that bonds issued as compensation should be divorced entirely from the industry and normal Government stock should be issued, carrying a fixed rate of interest.'

In this way the State-owned industry would be freed from the direct profit motive and so avoid one of the worst defects of such schemes as the London Passenger Transport Board.

COLLABORATION THROUGH INDUSTRIAL BOARDS

From this point on, however, the Report goes to pieces. Over the wide field of industry, still left in private hands after the basic industries have been nationalised, the Report advocates wholehearted collaboration with the employers through the medium of industrial boards, intended to be largely self-governing bodies within each industry.

These boards would rule over the following industries: heavy chemicals, cement, rayon, soap and margarine, non-ferrous metals, rubber processing, grain-milling and tobacco, motor cars, aircraft, railway locomotives and rolling-stock, and shipbuilding, furniture making, clothing and finished textiles, boots and shoes, processed foods, domestic utensils, and electrical and mechanical appliances for the home. It is proposed that these Boards should be composed of representatives of the trade unions and the Employers' Federation, or the Trade Association of the industry concerned. Over each Board would preside a chairman appointed by the appropriate Minister, with a tenure of office of a fixed number of years and paid by the State. Once a Board has been established it would be necessary, in the words of the Report, to 'secure its authority by giving statutory sanction to its collective decisions when such sanction seems desirable in the public interest.'

In addition to these Boards for each industry, a National Industrial Council is suggested, consisting of representatives of the unions along with persons appointed by the Federation of British Industries and Employers' Confederation. As the Report says, 'a properly constituted council of this kind would provide the Government with detailed industrial experience upon which to draw in the formulation of policy. It would also materially assist in the application of economic policy to industry.'

These Boards, among other powers, would be enabled by Act of Parliament to impose levies on industry for the administrative expenses.

Having got themselves into that situation, the General Council of the Trades Union Congress go on from one muddle to another. The clarity of mind and directness of reasoning which distinguished their approach to the publicly-owned industries desert them altogether once they commit themselves to collaboration. For example, they realise that the unions may be compromised in the discharge of their function as protectors of the interests of their members. All they can say is that the unions must be careful to avoid entanglement. But how can they avoid it if they accept membership of these Boards and therefore responsibility for the policy of the employers? How can they expect to sit on these Boards in the morning, making production policy, and then, in the afternoon, meet the same employers to discuss wages and conditions with any independence of outlook and action?

In such circumstances the union leaders will feel it their duty to induce the workers to accept the joint decisions already arrived at by the Boards. This is indeed the Fascist Labour Front with a vengeance. Once collaboration is established it must go the whole way. It is useless to say, as the Report does, that the unions must keep themselves free to 'advance in the public interest, authoritative and independent criticism or conduct of the industries in which they operate.' How in the name of common sense can they criticise the policies of which they themselves will be part authors? To do so would be a violation of their partnership.

The General Council want to have it both ways. They want to share power with the employers and yet persuade us they can be relied upon to protect the general interest against these same employers. The unions may decide, if they wish, to become assimilated into the machinery of private industry, but they must not expect us to regard them, at the same time, as reliable protectors of the workers, nor as watchdogs of the public welfare.

WHAT BECOMES OF PARLIAMENT?

As the Report itself says: 'Public undertakings must be directed to the public service. Private undertakings must necessarily operate by reference to the interests of their owners.' Precisely. As I have already pointed out, the union leaders were clear in their minds that the Miners' Union, for instance, could not accept managerial responsibility for a nationalised mining industry without loss of its independence, and they advise against it. Surely it is even more difficult for a union to maintain its independence if it accepts trade, commercial, and production responsibilities in privately owned industry. Such an attempt to have a foot in both camps would reduce the unions to nullity.

If these Industrial Boards and the National Industrial Council are set up, what becomes of Parliament? Apparently the unions expect Parliament to perform the functions of referee. The Report says: 'Any proposal to fix minimum or general prices or restrict production, or entry into the industry should be subject to stricter examination by an appropriate public body and to approval by the Government, possibly by Parliament.' I like that 'possibly by Parliament.' It comes in as an afterthought, which, indeed, would be its status if this Corporative State apparatus ever eventuates.

Consider the position of the House of Commons in the conditions envisaged by this document. The Boards will have made up their minds what they want, and their decisions will tie up the individual unions and groups of employers affected. On top of that, the National Industrial Council, consisting of the national representatives of the same bodies, will have endorsed them. The total result is then presented to the House of Commons. What earthly chance is there for Parliament to arrive at an independent judgment on the issue? A large group of M.P.s will be closely associated with the unions. A still larger group will be connected with the employers' interests. The issue would be prejudged before Parliamentary consideration began. All the House of Commons could do in those circumstances would be to rubber-stamp the policy already decided by its masters.

All this goes to show the fallacy of the basic assumption that effective public control can be exercised over private industry when the latter is given collective organisation and the restraints of competition are consequently removed. The union leaders are correct in their contention that modern industry needs collective organisation and direction. They are wrong in their belief that this can be done whilst leaving industry in private hands, and at the same time evade the risks of Fascist developments.

When private interests organise themselves in the fashion recommended by the T.U.C. Report they take over the apparatus of the State itself. The result is not control of industry by the State. It is the control and domination of the State by private interests, disciplined and organised by the necessities and technical requirements of modern industrial society. The T.U.C. are perfectly right in laying stress on the fact that cartels, trusts, trade associations and similar combinations have destroyed the protections afforded by the competition and small-scale enterprises of the 19th century. The conflicting interests of different groups of capitalists left a considerable degree of freedom of action by the Government. The State could be, and was, manipulated by the capitalist class as a whole where and when its general interest was involved as in conflicts with the working class and in waging war. But a particular section of capitalists found it difficult to use the State apparatus in its own narrow interests without coming into conflict with other sections of capitalists. This led many people to the superficial conclusion that the State was above the battle, and able to intervene without regard to what the Americans describe as pressure-groups. It is this delusion that the T.U.C. perpetrates in its Report.

Indeed, its error is even more crass. It appears to think it can facilitate the creation of collective capitalist industrial organisations and yet preserve the power of the State machine to impose concern for the public welfare upon them. In addition to that it imagines it can identify the workers' organisations with this new capitalist collectivity without affecting the 'purity' of the State machine. Where, in these circumstances, do they think the Government is going to derive its power and authority to impose the public will – assuming one can be created in such circumstances?

DEMOCRATIC INDIGESTION

It is this theory of the immaculate conception of the State which lies at the root of the T.U.C.'s confusion. It leads them to believe it possible to build up a Fascist social content and adapt it to the forms of a modern political democracy. Of course, the result is democratic indigestion, which becomes chronic at a time of economic difficulty – as in Germany – and it finds the institutions of democracy too debilitated to put up an effective defence of itself when Fascist elements carry the logic of the situation to the point of liquidating the then moribund State apparatus.

The conclusion the T.U.C. should have reached is this: When collective industrial organisation is the only means by which the technical resources of industry can be properly utilised then the point has come for the socialisation of the industries concerned. It is not the democratic State apparatus which becomes redundant in those circumstances, but rather the private ownership of industry. The T.U.C. proposals attempt to place the benefits of collective organisation at the disposal of discredited private ownership. That is the very essence of the Corporate State. I am convinced the T.U.C. are not travelling that road with their eyes open. But it is scarcely comforting to know, when you reach the precipice, that you did so because your eyes were closed.

The Fatuity of Coalition – 13 June 1952

One of the most fascinating exercises is drawing up election programmes. It is also one of the most frustrating. It is not merely a problem of what to put in and what to leave out. The chief difficulty arises from the fact that a catalogue is not a description. If the enumeration of a list of specific proposals is not to have the effect of a banal anti-climax then they must be related organically to the central purposes they are intended to serve. The failure to appreciate the truth of this was partly responsible for the stark inadequacy of the Party's 1951 Election Manifesto. No one could be expected to be wildly enthusiastic about the mutualisation of insurance and the nationalisation of sugar, cement and water. When sufficient time has passed it may be possible to explain why we descended so steeply from the inspiring heights of the 1945 Election Programme.

The unity which binds the different parts of a programme together and gives it coherence and dignity is the philosophy that lies behind it. If this is clearly seen and firmly applied then the particular proposal, however prosaic in itself, receives illumination and stature from the main principles that led to its selection in the first place. Thus the proposal to nationalise water supplies did not merely flow from the greater efficiency and tidiness of a machinery for water conservation and distribution that more closely correspond with natural conditions. It was intimately related to the attack which will have to be made to increase food production from our own land.

This necessity is now sharply underlined by a worsening in the balance of payments crisis. If the over-riding importance of this is kept in mind then it reduces the resistance of certain municipalities to the parochial status to which it belongs. It is all very well for certain cities to take pride in their water undertakings. But this pride will not long survive the semi-starvation which awaits our urban populations if we continue to fail to bring about a healthier balance between urban and rural life.

I am led to these reflections because once more the Labour Party is in the throes of policy making. Nor have we as much time as some people seem to think. The authority of the Government is gravely inadequate to the crisis in British affairs. This will become increasingly apparent as the months go by.

In the meantime our self-confidence will be assailed from two separate directions. There are those who will suggest – they are already suggesting it – that we should set aside our distinctive Party approach to the national economic crisis and adopt a bi-partisan policy in domestic as well as in foreign matters. Once more we shall hear the familiar call for national unity, although nothing could be more irrelevant to the economic situation. A primitive tribal reaction to the difficulties of industry and finance is as much use as a tomahawk against an atom bomb.

If we are to surmount our economic difficulties it can only be at the expense of industrial and financial interests which are deeply entrenched. Unity with these can be achieved only by the abandonment of the very solutions most urgently needed. Indeed, the cry for national unity is their sole protection against the urgency of the national emergency.

In 1931 the Labour Party was swamped by the herd cries of the Old Men of the tribe. A National Government of all the talents was formed. But it solved nothing. And this was by the very nature of its being. It included within itself all those whose interests would have to be sacrificed to radical solutions. A typical example was the steel interest. Instead of modernising and expanding British steel production they demanded and got protection against steel imports. The result is that even today we are having to buy dollar steel, thus adding to our balance of payments deficit.

But, I may be told, are we not in danger of being once more swamped by a recurrence of the same herd panic and, therefore, would it not be much better to be inside and therefore have more influence on the course of events? There are two answers to that. First, there is little danger of a repetition of the 1931 pattern. Events do not repeat themselves with fidelity. In the second place, what is the use of a combination which denies the remedy? The result would be to engulf the Labour Party in the common failure and so expose the nation to the most desperate courses. Democratic processes demand the availability of alternative governments. If all those besmirch themselves in a combined futility then the stage is set for neo-fascist elements.

The second danger to which we shall be exposed comes from what may be called the Fresh Thinkers. I use capitals because I want to distinguish Fresh Thinking from the perfectly proper desire to keep our minds alert and adaptable. Perhaps a better term would be Socialist Revisionists. These are people who want to substitute novel remedies for the struggle for power in the state. They suggest that an extension of public ownership is an old-fashioned and outdated idea. Now that we are engaged once more in policy making it is essential that we should keep clear before us that one of the central principles of Socialism is the substitution of public for private ownership. There is no way around this.

The Tories understand that perfectly. That is why they are prepared to fight over transport and steel. The success of the Labour Government of 1945–50 consisted in the fact that it recognised the inner character of the struggle and kept firmly to the extent of its mandate.

The Socialist Revisionists are frightened by the administrative difficulties which accompany the nationalisation of major industries. These are the problems of transition and should be seen as such. They are the inevitable result of attempting a revolution by consent and especially of having to nationalise often with hostile elements in the industries concerned. Part of the remedy is probably a greater ruthlessness in the selection of our administrative agents and a wider application of the principle of industrial democracy.

Courage is as important in politics as ingenuity. So also is vision. And without a coherent philosophy with which to inform our conduct our courage will falter and we shall fumble amongst a variety of unrelated proposals. Each will have its own meretricious attraction but taken altogether they will fail to add up to what should be our distinctive Socialist contribution.

Can Parliament do it? – 26 November 1954

READER'S QUESTION: CAN SOCIALISM COME BY CONSTITUTIONAL METHODS?

There is no constitutional obstruction to the achievement of Socialism in Britain. In the last analysis the will of the House of Commons is supreme. The power of the House of Lords is one of delay and that has now been reduced to one year dating from the Second Reading of any bill in the House of Commons.

Some people talk of 'reforming' the House of Lords. They advocate a re-constituted Second Chamber, more rational and up-to-date than the existing one. If this were done, it would then be used as an argument in favour of giving it more power.

I am not suggesting that all who want a reformed Second Chamber are thinking of some way of thwarting or checking the will of the people as expressed in the House of Commons. But many of us feel that any attempt to bring the House of Lords 'up-to-date' carries with it the danger of a bicameral constitution and this usually confuses and obstructs the processes of legislation.

The long and often tedious passage of measures through all their stages in the House of Commons already provides sufficient time for reflection and amendment. The demand for 'second thoughts' usually conceals a wish for a second wind for the vested interests opposed to the legislation in question.

Where there is a written constitution that can be construed by the courts, limits are imposed on what can be done by the legislative assembly. There is always danger in such a situation.

The necessities of contemporary circumstances cannot always be expressed in the letter of the written constitution or anticipated when the constitution was made. It therefore sometimes happens that legislative action is caught in a clamp of legal terminology and the elected representatives of the people are compelled to wait whilst the lawyers argue the limits of their powers.

If the issue involved is sufficiently urgent, the danger of a collision between court and Parliament exists. The danger is sometimes avoided by a biased selection of the judges having the right of interpretation. This is an unhealthy relationship between Parliament and the judiciary. We are fortunate not to have this obstacle in our way.

In conclusion, we cannot say that we have inherited a constitution that bars the approach to Socialism. But, of course, this is assuming that Socialists do not raise barriers in their own spirit, that we pursue our policies with sufficient dedication and robustness.

Automation: The Socialist Answer – 8 July 1955

Automation is an unlovely word, but I suppose it has come to stay. Like the thing for which it stands, it compresses many meanings into one expression. Spelt out more extensively, it means the machine that manages and controls the machines. It carries the substitution of human labour by mechanical agencies a stage further.

Stated in these terms, it does not sound very disturbing. It is a process with which we have become familiar ever since the beginning of the Industrial Revolution. But the significance of automation lies in the enormous acceleration of the process.

The field of its operation is the factory, the office, the oil refinery; the impact of its arrival is in society and in the homes of the workers. The question for us is whether our society will be able to digest its impact without causing unnecessary suffering and dislocation.

Automation is the product of scientific and technical brilliance. Whether it becomes a benefit or a curse will depend on our collective intelligence. There is no need for alarm but there is every need for forethought and preparation.

***

At the moment there is altogether too much complacency. 'In the long run', we are told, 'the substitution of machines for human labour has brought great advantages'. Yes, but how long is the run? And, in the meantime, how high is the price, and who will be called on to pay it?

Our experiences, both remote and recent, provide no justification for smugness. We are still far from clearing up the mess caused by the early industrial revolution, as can be seen in all the older industrial centres of Europe.

The ugly, dreary, squalid, endless miles of back-to-back cottages and tenements, the careless dumps of industrial waste, the poisoned rivers, the senseless slaughter on our inadequate highways, the silted canals, and innumerable other appalling legacies of a failure of social and political adaptation to swift technical change – these all point to a breakdown of collective intelligence and will.

Technical maturity and political adolescence is the verdict any thoughtful person must pass on the history of the last two hundred years.

***

Are we any better prepared to assimilate the social impact of automation? There is no evidence of it as yet. On the contrary, the outlook could not be gloomier.

Britain has just emerged from a general election where the Tory principles of industrial and social anarchy were triumphant. Public ownership and the communal accountability that should accompany it are sneered at and derided, often by the same people as warn us of the new challenge of automation.

In the absence of the social controls that an extension of public ownership would give us, there is a demand for the complete restoration of price competition. And this is at the same time that the enormous capital outlay on automation will progressively squeeze out all smaller enterprises in the industries where the robots will take charge.

The movement towards monopoly is inevitable where great capital expenditure is needed. The real answer is not to attempt to restore the authority of the market where this is manifestly at variance with the needs of capital expansion but to restate, in modern terms, the proper relationship between public and private enterprise.

Where price-fixing arrangements are resorted to in an attempt to rig the market against consumers, and to maintain high profits with low productive efficiency, an insistence on the discipline of price competition should be an essential corollary of private enterprise.

But where capital investment is on a vast scale, as for instance in steel, oil and chemicals, the remedy is not an increase in market uncertainty but an extension of public responsibility by taking them into public ownership.

***

If the frontiers dividing private and public enterprise were drawn in this way, the relationship of both would be more intelligible and a new social synthesis made possible.

This is the path of democratic socialism as it is also the way to the smooth assimilation of automation into the national life.

It is also the most effective way to guide new investment where it is most needed in the national interest, in place of the clumsy, indiscriminating and often unjust manipulation of the bank rate.

If new sources of employment, and therefore of higher standards of consumption, are to be sought when automation causes labour displacement on the scale now anticipated, they can be found only by careful preparation beforehand, not by waiting until unemployment inflicts hardships on the workers.

The greater the scale of operations and the higher the capital expenditure involved, the slower is the pace of adaptation in the hands of private enterprise.

And it is the pace of economic and political adaptation that is the secret of dealing with the problems arising from automation.

It was the speed of technical advance that baffled 19th century Europe. Political and social institutions were geared to a slower tempo. The technical displacement of the industrial revolution found our forefathers unprepared.

It is no answer to point to the United States as an example of a more athletic private enterprise economy, for in that country the role of the state as an employer of labour and as a spender of money is much greater than many people imagine.

***

The retreat from Socialism, in places where it should be least expected, is therefore the abandonment of collective intelligence at the moment when it is most needed. It results in political indifference and social anarchy under conditions where automation demands sustained communal action.

A high level of employment has become a substitute for an intelligent direction of employment. If that continues we shall be cheated of some of the best results that can be expected from automation, because the economies achieved in the workshop will be wasted through lack of social planning.

An outstanding example of this is to be seen in our great urban sprawls where workers spend shorter hours in the workshop only to waste the time so gained in weary journeys to and from their places of employment, often more jaded by travelling than by the work itself.

In face of the experience of the last two hundred years there can be no excuse for us if automation finds us unprepared. If our individual experience is deficient, there are social memories to guide us. If our young men and women want a problem to get their teeth into, here it is.

Automation can be turned from a threat into a challenge and an opportunity. What we dare not do is to wait until it is upon us and then hope to muddle through.

Tory gamblers pour £1,500 million down the drain – 7 November 1958

Parliament has this week debated the country's economic situation. This discussion had for me a curious air of unreality. It was as though we were discussing some obscure aspects of a natural phenomenon into which human knowledge has so far only very dimly penetrated.

Yet, in sober fact, what we were really talking about was what men are consciously doing to themselves and to each other.

One would have thought that we would know what we are about. Certainly we might have been expected to estimate what would be the sum of our actions. But, in the capitalist societies of the West, the opposite is the case.

MYSTERY

Private economic adventure – miscalled 'private enterprise' – insists upon mystery. If the behaviour of market forces could be predicted, capitalism could not survive.

It depends for its survival on the deliberate cultivation of unpredictability. It is wholly opposed to the scientific spirit of the age, which strives to understand and to control what is happening around us.

A debate on economics among Western economists is rather like a peculiar kind of crystal gazing. They anxiously read the portents, trying to perceive the significance of almost wholly unknown phenomena. It is impossible to reconcile a belief in economic mystery with the search for predictability.

Some people say that the changes which have occurred in the economies of the West are so profound that they make them fundamentally different from what they were, say, at the turn of the century.

MARKET FORCES

Changes there have been, both qualitatively and quantitatively, but the essential and fundamental character of the system has remained unchanged.

Its dynamism is governed by the market forces. These in their turn are the product of individual economic decisions, often made without reference to each other.

The ablest of the capitalist economists are engaged in a persistent search to find out which particular piece of this chaotic economic system is most significant and likely to indicate reliable market trends.

So far they have not had much success. If they did succeed they would destroy that gambling and speculation upon the future which is the essence of an economy based on private economic adventure. You cannot gamble on the temperature of the water if the thermometer is always to hand.

Mr. Macleod, the Minister of Labour, has been speculating on the levels to which unemployment will rise before an improvement can be expected. But it is no more than a speculation, for the factors are outside his control.

REAL CRISIS

It is argued that the reason for this is that the British economy is subject to so many movements in world commerce. But this argument is not really valid. The same atmosphere of mystery surrounds the American economy, which is not affected by world trade to anything like the same extent.

Furthermore, important though they are, the figures of unemployment are no longer in themselves a true measure of the underlying crises in the Western economy. This crisis consists in the failure to bring the productive forces into full operation without almost certain price inflation.

The failure to tackle this problem, in the case of this country, has resulted during the last three to four years in stagnant production and, more recently, falling production. That is to say, the annual increment of wealth stopped more than three years ago.

To put it another way, increases in national wealth, made possible by new scientific and industrial techniques, have been blocked by the social and political peculiarities of capitalist society.

Various estimates have been made of the extent of this material loss. Conservative calculations put it as amounting to £1,500,000,000 a year. This is a sum equal to the total expenditure on arms.

Others have put it much higher. What the figure is for the United States, I don't know. It is certain to be of staggering proportions.

The old Marxist thesis stated that a time would be reached in the development of capitalist society when property relations would limit the expansion of the productive forces.

That analysis was too austere. The position today is not that capitalist society is plunged into an epic economic crisis. Instead, the economy functions but in an enfeebled condition, like a patient with a persistent low fever.

We are not in the old phase of boom and bust. There is never a real boom and never a real bust. There is only a persistent sabotage of productive potentialities.

CONFESSION

The main reason for the fact that the swing of the economic pendulum is not as violent as it once was is to be found in the fact that quasi-Socialist principles have been inserted into the economy.

Take, for example, this comment by the *Daily Telegraph* on the House of Commons economic debate: 'The main engine for expansion is to be the increase in investment of the public sector.

'This increase – decided on, the Chancellor has now revealed, some time in the summer – is already under way ... For the whole of 59/60 public investment should be 125 to 150 million pounds above last year's level of £1,425,000,000. Moreover, this increase, which is estimated to provide jobs for 150,000 workers over two years, is expected to fulfil two functions.

'First, it will take up the slack created by a probable fall in private investment next year; then, as it stimulates demand, it should start private investment rising again in the following year.'

This is a classic statement by an ultra-Conservative journal, of how past Socialist success is now relied upon to rescue capitalism committing suicide.

The only part of the economy which is under public control and where, consequently, the element of predictability exists, is in the public sector. Through this sector fresh demand can be inserted into the economy, bringing about an expansion of demand eventually reaching the inert private sector.

Thus a blood transfusion takes place from the Socialist to the private sector.

In Britain the public sector consists in the main of coal, electricity, roads, railways, airways and, to a partial extent only, steel; and, of course, the National Health Service and schools.

There is no mystery about what to do with these. In them, the levers are to our hand. They can be expanded or contracted at the public will and in the service of national objectives. They constitute the rational element in an otherwise irrational society.

In the ethos of capitalism, mystery is equated with liberty. Yet it is just in that part of the economy where conscious intention can be an instrument of economic activity that the British people are free to bring about an oasis of progress amidst the surrounding chaos.

Bevan on Parliament – 5 June 1959

Several newspapers, have been carrying a considerable amount of comment during the past few weeks about the relations between Parliament and the people. It is alleged that the prestige of Parliament has reached a low level.

It is difficult for one like myself, who has now spent more than 30 years in Parliament, to express an unprejudiced opinion. It is not easy to believe that the institution in which you have spent most of your life now commands so little interest.

A great deal of the criticism comes from journalists for whom exciting debates are one of the principal sources of their material. A crisis a day keeps the editor at bay, so to speak.

Of course, if there were any substance in these accusations it would indeed be very serious; serious not only for the British people themselves, but for all those, especially among the new nations, that have followed the example of Britain in creating and fostering parliamentary institutions.

The first question to ask is whether the charge is true; whether these allegations of a decline in the affection and esteem of the British people for their Parliament are well founded. I believe the fair answer to be that the reputation of Parliament as such stands as high as ever it did, but that this particular Parliament will go down in history as a pretty poor affair.

The truth is that after the crisis of 1956 this Parliament received a mortal wound. It has been carrying on a miserable existence ever since – tepid and uninspired, guttering up now and again into a feeble flame under the influence not of its own initiative, but of the sheer necessity to look alive somehow.

And this for one reason and one reason only. The Conservatives have hung on to parliamentary power from week to week, and month to month, in a sustained effort to repair their fortunes and seize a favourable opportunity to appeal to the country.

It may be said: who can blame them for that? After all, the governing party of the day is entitled to go to the country when it thinks it has a favourable chance of being returned by a majority.

This may well be so, but in the meantime, while that operation is being carried out, this particular Parliament is unrepresentative. It is scarcely likely that an electorate which has already rejected the Parliament of the day could continue to take an avid interest in its conduct.

For the Conservatives, the years since the conclusion of the Suez debacle have been a period of holding on. A Conservative MP, Mr. David Price, writing in last week's *Spectator*, threw considerable light on this aspect of the question.

He was writing about the tedium of long, boring debates, and of hanging around the corridors of the House of Commons merely in order to cast a vote, the purpose of which, as he himself said, was not so much to express an opinion on the issue in question, but to keep the Government going.

He quotes a statement by Mr. R. A. Butler. Where Mr. Butler made the Statement Mr. Price does not tell us, but it appears to have been made after he had been approached about the boredom and sufferings of his back bench supporters.

According to Mr. Price, Mr. Butler said, 'If we are to be realists, we must suffer a certain amount of discomfort in achieving that realism. I say this on purpose, because outside it may seem very bad, and inside it may seem ridiculous that we should hang about these passages. But if we were to relax, we might lose the very point of the struggle – that is, the preservation of power.'

So there we have it. Not in elegant prose, perhaps, but still sufficiently clearly to expose the nature of the Conservative attitude to politics.

For the Conservative, political power can be said to be almost an end in itself. The party's main object is to preserve the *status quo* in society. Its main strategy is to make concessions as belatedly and as grudgingly as possible, but with such dexterity as to preserve the reality of continuing power.

If the Conservative finds that his opponent has attracted support for this or that idea or reform, the tactic is not to oppose it outright, but to adopt as much of it, or appear to adopt as much of it, as takes the edge off the opposition assault. In this art the Conservatives are exceedingly skilful, but it cannot be said to make for dramatic clashes. Theirs is the art of avoiding sharp conflict, of muting and smothering the struggle, of encouraging the obscurity which makes the frontiers separating the two parties appear to merge into each other in a sort of grey mist.

In this they are powerfully assisted by the popular press, where the dissemination of ideas is always subordinated to gossip about personalities.

Judged against this background, what the critics are really saying is that Parliaments always tend to be listless, unexciting and unfruitful when they possess Conservative majorities.

A Tory Parliament is, therefore, a negative Parliament, unless it has the misfortune to be the occasion of a piece of tragic and colossal folly like the Suez adventure.

The critics of the present House of Commons might interest themselves in a comparison sufficiently recent to be a witness worth examining. Compare the Parliament of 1945 to 1950–51 with the Parliaments since.

Can anyone seriously say that the Parliament immediately after the war was listless, uninspired and unfruitful? Of course not. That Parliament concerned itself with almost every aspect of national life. However controversial its measures, they ignited the imagination of the country, aroused and held political interest, and by so doing, grounded Parliament in the esteem of the British people.

In the last analysis – and this is no extenuation of the Opposition – the vitality or lack of vitality of Parliament is an expression of the vitality of the ruling party.

Stabbing water is an unrewarding exercise.

2
LABOUR AND THE UNIONS
Wanted – A New Drive For Wages – 22 July 1938

THE LABOUR Movement will have to do something about the problem of unemployment, and that soon. For there is no doubt about it that we are failing to provide suitable agitational expression for the vast body of workers, who are either unemployed, or continually on the verge of unemployment.

This view was brought home to me with added force on Monday night, when we had one of our infrequent discussions on unemployment.

If there is any truth in the suggestion that the public are not concerned with the questions of Parliamentary Privilege, which were raised in the Sandys case, it is because Parliament is failing to stage with appropriate dramatic force the domestic and economic conditions which oppress millions of our fellow-countrymen.

BELOW 48/- A WEEK

When the Leader of the Labour Party rose to speak on Monday night it was to an almost empty House, with the exception of the Labour Benches, which were reasonably full. Why is this? It is because unemployment is too cheap.

It is not enough to say that in some parts of the country unemployed men and women are a little better off than they were, for the economic resources of the country are immeasurably superior to the position, even as recently as ten years ago, and can, therefore, afford to carry a much larger burden of unemployment.

One figure mentioned in the debate seemed to me to be the key to the situation. Queerly enough, it was a Conservative who mentioned it. He pointed out that 12,000,000 incomes in this country are below 48/- a week. There are roughly 18,000,000 workers employed in Great Britain.

I invite the reader to study these facts. What do they mean? They mean that unemployment is too cheap, because labour is too cheap. The standard of living of those who are in work is so low that the difference between their conditions and the conditions of those unemployed is not wide enough to shock the conscience of the nation.

At the same time, in many parts of the country, the low level of wages is keeping unemployment assistance lower still, although both are admittedly below the level of subsistence. So long as this condition of affairs persists, agitation among the unemployed is hampered.

In the House of Commons, on Monday night, Labour speakers naturally said that the way out was not to lower unemployment assistance, but to raise wages. But the fact must be faced that it is psychologically difficult, if not impossible, to raise unemployment assistance above the normal level of wages.

EXPOSED TO ATTACK

This state of affairs has already resulted in lowering the standards of the unemployed in South Wales, and Durham and other places, because of the appalling level of wages in East Anglia, Lancashire, and among the new industries of South and South-East England.

The divisional inspector for East Anglia reported that many applicants for assistance to the Board largely confined their efforts to find work to the local authorities, where the wages are 55/- per week.

All this means that the political section of the Labour Movement is doing its job better than the industrial section. The natural protectors of the unemployed are the employed, and the employed workers are exposing the unemployed to attack, because they are not sufficiently successful in maintaining their own wage standards.

The time has come for the trade unions to review their whole wage strategy, or it will become increasingly difficult to maintain the Parliamentary position. The agitation for family allowances is an ominous development, for it implies an attempt to redistribute the amount paid in wages to the working class, rather than to increase the total.

In this situation Parliamentary discussions on unemployment are listless and academic, lacking the driving power which comes from industrial agitation.

Over and over again discussion of the conditions of the unemployed spilled over into references to circumstances of the employed. In many ways this is all to the good, for it brings into relief the general standards of the working class.

REDUCING YOUR SHARE

Nevertheless, the situation has its dangers, both for the employed and unemployed. We are running into a trade depression; indeed, we are in it. That it has come so early is due partly to the fact that wages did not keep pace with rising production during the so-called boom. If the usual thing happens and wages are attacked, then an attack on unemployment benefit and assistance is almost certain to follow.

Indeed, the attack has already started. In almost seven thousand cases benefit and allowances are less than the amount provided by the scales, because the former would be above the wages earned by the applicants when they were in work.

The attack would have extended and widened if it were not for the fact that the restrictions of a balanced Budget have been temporarily removed by the requirements of the rearmament programme.

But there is already ample evidence to show that British capitalism is becoming alarmed by the financial outlook. The exponents of the rival schools of economies and inflation are raising their voices, and both have the same end, to reduce the share of the national income which falls to the workers.

TAKE THE OFFENSIVE

This situation should be anticipated by the leaders of the trade unions. The General Council of the Trades Union Congress should meet and prepare their plans. Part of this plan should be an all-round increase in wages, and to this end a national campaign should be launched, having for its objective industrial action, should the demand for increases be refused.

It would be a change from the wearisome political campaigns from which immediate action could not ensue. It would put labour on the offensive at a moment when it is about to be the subject of attack.

And it would bring an air of reality into Parliamentary discussions, which now consist of excellent speeches, thrown like stones into pools of silence.

A job for the trade unions – 23 August 1940

The builders of the Holy City built their walls with the sword in one hand and the trowel in the other. That story is the synopsis of all the history of mankind. Men have never been able to go about the ways of peace without keeping an eye on their enemies. War, either active or imminent, always troubled their minds and if they laid the sword aside for a moment it was never far away. It has therefore never been possible for men to turn away from the thoughts of war and dedicate themselves wholly to peaceful pursuits, for both war and peace are woven together inextricably in the pattern of human history. It would seem to follow from this that if in times of peace the shadow of war marches by our side, so also in time of war we must never abandon the dreams, ideals and ambitions of peace. To do so would be to give war a mastery it has never had.

Beware of the people who tell the workers that they must forget everything else and concentrate on the one task of beating the Nazis. This is to ask the workers to adopt an attitude of neutrality to every social question except fighting. It is a neutrality which does not exist in the City, the banks and the employer's office.

It seems to me that never was this more true than at present. The participation of Labour in the Government creates a situation of peculiar danger for all those associations and activities, Liberal, Labour, the trade unions, etc., from which have come the main social drives and inspirations of the 20th century. Of all these the most important are the trade unions. If they emerge from the war, fresh, vital, independent and retaining the respect of the workers, then the atrophy of the local Labour parties, which seems to have occurred throughout the country, will not prove fatal to the Labour Movement. But if, on the other hand, the trade unions share this atrophy, and not only become passive, but allow themselves to be drawn into the machinery of government, then the outlook for the future will be black indeed.

The problem is admittedly a difficult one – how is it possible to share responsibility with the Government for the conduct of the war and at the same time maintain active agitation among the masses of the workers?

The leader of a trade union is not like the director of a limited liability company – although I am bound to say that many of them look and behave as though they are. The leader of a trade union is primarily an agitator. When the functions of administration overwhelm those of agitation the trade union is beginning to die.

In the last war the situation was comparatively simple. The unions were kept alive by two factors. One was a strong anti-war element which fostered an independent attitude to many questions and resulted in considerable and successful struggles and agitations about wages and conditions. The other was the shop steward movement which helped to compensate by rank and file control for the Jingoism of many of the national leaders. From these two main streams many sympathetic activities sprang with the result that the end of the war saw the trade unions in a stronger position than they had ever enjoyed.

The situation today is not nearly so favourable on a long view. The trade unions, through their intimate association with the Labour Party, are in direct partnership with the Government and therefore to some extent become apologists for many unpopular features of the Government's policy. Further, the shop stewards hardly exist in many places, and where they do, they are more 'official' than they were.

Another factor which assists to 'passify' the unions is the many arrangements which exist by which membership of the union becomes almost automatic. There is always an element of danger in a situation where trade union dues flow in without the constant education which makes membership a voluntary and conscious decision. In addition to all these there is the over-centralisation of the unions, which reached an advanced stage before the war, and which enormously reinforces the powers of 'discipline' in the hands of the head offices. It is more difficult for the rank and file to rebel and easier for the bureaucracy to control.

Another powerful factor has been added recently in Mr. Bevin's policy of compulsory arbitration. Whatever may be said for it there can be no doubt that it stresses the administrative as against the agitational activities of the trade unions.

No one anxious for the future of the British trade unions and the welfare of progressive institutions can review all these conservative agencies without misgivings. If they are permitted to discharge themselves upon the Labour Movement without some counteracting force then we are heading for a situation in which the organisations of the Left will degenerate into lethargic and lumpish mechanisms, falling progressively out of touch with the actual life of the people. One breath of fascist reaction would blow them away.

In all this the key is the attitude of Labour to the Government. If Sir Walter Citrine's view prevails – which seems to be that the terms of an immutable Covenant were agreed upon between Labour and Mr. Churchill which fixed their mutual relations for the duration of the war – then Labour has received a set-back from which it cannot recover. I am sure his view does not represent the opinions of those who voted for Labour to enter the Government when it was discussed at the Bournemouth Conference. Most of the delegates there looked upon it as a provisional arrangement leading to more and more Labour control of the Government. Are Labour's relations to the Government to be static or dynamic?

Or the question can be varied slightly. Are the Labour Ministers the delegates of the Labour Movement within the Government or do they, with the rest of their colleagues, form the Government of Labour? The question is crucial. If they are the delegates of Labour then we have only a limited responsibility for what the Government does and we are entitled to be consulted by the Labour Ministers and to instruct them upon the policies which they should press upon the Government. This carries with it the right of agitation in the country and in Parliament so as to provide us with the influence essential to put forward our views.

What is quite intolerable is for the Labour Ministers to present to the Labour Movement a set of policies arrived at in Cabinet meetings in which they are in the minority and ask us to accept them as the inevitable price of our participation in the Government. That would be a method by which the Tory majority in the Government would govern the Labour Movement. Instead of introducing Labour principles into the Government it would be the infiltration of Labour by Tory principles. That is an intolerable position, fatal to the successful prosecution of the war and to the Labour Movement. We must make up our minds now before we reach a position of helplessness in the Government and impotence in the country.

M.P.s' tongues must be loosed – 21 March 1941

There are three great instruments of democratic expression in Britain: the B.B.C., the Press, and Parliament.

In a recent article in the *Tribune* I attempted to show that the newspapers of Great Britain can no longer be relied upon to do any other than express official views. Mr. Herbert Morrison, in shutting down the Daily Worker in the way he did, did much more than silence the organ of the Communist Party; he frightened the rest of the British daily press into subservience to Government pressure.

Then there is Parliament; an old Parliament elected more than five years ago on an issue so remote that it no longer has relevance to existing realities; composed of 615 members who may or who may not represent opinions in their constituencies; and a Parliament which is not refreshed or invigorated by the freshets of contested by-elections. Yet in the hands of these 615 men and women the ultimate authority and destiny of British democracy repose.

***

The vitality of Parliamentary institutions depends, to a very large extent, upon its close contact with public opinion, and that opinion is formed and communicated to it, and it in its turn educates and directs public opinion, by means of the newspapers and of the B.B.C. The stultification of the last two reduces Parliament to an isolation from normal association with the people to a dangerous extent.

To all these disabilities another one is added. There is now no official Opposition in Parliament to check and restrain the Government.

***

It is in these circumstances that the Parliamentary Labour Party has been considering, in the last few weeks, its attitude to those of its Members who have been claiming the right to independent judgment and action in the House of Commons.

The problem was brought to a head by the action of 19 Members of the Party in voting against the official policy of the Party on the second reading of the Determination of Needs Bill. The Party had decided to support the Bill, as embodying a compromise with the Conservative elements in the Government. The Members of the Party who supported the Bill complained bitterly that they were being put in a false position by the 19 Members who opposed. It is certainly true that the vast majority of the Party would have infinitely preferred to see the Household Means Test abolished, but they felt that the negotiations which had taken place behind the scenes, with the Conservatives in the Government, had resulted in such reforms as justified them in supporting the Bill.

The minority, on the other hand, contended that much more could have been obtained by greater pressure, and that in any case they should be allowed to state their case on the floor of the House of Commons, and to vote for their opinions in the lobby.

***

It is not necessary at this stage to consider the controversy over the Determination of Needs Bill as any other than an illustration of the crisis which has now been reached in deciding what is to be the role of Parliament throughout the war.

The majority point of view of the Parliamentary Labour Party is a simple one. They say: 'The Labour Party has decided to form part of the Government and to support it. The Parliamentary Party, meeting privately, decides what its policy should be on each question as it arises, and when it has done so, its decision should be binding upon all members of the Party in the House of Commons.'

Consequently, when Parliament assembles, it would do little more than register the compromises and decisions which have already been arrived at by the parties forming the Government behind the scenes. This would have the effect of abolishing the intimate relationship between a Member of Parliament and his constituents, and substituting for it the Party decisions arrived at in secret with the other elements forming the Government. Parliament would therefore become nothing more than a rubber stamp, registering and endorsing decisions, reached, not by public discussion, but by secret negotiation.

I do not wish to under-rate the strength of the orthodox point of view. It appeals, in the first instance, to Party loyalty. It claims that since the Labour Party agreed for its leaders to join the Government, those leaders must be supported by the Party in the House of Commons; otherwise the agreement upon which the Government is formed breaks down, and in the very midst of war national unity is impaired.

Those who take the opposite view say that Parliament itself would then become no longer a forum of public opinion, but a registrar, emptied of all reality, and merely giving its authority to conclusions that it had itself no part in shaping.

In this fashion political parties become the enemies of Parliamentary democracy. All the parties who form the Government for the purpose of prosecuting the war, do so because they have agreed upon what? That the war is necessary in order to defend democratic institutions against the Nazi menace. Nevertheless, they plead that national unity to achieve this purpose cannot be maintained unless Parliament itself agrees to become a rubber stamp.

Such a state of affairs is obviously intolerable.

***

But there is no insurmountable difficulty in this situation. When the Labour Party decided to join the Government of Mr. Churchill last Whitsun, we supported the decision. We are still of the same opinion. The co-operation of the great parties of the State is necessary to achieve the national effort required to defeat the Nazi designs. No writer in the *Tribune* desires the leaders of the Labour Party to withdraw from the Government, because if this happened, British resistance would soon disintegrate, and a Nazi victory would quickly occur.

At the same time, there is no reason why the Party leaders should not, at the Party meetings, secure official support for the policies of the Government. But at this point I depart from the orthodox point of view.

Individual members of Parliament should be free, whether they be Conservatives, Liberals or Labour, to express in open discussion what they consider is in the interest of their constituents and of the country. Party discipline should end at the point where it impinges upon Parliamentary liberty.

There can be no more steady and insidious undermining of the national war effort, than to enable Ministers of the Crown to believe that they need no longer face the possibility of hostile criticism in the House of Commons. When all else has gone this citadel should remain. There will be occasions when free and frank discussion in the House of Commons will expose Ministers to embarrassment, but it is better that Ministers should be embarrassed than that Parliament should die.

***

In Germany democracy died by the headsman's axe. In Britain it can by pernicious anaemia. The end is the same no matter what weapon is used. If those who put unstinted and blind obedience in Party decisions before free discussion in Parliament, get their way, in six months Parliament would sink so low that no one in Britain would be prepared to die to defend it.

Social institutions, like muscles, depend upon their use. If they are not used they become atrophied. No one wants to make any sacrifices for something which is dead. If the people of the country know that their representatives in Parliament are safeguarding their interests, and valiantly and fearlessly espousing their cause against the encroachments of bureaucratic appetite and the assertions of private property they will defend them, and regard Parliamentary institutions as being still worth the sacrifices they are called upon to make. But if their Members come back to them and excuse themselves for their negligence and silence on the ground that to have spoken would have been to violate their allegiance to their Parties, then the people of the country will reply: 'We did not enter this war for the purpose of preserving the Liberal Party, the Conservative Party, nor the Labour Party, but for the rights of ordinary men and women, through their representatives, to have their grievances redressed, their wrongs righted and their aspirations woven into the policies of the State.'

***

War demands supreme exertions and many sacrifices, but there is one sacrifice that war should never ask the nation to make, and that is to give up the prize for which alone the war is being fought.

To any Labour Delegate – 11 June 1943

Dear Comrade,

This letter has given me more trouble than anything I have attempted for many years. It was with great difficulty that I could persuade myself it was worth while writing it at all. What is the use, I said to myself, of trying to influence what the Labour Party Conference will do this Whitsun? It is clear what will happen. The application of the Communist Party for affiliation will be rejected. The Electoral Truce will be reaffirmed. Common Wealth will be put on the black list. The Beveridge Plan will be approved in its main outlines, and the Labour Ministers who voted against it will be assured of your confidence. To round it off, the declaration of the Executive on 'The Labour Party and the Future' will be adopted after a number of quite excellent speeches from the platform backed up by a few from the floor by carefully selected delegates. All this having been accomplished, you will go home and report what you have done to your local party. It is this deadly conviction that nothing I nor anyone else can say will alter your conduct that makes it so difficult for me to convince myself it is worth bothering to write to you at all.

Nevertheless, I am bound to do it because, in the absence of trying to change your point of view, I can see no alternative but to wait for the inevitable eclipse of Labour during my lifetime and the defeat, if not the destruction, of all the decent values to which I and so many like me have attached such dear hopes. It is this which makes the Labour Party Conference so important. Millions of people who know nothing about its machinery, nor of its devious cross-currents, look to it as the final expression of the creative forces in the political life of Great Britain. There is nothing else comparable with the Labour Party. It comprehends within itself all the organised elements of progressive thought and it articulates through its industrial and political activities the aspirations and traditions of the ordinary people of Britain. That is why you carry so heavy a responsibility, and that is why, despite so many misgivings, I ask you to consider one or two things before you leave the Conference behind you and return to your home.

THE ACHIEVEMENT OF POWER

The first thing you should do is to look at what you are asked to approve about the 'Labour Party and the Future.' With most of it you will be in enthusiastic agreement, as indeed, I am myself. But how is it to be accomplished? In co-operation with the Tories? Do you seriously believe that the Tories will help us to bring the 'essential means of production under public ownership and control,' and 'military authority under the effective control of an authority of world-wide scope?' Of course you don't. But if not, how does the leadership of the Party propose to accomplish these aims? Look through the whole of the proposals placed before you and ask yourself where, in any of them, is there the slightest suggestion of a way in which Labour might get the power to put its own plans into effect. I challenge you to find it. Nowhere in the dreary expanses of wasted paper produced by the Executive for the bemusement of the Conference is there the tiniest evidence of even an approach to the problem of how Labour is to get the power to put into practice what it preaches. If you don't want to face that question, then in the name of decency shut up and go home and don't go on deceiving people into thinking you are serious in what you say you want to do. There is nothing more damaging to democratic politics than to talk big and then act small. Labour has been doing that now for many years, and the result is cynical contempt among large numbers of workers. Listen to what the Executive says and what they ask you to approve:

> 'Unless victory leads to a new assurance of Peace, Prosperity and Democratic Liberty, we shall have lost the Peace; and without a wide extension of Socialist principle and a limitation of national sovereignty, that assurance will be impossible. Civilisation will not escape yet another disaster unless this war results in victory for our Socialist and Internationalist Cause. This is a conflict of principles, and Labour will strive with might and main to ensure that the right Cause will win.'

SAVING CIVILISATION

How? I bring you back again. How? I know it is very unpleasant to have to face it. If it is true – and I believe it is – that civilisation will not escape disaster unless the war results in victory for our Socialist and Internationalist

Cause, then it is proper to ask how do you propose to realise that victory? Ask your leaders. I promise you they haven't an answer. Look at the problem again. To save civilisation the war must end in a Socialist peace. That is what our leaders tell us. Right. The Tories won't help us to get that, and they are in a majority in the House of Commons. Nevertheless, we are told, we must continue to co-operate with the Tories. There is only one conclusion to that. It is obviously more important to co-operate with the Tories than it is to save civilisation. That is the kind of ridiculous position the Labour Party leadership has got itself and us into. Of course, they are not as silly as that position would seem to reveal them to be. They are not silly. They are either deceiving us or themselves. They go on mouthing Socialist phrases in which they no longer believe because it is necessary to do so in order to persuade you into continuing to give them your confidence. But these phrases now conflict so sharply with their practice that only a fool could be deceived. I am sorry to put these things so bluntly. But, really, the time has come to talk bluntly.

It is you who are really responsible. You will neither drop your Socialism nor fight for it. Consequently your leaders are compelled to use the language of Socialism although it is made nonsense of by what they actually do. It is more your hypocrisy than theirs. It is you who carry resolutions about the nationalisation of coal mines and then support the bastard arrangement under which miners are sent to gaol because they find their employment intolerable. It is you who talk big about a decent living for old age pensioners and then support the very leaders who refuse it. It is you who send men into the Army and then tolerate semi-starvation for their wives and children. It is you who weep about the workers being mangled in industry, and then applaud leaders who connive at rates of workmen's compensation which drives the recipients to the Poor Law. It is you who demand that international Socialism should be kept in the foreground of our declared aims, and then lavish maudlin praise on a Prime Minister and on leaders who put bloody-handed Darlan in power in North Africa, and made nonsense of everything we have said since the war began. There was a time when you could blame all these things on the Tories. You can still do it to some extent, but your own fingers are dirtied now. Your own leaders hold key positions in the Government, and for many of these things they are directly responsible. Therefore, I blame you, for you are the source of their power and influence. The lie is in your soul, for you will go on saying – saying what you don't really mean.

Now I know there is one good excuse you can advance for what you are doing. You can plead that the fault does not actually lie in you but rather it is embedded in the unfortunate fact that there is a Tory majority with whom we must perforce co-operate, so as to prevent a Nazi victory. Once that menace is removed, you say, then we will take the gloves off and deal once and for all with the Tories. Are you quite sure? Do you seriously think you can continue the Electoral Truce for five or six, or more, years, and then be ready to take the political field when the war is over? You know better than I do that the Truce is sucking the guts out of the movement. Our Party is no longer attracting the young people, and when that happens it is only a question of time before the end. Young people want to fight for what they believe, and the Labour Party doesn't fight. For many years it has substituted discipline for enthusiasm, until the Annual Conferences have degenerated into a stale parade of political marionettes.

LEADERS CHOSEN BY ENEMIES

If the Electoral Truce is continued much longer the Party will be forced to continue its association with the Tories, for it will be too weak to stand on its own feet. Indeed, the time will come when the Tories will kick it out contemptuously if it suits them to do so. The time has already arrived when the Labour Party is unable to defend its own representatives. Churchill kicked out the Deputy Leader of the Party – Mr. Arthur Greenwood – from the War Cabinet, where he was put by the Labour Party Conference at Bournemouth in 1940, and not even a whimper of protest has been raised on his behalf. If Churchill could do that last year, what will he do after the Party has further weakened itself by its fawning sycophancy? What can be said for a Party which allows its leaders to be chosen by its enemy? Yet that is what now occurs. Churchill is the leader of the Tory Party, and it is he who now chooses Labour's representatives in the Government. Do you wonder why I write so bitterly? It is not pleasant to have spent all one's life working for a cause which has sunk to such a pitiable condition.

But if you cherish the thought that when the war is over Labour will be able to recover its independence then you had better wake up. That is not the intention of many of your leaders. In what part of your leaders' recommendations to you are you asked to declare that when the war is over Labour will fight as an independent force? Of course, if you were asked so to declare you would unhesitatingly do so. That is precisely why you are not asked. Your leaders don't want to fight the Tories now, so they recommend the Electoral Truce. Some of them anticipate that they may desire to keep with the Tories when the war is over, so they don't want to be tied by a Conference resolution against it.

Consider the terms in which the Executive are recommending the Electoral Truce. They assert that it is necessary for Labour to stay in the Government now in order to prepare plans for the future. You observe how the argument shifts. At first it was necessary to join the Government in order to wage the war. Now we must stay in so as to plan the peace. The next stage is to continue the Coalition for the purpose of implementing the plan. Cannot you even now imagine the speeches that will be made to you? You will be told how absurd it is to instruct the Party leaders to co-operate with the Tories in the preparation of post-war plans and then to leave these to be spoiled by the Tories. Do you think this deduction is far-fetched? Well, if so, consider what Mr. Garro Jones, M.P., Parliamentary Secretary to the Ministry of Production, said at Oxford on June 4th last. It is headed 'Plans for Post-War Election,' and is taken from the *Daily Herald* of June 5th. Mr. Jones said:

> 'The most practicable programme which could be offered to the electors would be one based, in the main, on plans now being hammered out between Labour and Conservative Ministers in the Government and their experts. It would, of course, be open to the Labour Party to repudiate, if they so decided, the plans which their leaders had provisionally approved. If they did that, and decided to fight on the basis of purely Party programmes, the position of the Labour Ministers, who would necessarily be identified with the prepared policy, would be one of embarrassment, to say the least.'

Mr. Jones went on to say, 'In any case, the personality of the Prime Minister would certainly obscure, and might transcend, other issues.'

No one can complain about that speech. It is clear, it is logical, and it is brave. Garro Jones faces up to the issues you are hoping to dodge. At the same time that you are declaring that the preservation of peace and the future of civilisation depend upon the application of Socialist principles your leaders are presumably digging the grave of peace and civilisation in conjunction with their Tory colleagues in the Government. Unless, of course, the Tories have been converted to the application of Socialist principles after the war, in which case the simplest course would be to join the Tory Party and have real national unity.

Reflect a little on the position into which you are now being adroitly manoeuvred by certain of your leaders, and for heaven's sake don't say afterwards that you didn't know, because I am telling you now; and although I may not be able to sway your judgment, the facts should. You say to your leaders, stay in the Government and help Mr. Churchill to win the war. With no discernible reluctance your leaders agree. Then they say to you: But if we stay in the Government we must co-operate in the preparation of post-war plans, for we cannot leave everything to the last minute as it was left during the last war. That sounds reasonable, so the plans are got ready. But if you carry out your present intentions and fight the Tories when the General Election occurs, you will be fighting your own leaders' plans, not to speak of the glamour of Churchill whom you are helping to build up into a formidable Tory election asset.

JOCKEYED INTO SURRENDER

Therefore, face the fact that you are not being asked merely to confirm the Electoral Truce for the duration of the war. You are being jockeyed into the surrender of Labour's independence for an indefinite period. The irony is that some of those who are guilty don't even know what they are doing because their 'practical common sense' prevents them from looking more than two steps ahead.

What, then, should we do now? Leave the Government? Of course not. That would be open to the gravest misunderstanding in the country. What we should do is to make it clear that after the war we are going to recover our independence. In the meantime, we should recover our liberty to fight by-elections.

Having made our position clear, we should take our stand on some principle of fundamental importance, and, if necessary, leave the Government on it. Anything less vigorous will not give us back the initiative we have lost.

Coalition of the Left – 18 June 1943

Last week I addressed a letter to 'Any Labour Delegate.' This week I limit what I have to say to *some* Labour delegates. The reason is obvious to anyone who has watched the Labour Party Conference at work. It is clear that a number of delegates, mainly from the trade union sections, might just as well have been attending a darts club, or a Wings for Victory Week demonstration for all the Socialist intelligence they have displayed. I do not blame them for that. It is a normal feature of every Labour Party Conference, and it is part of the price we have to pay for the silly assumption that because a man pays his trade union dues he is thereby entitled to influence the decisions of a Party to which he has given less of his grey matter than he devotes to the local greyhound race or to the Derby. He rejoices, quite naturally, in a week's holiday in London, and he gawks with understandable thrills at the personal appearance of prominent political personages whose names he has seen in the daily newspapers. I sympathise with his pleasure, although I deplore the occasion for it. But I do not address myself to him because he is a subject for long term education, and that is not my purpose at present.

Nor do I address myself to those, more sophisticated delegates, who owe their wages, their status and their possibilities of future preferment to the maintenance of the Labour Party machine. They have their uses and they are indispensable to any form of organised social effort. But it is of no use talking to them, for the barriers of self-interest are too formidable to justify me in hoping that anything I can say will cause them to pause in their pedestrian devotion. The Russians have a word for them. They call them 'apparatchiks,' and the Russians should know, for they have produced an astonishing number of them all over the world.

Nor, again, do I address myself to what is usually called the 'Platform,' for they have a vested interest in the perpetuation of their own folly.

BURIAL EXPENSES

No, I speak to you, the aware and concerned Socialist, in the trade unions and in the local Labour Parties whose spirit must have been depressed by the monstrous farce of this Conference. I am writing this on Wednesday morning, before the debate on Communist affiliation, but it is already clear that the Conference promises no surprise decisions on any issue of importance. What I predicted last week has come to pass in every monotonous particular. The Electoral Truce has been confirmed with a smashing majority. Common Wealth has been proscribed after a perfunctory debate. The application of the Communist Party for affiliation will have been rejected before this appears in print, and the attitude of the Party towards the Beveridge Report has been proclaimed with quite bewildering ambiguity.

All these momentous issues have been voted upon after debates which reached a new low in Labour Conferences; and how could it be otherwise? All the opposition speakers knew beforehand that the unions would be against them, and they therefore made their speeches with the obvious consciousness that nothing they could say would influence the bovine, inert and irresponsible weight of the trade union vote.

I spoke to you bluntly last week. I am going to be even blunter this week. The trade unions are no longer paying affiliation fees to the Labour Party. They are paying its burial expenses. It is no consolation to realise that they are also responsible for its death.

CONTEMPT FOR PARLIAMENT

Consider the ignominy to which you were reduced over the issue of the Trade Disputes Act. The Chairman read out a long statement setting forth the history of the Act and the reasons which led to the Trades Union Congress' decision to defy the Government and accept the affiliation of the Civil Service Unions. For weeks past the national Press has been full of the implications of this action, for, of course, it is a direct defiance of the law, and it raises questions of such magnitude as might lead to the withdrawal of Labour from the Government. Nevertheless, the Trades Union Congress took this step without consulting either the Executive of the Party or the Parliamentary Labour Party. Since they took their decision they have met the Executive in order to make known their position, but to this day the Labour Members of Parliament have not been consulted about a matter which concerns them in the first instance.

There has never been an example in the history of the Labour Movement of such impudence and arrogance on the part of a number of trade union leaders who have become too big for their boots.

They have reduced the elected representatives of the people to the status of mere puppets. They show a contempt for Parliament which is only equalled by the leaders of the German Labour Front. Indeed, representative institutions in this country are in almost as much danger from the irresponsible power which is now being wielded by a small group of highly placed trades union officials as it is from Fascist elements lurking in British society.

I could give instance after instance of how the Trades Union Congress have usurped the proper functions of the Parliamentary Labour Party. But the point I want to stress here is that the Labour Conference was prevented from discussing a position which can easily develop to a point which would make complete nonsense of everything the Conference decided this week. Of course, the Executive of the Party connived at this affront to the Conference because its majority is composed of the stooges of the trades union leaders. Can anyone wonder why it is that in these circumstances the local Labour Parties are unable to recruit any considerable number of young men and women? Why should young people pour their energies into a Party where they would be the marionettes of a clique of trade union bosses who owe their power to the cunning with which they manipulate the social democratic machine?

Now I ask you to face this situation fearlessly. The problem facing us all is how to so manage our affairs that the industrial strength of Labour is reinforced by the idealism which resides in the political awakening of the younger generation. No one knows better than you that this week's Conference has done nothing more than to throw into sharp relief the urgency of that problem. All the discussions have been overshadowed by that issue. It has formed the background of the Conference, and it has not been resolved by the merely negative decisions to ban Common Wealth and refuse affiliation to the Communists.

FEDERATION

Some of you think that Labour can succeed by reasserting its independence after the war, and fighting the General Election on its existing basis and programme. You can put that out of your mind. That way lies complete disaster. If you toy with that idea too long you will end by going to the country as an adjunct of the present Coalition, and the Party will live on the sufferance of the Tories. The issue before us is how to mobilise all the forces of progress in this country and launch them at the forces of reaction now getting ready to take the field. The Tories will not, if they can help it, fight a General Election as the Tory Party. They will disguise themselves once more as Nationals.

What must Labour do to meet that challenge with a chance of success? The answer is clear. Labour must make itself the rallying point of a Left Centre combination. The reply to a Right Centre alignment gathered around the Tories is a Left Centre grouped around the Labour Party. How is this to be brought about? The first suggestion which occurs to the mind is a pact or agreement between all the potential elements, like the Communists, the I.L.P., Common Wealth, and such members of the Liberal Party as would co-operate. Attractive though that sounds, it can be ruled out at once because of the insurmountable difficulty of allocating to each a due proportion of Parliamentary seats. There would be no basis on which to proceed, and the squabble to find one would upset the infant alliance almost at birth.

But I beg of you not to lose heart immediately, for on our success so much depends. There is a way of building up the combination I am speaking of, and that is to make the Labour Party into a real Federation of like-minded groups. In short, the Labour Party should return to what it was in its origins, a federation of trade unions and Socialist parties. It is still that to some extent. The unions belong to the Party on a federated basis. The miners, the transport workers, etc., are all members of the Party in blocs, and not as individuals. There is also the Fabian Society. Indeed, the Communists, the members of the I.L.P., and many members of Common Wealth are already in the Labour Party in a certain sense to the extent that their members are trade unionists. It is one of the ironies of the Party that many of its decisions are manipulated from behind the scenes by people who don't belong to it. This applies particularly to the Communist Party. The unions are responsible for this situation by affiliating as industrial groups, but they insist on being the only affiliations of that sort, and doing so they bring the Party under the sort of robot control we have seen at this Conference.

One of the difficulties of affiliating the Communist Party has been the danger that it would be the only agency of individual recruitment apart from the local Labour Parties, and once the Communists were in they would tend to dominate these. The answer to that is to affiliate at the same time the natural antidotes to the Communists, in the shape of Common

Wealth, the I.L.P., and a Radical Liberal Group formed of Left Liberals. Naturally there would be fierce controversy between these different elements in the Labour Party, but there exists enough common ground between them to form the basis of a programme sufficient for our lifetime. One of the chief merits of this proposal is that it is now apparently the only way by which the Labour Party can be brought into contact with the younger generation. Each affiliated section would make its own distinctive appeal to the young people and the final result would be to pour their enthusiasm and vigour into the now inert and moribund Labour machine.

In the constituencies the problem of allocating seats would naturally solve itself, for the adopted Labour candidate, in each instance, would tend to be a member of the dominant affiliated group. The important thing to keep in mind all the time is that such a combination would transform the political situation and face the Tories with the task of finding an answer. The country is moving and will continue to move Left. The Tories need us. We don't need them. They have only one asset, and we are partly responsible for it. That is Churchill. But he is already an old man, and we shall witness quite a number of changes yet which will tend to reduce the glamour of his name to rational and manageable limits. I do not believe that the Tories could retain power in this country in face of the combination I have described. The statement of the Chairman of the Conference that Labour is looking forward to the day when it will regain its independence does not move me. We had independence right up to 1940. What we must now go out for is real power, not illusory independence.

IMAGINATION, TOLERANCE AND COURAGE

Now I know what I have suggested may not commend itself to you at first reading. But please don't reject it out of hand. Consider seriously the alternatives. There is not one of the existing Left groups that could win power in this country under its own steam. The sole result of competition between them will be to put reaction in power for another decade. I realise, for example, that the Communists will condemn the suggestion with their usual extravagance. I beg them to moderate their language a little on this occasion, because within six months they will have to revise their whole attitude to British politics or pass into rapid decline. The Communists have not yet received the full delayed-action effect of the winding-up of the Comintern.

When that reaches them they will find it necessary to revise the methods which have reduced them to futility in one country after another. In any case it is quite certain they must face two facts. One, they will not be taken into the Labour Party unaccompanied by other groups, and second, they have not the remotest chance of getting power in this country by themselves. They must, therefore, choose their allies.

Now that the Conference is over and you are returning to your home do not take with you a spirit of defeatism because of what has happened this week. There is much to depress I know, but there is also great hope. For everywhere young men and women are thinking of the future more seriously than ever before. What we need now is imagination, tolerance and courage, and if we can achieve these we can save our Movement and at the same time give to this country the moral leadership of the world.

Trade Unions and the Labour Party – 23 July 1943

Since the Whitsuntide Conference of the Labour Party a number of Trade Unions have been holding National Conferences. The results of these have surprised many people who are not familiar with the structure of the Labour Party. In some instances the union delegates reversed the decisions which were made on their behalf at the Labour Party Conference. On the face of it the general public are entitled to feel astonished that within a few weeks of the Annual Conference of the Labour Party, the big unions should be consulting their membership on the very questions about which their votes have already been cast. They are even more entitled to be amazed to find that the union leaders cast their votes, on some issues, against the wishes of their own members.

Nevertheless, to those of us who are acquainted with the relations between the Trade Unions and the Labour Party there is nothing surprising in the apparent frivolity with which the union leaders cast millions of votes on first-class issues without taking the trouble to find out what their members think about them. These recent examples only serve to bring into sharper relief a situation always bad, but which would now be farcical if it were not so full of peril for the future of progressive politics in Great Britain.

DECLINE IN MEMBERSHIP

First, however, let us get the essential facts straight. The Trades Union membership in this country is six million. Since the beginning of the war the number of trade unionists has increased steeply, due, of course, to the greater percentage of the population drawn into industry. This has more than offset the drain from industry into the armed forces. It must be understood that the unions do not affiliate to the Labour Party on the basis of their total industrial strength. Only those trade unionists who 'contract-in' to pay the political levy are affiliated to the Labour Party, and it is only in respect of these that the Trade Unions vote in the Labour Party. The rest of the membership of the Labour Party is drawn from the local Labour Parties, the Fabian Society, the Royal Arsenal Co-operative Society and a few other small affiliations of no great importance. I will give a few figures to show the distribution of the membership of the Labour Party. In 1942 the total individual membership of the Labour Party outside the Trade Unions was given at 423,000. This year it is given at 247,723, a reduction of 175,277. In 1942 the Trade Union affiliation was shown at 2,226,000, This year it had fallen to 2,206,209, a reduction of 19,791.

A number of interesting conclusions follow from a study of these figures. First, the Trade Unions fail to persuade more than about a third of their members to affiliate to the Labour Party.

Indeed, their political affiliation falls even as their industrial membership rises. It seems, therefore, that the unions are failing as a source of political education and recruitment. The unions would plead in extenuation that the Trades Disputes Act raises difficulties, in the way of 'contracting-in' their new members. But the fact still remains that as a venue of getting additional Labour Party members the unions cannot be relied upon. As a means of political identification with the contemporary political struggle the unions – as at present constituted and conducted – do not appeal to a growing number of industrial workers. This fact alone should begin to cause headaches to Labour people.

But the fall in individual membership is even more ominous. A decline of 175,277, or almost half in one year is calamitous. This means that, like the Trade Unions, the local Labour Parties also are ceasing to appeal to the present generation as an instrument of political agitation and struggle.

UNION DOMINATION

It will be argued that the local Labour Parties are among the first to suffer from the demands of the Services and the disturbance of the industrial population. This would be a sufficient answer if it were not for the fact that the Communist Party is winning new members in large numbers, and that this is the same period and condition when Common Wealth appears on the scene and also attracts a growing and enthusiastic following.

I shall be told that all, or most of this, is the result of the political truce, and that when the Labour Party is free to take independent action once more the situation will change and the Party become re-invigorated. It may be so, but I doubt it. The decline in Labour politics dates before the war. The period between 1931 and 1939 is the story of complete lack of resilience and adaptability on the part of the leadership of the Labour Party. It was already failing to attract the young in any numbers. The United Front and Popular Front campaigns, and the Civil War in Spain revealed the Labour Party like a ship, uncertain of its port, and drifting sluggishly along, at the mercy of any current, because its engines had stopped. What has now happened is that the Labour Party has come to anchor in the Coalition Government, and unless it takes care the engines will rust to the point when they will never start again. Coalitions are never kind to their Left members.

The outstanding fact is that the Labour Party is dominated utterly and completely by the Trade Unions, and consequently it is in the policy and conduct of the unions that an explanation for the condition of the Party must be sought.

The justification for Trade Union affiliation is that it provides the Labour Party with a broad industrial basis among the masses of working people, brings to Labour the invaluable advances of traditional loyalties and the refreshment of practical urgencies in everyday life. This is unquestionably the case, and it helps to explain why it is that the Labour Party has survived the mistakes of its leadership. But the facts I have already set out show that the Trade Unions no longer bring the impact of the masses to bear on the making of Labour policy. Each union is affiliated as a national body, and this has the effect of bringing the Party not so much under the control of the membership of the union as under the influence of its official apparatus. In short, the union as an institution is enfranchised within the Labour Party, but the union membership is not. The result is you get union politics, in which a handful of Trade Union leaders can move their votes about as on a chess board, until one day you wake up to find that their behaviour bears not the slightest relationship to what their members believe.

REMEDIES

It is this which is responsible for the fact that the Labour Party is compelled to take short views where the ability to take a long view is the very essence of successful political strategy. It may even be necessary for a political party to risk temporary eclipse as the price of fidelity to a principle, confident that time will reward its integrity. But the trade Union Leader is tied by nature of this function to day-to-day expedients, for he cannot expect his union to await 'far off interest of tears'. It is essentially this difference of function which makes it fatal to give the union, as an institution, an undue political weight through the personalities of its chief executives.

I cannot hope within the short compass of an article to exhaust the subject of the relations between the Labour Party and the Trade Unions, and I must therefore leave many important things unsaid and hurry on to a discussion of suggestions for a way out of the difficulties.

The first suggestion I make direct to trade unionists themselves. The remedy lies in their hands. All they have to do is to insist that their affiliation to the Labour Party should be exclusively through their Trade Union branch to the local divisional Labour Party and not through the head office of their Trade Union. This would have the immediate effect of shifting the centre of political gravity from the head office to the branch. The political funds of the unions would be distributed throughout their branches, and consequently political unity would be under the direct control of the rank and file. I am bound to warn you that the national leaders would fight this bitterly, for it would destroy their own political status and elevate that of the rank and file. After all there is nothing wrong in this, for why shouldn't he who pays the piper call the tune? If this were done the Labour Party would become a mass party at a stroke.

It may be urged against this proposal that many of the Trade Union branches would affiliate to nobody, and would therefore remain in spiritual isolation; or they want to affiliate to some other political organisation. Well, what of it? Nothing would have a more healthy effect on Labour than for the local Labour people to have to state their case at Trade Union branch meetings. The harvest in political education would be invaluable. It would convert the Trade Union branch into a forum of political discussion on all the vital issues of the day, and make it a place that young men and women would want to attend. This quite apart from the fact that the more affiliations the divisional party got the sounder its finances.

With these finances at their disposal the local Labour Parties would be able to select young men and women as Parliamentary candidates, and not be dependent upon 'official,' and often elderly, nominees possessing the meretricious attraction of commanding finances from the national political pools.

No Socialist can doubt that the unions are an essential, indeed an indispensable instrument in the social changes which must be made if we are to save ourselves. This makes it all the more necessary that they should be renovated so as to bring them under the control of the younger generation.

If this proposal is rejected and the unions insist on the Labour Party remaining a federation of affiliated bodies, then let it be wholly so and federate all the Left organisations which can legitimately claim to be such. I advocated this in a recent article in *Tribune*, and it brought me a mass of correspondence, most of it in support. A few of my correspondents complained that if this were done the Labour Parties would be swamped by the others. There is not the slightest reason why this should be so. On the contrary, their membership should increase, and their influence and status be protected by adequate representation on the national executive of the Labour Party.

UNITY

I know there are uncertain timid ones who shrink from bringing into the Labour Party all the elements now quarrelling with each other – the I.L.P., the Communist Party, Common Wealth and the Radical Liberals. I promise them they will have to face much more drastic things than that if we are to defeat the black reaction which is rearing itself once more in the world. There is one master word from which alone the moral reserves can be found to arm us for the struggles which lie ahead, and that is Unity. But those who make it their slogan refuse to face its implications. It is one of the ironies of politics – of which a few of us have been the victims as well as the witnesses – that it is quite often the very people who defend the 'purity' of their politics by refusing to join with others on the Left yet find no difficulty in making common cause with elements on the Right.

It is the peril of progressive forces just now that the poisons of decay and disintegration which rise from the dying social order invade and debilitate the organisations destined to save us. Let us strive to expel them and find amongst us common ground for a united effort.

Rubber stamp M.P.'s – 20 August 1943

Readers of *Tribune* are sufficiently well informed about the differences between the Government and the T.U.C. over the Trades Disputes Act of 1926. Nor should it be necessary for me to spend much time stating my own point of view. I took part in the campaign for the repeal of the Act, and I regard its existence as an affront to Labour and as an example of Tory class legislation. With the merits of the issue, consequently, I do not propose to concern myself in this Article. I intend to take this instance, and also the Bill for an amendment of the Workmen's Compensation Acts now before Parliament as illustrations of the relations which exist between the T.U.C. and the Labour Party in the field of parliamentary action.

In passing I feel bound to express a sense of humiliation at the complaints of the Labour Press with the attitude of the Tories on the question of the amendment of the Trades Disputes Act. It complains that the Tories show no gratitude for the co-operation which the trade unions have so generously given during the war, and last Sunday's *Reynold's* leader went so far as to chide Mr. Churchill for considering the interests of the Tory Party rather than the unity of the nation. Since when have labour reforms been advanced by the gratitude of the Tories, and in what instance has Mr. Churchill set aside the special claims of the Tory Party where these were in conflict with the welfare of the nation? It is the core of ruling class strategy to represent its sectional interests as synonymous with those of the nation; it has never meant anything else by national unity. It is its special technique to conceal the skull and crossbones of organised pelf behind the folds of the Union Jack. For Heaven's sake don't let Labour plead for improvements in its position as a reward for good behaviour. It is not only undignified, it is also fruitless.

It has always been the claim of speakers on Labour platforms that the Labour movement embraces both the industrial and political arms, and that both are welded in unison for the attainment of the objectives of the movement. In the main this claim was justified, but it is doubtful if it is any longer valid. In the two cases I have mentioned the industrial arm acted without consultation with the political. In the case of the Trades Disputes

Act the T.U.C. decided to challenge the Government without, in the first place, even informing the political side of their intention. In the case of the Workmen's Compensation Bill the General Council of the T.U.C. agreed to the terms of the Bill without consulting the Parliamentary Labour Party. Both these decisions are primarily political, for both involve parliamentary action.

It is quite true that the Trades Union Congress asserts its right to pronounce its policy on all questions, and allows an equal right to the Labour Party. So far so good; but the trade unions also dominate the Labour Party by way of block affiliation, as I pointed out in a recent article in *Tribune*. In practice, therefore, the decision of the trade unions becomes an instruction to the Parliamentary Labour Party, and a Labour Member of Parliament is reduced to the status of a rubber stamp endorsing the conclusions of the General Council of the T.U.C.

The last Conference of the Transport and General Workers Union made no bones about it. Its spokesmen roundly abused the Parliamentary Labour Party for daring to hesitate to pass into law the amendments to the Workmen's Compensation Act which the T.U.C. had negotiated over its head.

If this is to be the position then Labour election addresses in the future will be very much simplified. All they need say is that Labour candidates agree to pass such legislation in such terms as the General Council of the Trades Union Congress may at any time determine. For their part the Tory candidates will say the same for the Federation of British Industries, and we shall have merged quite peacefully into the Corporative State. All that will remain to be done will be to pass legislation enforcing trade union contributions from the pay packets of the workers and to incorporate the Federation of British Industries, with powers to make by-laws to regulate relations with its members. Both developments have already made a start. Is this the Brave New World the war is being fought to establish?

In such a world the trade unions will negotiate legislation directly with representatives of the employers; Parliament will be instructed to put its imprimatur on the final result.

This may appeal to some people whose knowledge of political first principles is of the most rudimentary nature, but it will certainly frighten those whose political insight is a little deeper. In practice it would lead to the enslavement of the workers. Political democracy in a society based on private property, is an instrument which exposes the rich to the attack of the poor. Any method which impedes or by-passes that attack is inimical to the poor, renders them weaker, and exempts the rich from having to justify its claims before the bar of an instructed public opinion.

Take the proposed amendment to the Workmen's Compensation Act as a case in point. It has been negotiated behind closed doors with the interests concerned. At no stage have the Government, the employers or the insurance companies been compelled to justify their attitude in open discussion.

The nature of the amendments bears the imprint of this procedure. No single man will have any increase in compensation rates for the first thirteen weeks, and after then only five shillings per week. That is to say, more than 90 per cent. of accidents in this class will carry no increase in compensation. Married men without children will have an immediate increase of five shillings, but no more until the expiry of thirteen weeks. In both cases a maximum of two-thirds of average weekly earnings will operate, so that in numerous instances even the suggested small increases will not wholly apply. Married men with children will be better off, for there is an increase to five shillings for each child up to fifteen years of age, but even here there is a maximum of seven-eighths of pre-accident average earnings. It will be difficult, if not impossible for many old-standing cases to qualify for an increase. There are small additions in certain categories of fatal accident. I have not enough space to examine all the proposals in detail, but I have explained enough to show the essential meanness of the proposals.

Consider their effect on the mining industry, for example, where it is already a problem to persuade the younger men to stay in the industry, much more so to prevail on young men to enter it. How can a Labour Member of Parliament justify such proposals to his constituents?

Nevertheless, he is in a dilemma. If he opposes the Bill he is attacked for holding up such advantages as it contains, whilst his chances of improving it during its passage through Parliament are heavily compromised because it has the approval of the T.U.C.

There is no reason why this conflict should have arisen between the Parliamentary Labour Party and the T.U.C. if the latter kept to its proper functions. Those are to make representations to the Government as to the nature of the improvements it desires in laws bearing on industrial questions. In no circumstances should it reach agreement with the Government, but should leave the Parliamentary side free to choose its own methods of making still further improvements when the proposals come before Parliament.

No other method is consistent with the maintenance of a Parliamentary democracy. Certainly there is no other way in which the people can maximise their strength in struggling with the forces of vested interests.

It would be tragic if the industrial and political organisations of Labour should come to loggerheads over an issue which is essentially so plain and so straightforward.

All set for a new thrust forward – 26 September 1952

No member of the Labour Party can complain that this year's annual conference has been neglected by the press. If publicity is akin to flattery, then we are indeed in danger of having our heads turned. Of course it is normal and natural that the Conference should take the centre of the national stage as its turn comes round. It is even more so this year, because the narrow margin that divides the Opposition from the Tories in Parliament gives a special edge to public interest. But there will be few of us who can recall such an intense, detailed, intimate and prolonged preoccupation with our affairs as we have experienced over the past twelve months.

In all this there is a significance we should be careful to understand. It would be a mistake to dismiss it merely as the usual journalistic hunt for exciting news and sensational headlines. There is that, and plenty of it, and, of course, we have had the customary personal abuse and smear campaigns.

NATURE OF THE SHIFT

These superficialities tend to obscure the real nature of the shift of emphasis which is now occurring in British politics. Today the centre of interest is not the differences between the two great parties but the conflicts, real and imaginary, inside the Labour movement. The quick reply that leaps to the lips is that 'splits' or the possibilities of splits make news, and are therefore likely to be written up with as much circumstantiality and lack of scruple for the truth as the character of the writer will allow.

But differences of opinion within the Tory Party don't arouse anything like the same interest, and they are very real indeed, as we at Westminster know quite well. Nor is it an answer to say that conflicts inside the Tory Party never really threaten it because of the passionate loyalty of the Tories to their party and class interests. Such a view is borne out neither by remote nor recent history.

UTMOST FIDELITY

The record of the Parliamentary Labour Party since 1945 especially, and certainly during the period of small majorities, has been one of the utmost fidelity whenever the survival of the party has been involved. Indeed so overwhelming is the appeal to unity inside the Labour Party that there is a real danger of its being used to smother critical views and experimental moods, which must be encouraged to express themselves if the party is continually to renew itself against the challenge of changing times and issues.

The fact is that the Tory Party arouses little interest and speculation about its factions, quarrels and differences because these don't add up to anything relevant to the problems of the times. It is moribund. The intellectual and political initiative has passed to Labour, and the interest taken in us is evidence of that fact. Everyone now knows that nothing can be expected of the Tories but a repetition of past mistakes and a barren rearguard fight in defence of vested interests and against innovations and progressive policies.

The year that has just gone shows clearly that this situation has many dangers for the Labour movement. Elements outside the Labour Party are now attempting to take a decisive part both in shaping policy and in selecting the persons to whom the party entrusts the carrying out of its plans.

With one of these elements, the Communist Party, we have long been familiar. We know both its methods and its intentions. It is because we know it so well that the Communist Party has been reduced to a nullity in British politics. Its relationship to democratic institutions is that of the death watch beetle. It is not a party. It is a conspiracy.

JUDGE BY MERIT

It bores and penetrates, enabling the institutions of democracy to maintain their outside appearance of solidity until the testing time arrives when the whole apparently massive structure collapses and the Communist alternative emerges, disciplined, ruthless and purposive. That is to say, when it does not prepare the way for the triumph of fascism.

But there has always been a danger that the Communist Party would triumph as much by negative as by positive means. They kill many a good cause by making it their own. But if they are allowed to do so it is our own fault. It is no answer to a proposal to say that it is backed by Communists. Nor that if it is adopted they would acclaim it as a victory for themselves.

If a number of reasonable propositions are rejected because those supporting them are otherwise unreasonable, then the latter will soon appear reasonable. Thus we should be weakening ourselves at the same time as we strengthen our enemies. Nor should we ever lose sight of the fact that nothing is more mentally enervating than to win easy votes by mobilising emotions against Communists.

Let us take proposals on their merits, and if they commend themselves to us adopt them. In this way we shall be in charge of them, for by rejecting them solely on account of their authors they will be in charge of us.

However it is not only the Communists who are now attempting to influence our decisions. As I have said, we know, or we should know, how to deal with them. A far greater danger arises from the extent to which Tories and quasi-Liberals, along with their newspapers, are taking a hand in our affairs.

This they do in a variety of ways. The first and the most immediately dangerous is the way in which they seek to inflame arguments about policy into personal feuds. Thus no argument is approached except against a background of personal rancour carefully built up over the years and fed by distortions and plain lies. It is regrettable that a number of national newspapers of high tradition are now engaged in this disreputable task.

To this a new technique is now added. It is the technique of the smear. Up to quite recently this has been a prominent feature of American politics. It has now been imported into this country and the British counterparts have proved adept. If we are on our guard against it this weapon also will be blunted, but we should be unwise if we disregarded its subtle menace.

But the long-term aim of this unprecedented invasion of Labour politics by forces from outside our ranks is not primarily the elevation of this or the demotion of that particular leader. Its chief aim is the destruction of Socialism within the Labour Party. The Tories can no longer rely upon Socialism being defeated by Tory electoral victories. The last two general elections and the present mood of the country have clearly demonstrated that.

THE REAL STRUGGLE

The polarisation of British politics is not therefore as between Labour and Tory. The formal struggle will still be expressed in those terms. But the real struggle is for the soul of the Labour Party – and that consists in our Socialist purpose. In the last analysis the financial and economic vested interests of Britain would be perforce content with a succession of Labour Governments if these could be persuaded to drop Socialist policies. They would be ready to abandon the sweets of office if all the other sweets were left them.

It must never be forgotten that the heart and centre of Socialism is public ownership. The Tories are under no delusion about this. That is why they attack nationalised transport and steel. The effective defence of these is to add to their number. It would indeed be a poor defence of nationalisation if we proved laggard in wishing to extend the same principles to other industries. There is no point at which we can hope to consolidate our gains until public ownership is established in the main industries and services.

All evidence of reluctance to extend public ownership will be taken as doubt of the wisdom of what we have already done. This was seen with heartening clarity by the last Trades Union Congress when it passed the resolution demanding plans for further nationalisation. This resolution, taken in conjunction with the demand for the abolition of charges on the Health Service, means that all is now set for a new thrust forward on a wide front.

A democratic Socialist Party in a period of transition is always menaced by the invasions to which I have referred. It will be overcome by them only if it loses faith in itself.

If it substitutes expedients for principles, witch hunts for argument, and a passive for an active unity, then it will fail and it will deserve to fail. Fortunately there is every evidence that the mood of the Labour Party is vigorous, self-reliant and forward-looking.

Why we lost West Derby – 3 December 1954

READER'S QUESTION: 'DO YOU ATTRIBUTE OUR DEFEAT AT WEST DERBY TO APATHY OR LACK OF A UNIFORM POLICY?'

That there was apathy at West Derby is obvious. The question is what caused it? Each of us will answer this question in accordance with his own attitude to party policy. Those who think there is nothing wrong with the policy will blame the result on fog or on divisions in the party or on a combination of both.

LET US LEAVE OUT THE FOG

It was there of course. But there will always be some local situation or incident in a by-election on which to fasten by way of excuse.

About divisions. Let us be clear about this. There will always be differences of opinion among the members of political parties under a parliamentary democracy. The problem of leadership is how to adjust those differences without destroying the underlying unity of aim which must be there if the party is to exist as an effective political force.

In my opinion there are two ways of doing this. The first is to lay most emphasis on the common factor which binds us together and marks us off from our opponents. By this we achieve unity of action and distinctiveness of purpose.

THE COMMON FACTOR

What is this common factor which Labour people share and which sharply distinguishes us from Tories? It is Socialism. If it is not that then there is nothing, at least nothing worth bothering about. The more we play it down the less we differ from our opponents and the less reason there is for people to vote for us to get the others out. If we blunt the edge of the socialist case so as to capture the elusive 'floating voter' we produce apathy, for that is nothing more than the recognition of the absence of real difference between the parties. The fight for socialism unites and excites the party. To mute the fight is to disunite and deflate it.

The second way follows from the first. Discipline is called in when enthusiasm goes out. What we need are fewer proscriptions and more prescriptions. More 'let's do this' and fewer 'don't do that'. We can easily afford differences of opinion if these are not carried to the point of mortal combat. Standing Orders are all right in their place. But remember they are 'Standing' Orders. What we want is TO MOVE.

Aneurin Bevan gives his verdict – 3 June 1955

The General Election did not result in the sweeping victory the Government had expected and predicted. Its majority of 59 is a comfortable enough margin with which to govern the country and work the parliamentary machine, but it is, at the same time, small enough to restrain the Tories from excessive rejoicing. Taken in conjunction with the fact that the combined vote of the other parties exceeded that of the Government, it is clear the country withheld the overwhelming approval the Tories had hoped for.

NO CHANGE?

If the Government had put forward a number of proposals for which it sought mandate, it would be easier to be precise about the programme of action the Tories had been authorised to carry out. But this the Tory spokesmen carefully refrained from doing. Therefore, if the Government can be said to have a mandate at all it can only be described as one to avoid any major change in policy.

But it is an open question whether the Tory Party will so interpret the result of the election. Diehard Tories may feel they are now free to carry denationalisation still further, to make still more reductions in taxation, and in these and many other ways widen the gap between classes.

No doubt this is the mood of a large number of Government supporters, and however much Sir Anthony Eden and his immediate friends might wish to do otherwise they may find themselves too weak to resist.

Some factors in the situation may help them to resist. The country is in the middle of a wave of industrial unrest. If this keeps on mounting and leads to a series of strikes, production will suffer and industrial discipline will still further relax.

If the election had revealed widespread popular support for the Government, this by itself would prove sufficient to enable it to keep industrial unrest within bounds. The Tory election strategy deliberately played for a quiet, indeed tepid, election. There is consequently no fund of popular enthusiasm on which the Government can draw, such as the Labour Government of 1945 enjoyed.

NO RESERVES

It is all very well to refuse to adopt a programme on national action that might have ignited the imagination of the country and mobilised the nation's energy. But the consequences of this meditative attitude is that the Government has parliamentary power but lacks the moral reserves that are the main asset of great popular movements.

Why did the Labour Party fail in its electoral challenge? There is no one simple answer. Unlike the Tories, Labour did have a programme. It might not have been exciting or ambitious, nevertheless it was definite and practical. It was designed to carry the nation further along the road that had been marked out during the remarkable period of office Labour had enjoyed in the early post-war years. Why, then, did it fail to catch popular imagination?

The first answer is that Labour was the victim of its own success. The work of national reconstruction carried out in the five years after the war undoubtedly resulted in removing many causes of popular discontent. The most potent cause of unrest – unemployment – no longer existed.

For the first time within living memory a Tory Government managed to exist for more than three years without inflicting mass unemployment on the country at the same time. A generation has grown up in Britain that has not experienced the frustration and privation of unemployment. The old keen edge of attack on capitalist society was therefore blunted. Youth does not build its case on the memory of the old. It has its own emotional attitude to contemporary society and this is not compounded of the elements that make up the mental climate of past generations.

MEMORIES

Its fears cannot be evoked by possibilities that lie outside its own experience. Communal memories are overlaid by a new situation and their influence grows ever more remote and vague. Labour is essentially the custodian of those memories and they were not sufficient in themselves to form the basis of mass appeal.

The second main cause for Labour's failure was its inability to distinguish itself sufficiently from many of the Government's own policies, particularly in the field of foreign affairs. In the absence of any domestic issue of comparable importance this proved decisive.

At every point, Labour's attack on Government policy was blunted by its own involvement in that same policy. On colonial questions, for example, Labour's idealism on colour questions was tainted by its behaviour towards Seretse Khama and the equivocation of its attitude to British Guiana and to S.E.A.T.O. When the British Labour delegation visited China, hopes were raised that the Labour Party was at last about to take an independent line in South-East Asia and to challenge the whole course of American policy there.

Instead, it allows its attitude to become blurred once more, for at the last Labour Party conference a resolution designed to end isolation of Peking China was opposed by the official leadership. Labour was in favour of bringing Peking China into the United Nations and at the same time supported American policy aimed at keeping her in diplomatic quarantine.

On the burning question of West German rearmament, Labour had shown itself deeply divided. The argument inside the party was fierce and prolonged. The official leadership devoted an expensive and intensive campaign to the task of trying to win over the rank and file to its own view. It succeeded in obtaining a technical majority. The chief result, however, was to publicise throughout the country the fact that on such a crucial issue Labour was lined up behind Eden.

This in its turn weakened Labour's case for a reduction in the period of national service. To argue for an inquiry into the length of national service, in the belief that the inquiry would disclose a case for reduction, can scarcely be described as a robust attitude. Why have the inquiry if you believe the case has already been made out?

In face of these facts, it is remarkable that the Labour vote was not lower. There is a disposition to argue that the Tory Party organisation was superior to Labour's. That is so. It usually is. And Labour should always make its electoral machine as efficient as possible.

But no amount of technical efficiency can make up for deficiencies in policy. There is increasing doubt as to whether electoral campaigns change many votes. The mood of the electorate is usually set by the behaviour of the political parties on day to day issues between elections.

All the election campaign can do is harvest that mood for good or ill. An efficient machine can give an added cutting edge during the campaign, but it is this thrust of the shaft that really matters and that is determined long before the election date is fixed.

The party programme should always be an organic continuation and expression of the alignment of the party as revealed by its normal conduct. A good programme can never be a satisfactory substitute for a weak will and a vacillating mind.

It is, perhaps, inevitable for a post mortem to be held on Labour's defeat, but those who hasten to take part in it should keep in mind that it is a living body they are about to examine. Bleeding as a form of healing has long since been rejected in medicine. It is no more effective in public affairs.

The Struggle for Socialism: Why I am standing for treasurer – 7 October 1955

There has been much speculation and some downright lying about my decision to accept nomination for the Treasurership of the Labour Party.

Although the charges have been made in newspapers commanding millions of readers daily, I prefer to use *Tribune* as the medium for the expression of my own views on the subject. I do this because I wish to address myself in the main to members of the Labour Party, who are after all the people chiefly concerned.

Others may also be interested. The Labour Party is the second great party in the state and some day will again probably be entrusted with the government of the nation. It is therefore altogether natural that the policy of the party and of its leaders should be a matter of interest to everyone.

This especially applies to the political enemies of the party. They have two objectives always in mind. The first is to defeat the Labour Party; the other, if the party wins, is to try and see to it that its policies differ as little as possible from their own. Thus they seek to govern either directly or by proxy.

In the past few years, ever since 1950 in fact, Labour's political opponents have achieved remarkable success along these lines.

Indeed, they were getting a little alarmed lest Tweedledum should look too little different from Tweedledee.

***

It is the essence of Conservative political strategy to see to it that the appearance of political conflict is maintained while in essence the parties act on similar assumptions. Trivial differences are blown up into major conflicts, which, when resolved, leave the existing pattern of society fundamentally what it was.

Apart from the incidents of personal rivalries it was this development which led to the atrophy of the great Liberal Party, and the Labour Party entered the political vacuum which was left. The Liberal Party failed to challenge the existing social order in any fundamental respect and the electorate turned to another party which seemed to offer a genuine alternative.

Dissatisfaction with the ruling party is only one of the reasons why people seek a change of government. The other and more positive one is the desire to see, not only new faces in government, but also a more adventurous approach to the problems of the day.

It was the failure to offer an arresting alternative that was responsible for Labour's failure to bring out its supporters in sufficient numbers at the last General Election.

Undoubtedly there were also faults of organisation and it is wise to try to remedy these. But defects of organisation would not by themselves have kept Labour voters from the polls, and indeed Labour's organisation would long before have been keyed up for battle if it had been battle that had been desired and not merely the substitution of one lot of Ministers for another.

It is necessary only to recall that the whole of Labour's organisation was engaged for months in an attempt to persuade the membership of the party to adopt a foreign policy in all essentials little different from that of the Tory Government. As it was in the field of colonial and foreign affairs that public interest was most engaged at the time, it is not surprising that large numbers of potential Labour voters could not be inspired to go to the polls.

We may deplore their unwillingness, but it is essential to understand it.

Now it might be argued that Labour failed because the majority of people had little fault to find with the life they lived under the Conservative Administration, and that Labour's previous achievements had redressed most, if not all, of their old grievances.

If that is true, the answer should be another period of Socialist education, not a muting of the Socialist challenge.

Even if it is true that the Tories had stolen our clothes, that is a reason for wearing clothes worth stealing, not for adopting the same cut as our enemy.

If people desire no change, they will vote Tory, for Toryism is the defence of orthodox and traditional values. If people wish to entrust society to its traditional defenders they will vote Tory. They will certainly not turn to a party which by definition is out to transform society.

This is as true for so-called middle class people as for workers. A middle class voter does not turn his back on his old values in order to find similar ones elsewhere. He might just as well stay where he is, and that is in the main what he does.

But is it the case that the Socialist pulse beats more feebly than it did among the mass of Labour members? That is not my experience, and I have spent as much time going round the country as most.

I have been convinced for a long time that the great bulk of the membership in the trade unions as well as in the divisional parties is ready for a new forward thrust. The truth is that this thrust has failed to find effective expression in the upper reaches of the party.

I believe that the reason for this is a change in the structure of the Party or, at least, a hardening of tendencies that always existed.

The decisive element in the government of the Labour Party has always been the trade unions. They find the money for financing the central machine. It is the constituency parties on the other hand on which the bulk of the political and money-raising work falls in the localities.

This division of function always carried with it the possibilities of friction, if not of actual conflict. But until recently the dangers were kept in check and the party maintained in a reasonable state of equilibrium and co-operation by virtue of the fact that the union leaders at the national level did not exercise their power in an absolute fashion.

Moreover, the unions would frequently group themselves in different alignments on the various issues coming before Conference; the 'block vote,' therefore, did not operate always one way. This helped to mitigate the resentment against it that was always felt by the delegates of constituency parties.

As a means of collecting the political voices of their members the unions are not by any means an ideal instrument. Huge minorities are denied expression in the vote because affiliation is at the national level. Also the conference of the unions cannot give sufficient time or facilities for the consideration of political issues. These are consequently often deferred or reserved to the union executives.

It is not surprising in these circumstances that the decisions reached are – to speak most charitably – only rough-and-ready approximations of rank and file opinion.

Within recent years this state of affairs has been made worse by the emergence of the supremacy of the general unions. These require the support of only one or other of the other most powerful unions to enable them completely to dominate the party. And this is precisely what has happened.

Unless the rest of the unions combine against them, the general unions get their own way in every case. Because of their structure this means in reality that it is the leaders of the general unions who are in effective control of the Labour Party. No one with experience of the inner working of the party can deny this.

Apart from the seven members of the National Executive directly elected by the divisional parties and the member representing the Co-operative section, the rest of the twenty-eight members are in the gift of the leaders of the general unions, including the women's section of the Executive.

No serious person can regard such a situation as other than unwholesome. It is a travesty of democracy.

Important unions have never been able to secure a member on to the E.C. Even if they did they would soon be off it unless their representatives adjusted their views to those of the general unions. I have seen illustrations of this evil principle more than once.

The concentration of power in a few hands is always bad, and even if the political policies of the general unions were progressive, their ascendancy within the Labour Party would not be justified.

Of course, if they had pressed for Socialist policies their unrepresentative character would long ago have been exposed by the Tory press. But because their power has been used to debilitate the Labour Party they have passed virtually uncriticised except when their authority appeared unequal to the task of maintaining industrial peace.

For example, when my own expulsion from the Parliamentary Labour Party was under discussion certain leaders of the general unions made known their views of what the verdict should be even before the jury had had time to weigh the evidence. Rarely has there been such an example of interference with the freedom of Members of Parliament.

When I dared to suggest that this came near to being a breach of Parliamentary privilege I was accused of claiming the protection that has been built up by centuries of struggle against just such attempts to prevent the representatives of the people from freely expressing their views.

When I was interrogated by members of the National Executive Sub-Committee appointed to interview me I was even asked to give assurances that I would not in future attack trade union leaders; and this in face of the fact that I was under constant attack by them and that I had usually refrained from answering back.

A few months earlier the Editorial Board of Tribune was asked by the National Executive to explain how they could reconcile criticisms of certain leaders of the general unions with their membership of the Labour Party.

It is on the office of Treasurer of the Party that this conflict is now concentrated. It is not a personal conflict except in so far as some people like to make it so.

On two recent occasions two candidates for the constituency section of the Executive failed to secure election. The members of the Labour Party are aware of what happened on both occasions. The office of Treasurer was used to make sure that those rejected by the constituency parties were found seats on the Executive.

In one instance a candidate rejected by the constituencies was nominated for the Treasurership; in the other a contest for the Treasurership was avoided only when another means was found for ensuring to the defeated candidate a place on the Executive. No better illustration could be required of the political importance attached to the post; and of course, the Treasurer, once appointed, plays a considerable part in determining general political policy.

It seemed to me that here was an opportunity to challenge the assumption that what the general unions desired must be accepted by the party. So I accepted nomination for the Treasurership knowing that when I did so I would be inviting implacable hostility from the most powerful persons in the party.

Before and since I have been accused of unbounded ambition. It is a curious charge. I would have thought that ambition consisted in coming to terms with the powerful and not in challenging them at the very centre of their power.

I knew that, at least for some years, my defeat was practically certain. But it seemed to me then as it seems to me now that the party will never regain its health until the stranglehold of bureaucracy is broken.

It has been suggested that the office of Treasurer is not the symbol of the struggle for a Socialist policy within the Labour Party. It is worth noting that that is not how the enemies of our party view it. The Tories had taken sides long ago and they have employed every artifice to make sure that orthodox opinion within the party shall prevail.

I am aware of the deep desire of the party for unity, especially against the background of our recent electoral defeat. But unity must be achieved on the basis of policies which will inspire the party to fight, and not by slurring over the issues that divide us.

The Labour Party must have as its aim the establishment of a Socialist society. Otherwise it will have no significance in the future life of the nation.

It is in that faith that I have fought and will continue to fight so long as I have the strength to do so.

Being very, very practical – 24 February 1956

Almost alone among European nations Great Britain enjoys – if that is the right expression – a simple political alignment. The Tory and Labour Parties face each other across the floor of the House of Commons unhampered by the presence of other contestants worrying their flanks.

True there is still a Liberal Party, but it is now a remnant, with a leader who owes his election to the support of Tory votes.

The Communist Party fails now to get a single candidate elected to the House of Commons. This is a singular fact not to be accounted for by the association in the public mind of the Communist party with the Soviet Union. Soviet Russia is by no means so unpopular with the working masses of Britain as to constitute an electoral liability decisive enough to cause the rejection of every Communist candidate.

The explanation is twofold. Partly the Communists have failed to adjust their tactics to the realities of parliamentary democracy. Partly they have been thwarted by the success of the Labour Party in mobilising the support of the traditional Left vote.

If the Communists had addressed themselves patiently over the years to the winning of votes among the electors they might by now have won a substantial footing in Parliament. But, apart from putting up a handful of 'fishing' candidates, they have pursued the policy of attempting to capture strategic positions in the Labour machine and in trying from time to time to get that machine to support this or that aspect of contemporary Russian policies.

In the trade union sectors of the Labour Movement they have met with a measure of success and they might yet win more. But the price they have paid for it is the almost complete absence of any coherent body of Communist doctrine which could be said to be relevant to the British political scene.

Both the main Parties in Britain have therefore been successful in ridding themselves or in preventing the rise of serious rivals. It might be thought, therefore, that the British people are fortunate in being able to choose between two clearly marked bodies of political doctrine expressing themselves in equally clearly delineated programmes of action. However that has not been the case, at least in recent years. The most curious feature of British politics today is the blurring of the demarcation lines between the parties. Those who wish to preserve the vitality of British political institutions should be seriously concerned.

Of course the Conservatives are not disturbed by this development. 'No politics' means conservative politics; political inertia favours the maintenance of the existing social order. But if the progressive party is to succeed it must challenge the assumptions, intellectual or emotional, on which the existing pattern of society is based.

Against those assumptions it must state its own conceptions of what society should be like and its own ideas of how those conceptions are to be put into effect.

It is therefore compelled, if it is to do its historic duty, to evolve a distinctive social philosophy by which it can be recognised, both by its opponents as well as by its supporters, and which is, at the same time, its own touchstone in all practical affairs.

To the extent that this Philosophical attitude pervades its thinking it will develop its own intuitive responses to concrete political and social situations so that it is spared the self-conscious behaviour of the mere 'doctrinaire'.

Our Labour Movement has been manoeuvred into a state of doubt about its socialism. Siren voices lull us into a condition of intellectual torpor. We are being advised to be 'practical', 'pragmatical' and 'realistic'.

For example, the *Observer* recently offered us this advice. I set it out at length for it is a perfect example of what I have been describing.

'The root cause of all these troubles,' it wrote, 'is that the disappearance of the clear black-and-white divisions of pre-war days has left behind a ferment of frustrated political emotion. On both sides there is a bewildered and fruitless search for the certainties, the tribal mythologies and the ideological zeal of the old days. To our mind these are gone for ever, and they are no great loss.

'The problems we in Britain face today are more often practical than ideological. And, in our opinion, two teams of cool hardworking pragmatists representing real differences of interest within the nation are more likely to find the right answers than opposed cohorts of ideological crusaders.'

'For our part', continued the writer, 'we hope that neither Sir Anthony nor Mr. Gaitskell, in the crucial months ahead, will waste time, worrying about the political Rip Van Winkles who want a simple faith. They should spend their thoughtful hours finding real solutions to real problems.'

At the time when this was being written the Tories were completing the 'pragmatical', 'practical' and 'non-ideological' sale of the British steel industry back to private ownership. The transaction has been put through with scarcely a whimper of protest from the Labour Movement. Indeed, a few ex-labour leaders are assisting in the process.

No one, so far, has suggested any 'pragmatical', 'practical' or 'non-ideological' reason for doing it. On the contrary, under public control and subsequent public ownership, the steel industry expanded and broke all records.

Has the editor of the *Observer* protested? Not one word.

A highly successful sector of the public domain is being sold back to those who made a mess of it, on profitable terms to them and to the City which is conducting the transfer.

Henceforward the capital appreciation of British steel will help to swell the inflation which is universally regarded as the chief 'practical' pre-occupation of Britain. Instead of being canalised to where they would do most good to production, the future profits from steel will go where private greed dictates.

Meanwhile Labour is advised to enter a sort of intellectual twilight, where it is expected to grope about, looking for 'practical' solutions to 'real' problems. For Labour, intellectual disarmament; for private interests, loot.

It is perhaps unnecessary to mention that the Editor of the *Observer* is Mr. David Astor. As far as I know the Astor family has no direct interest in steel. It may be that all they have is an 'ideological' identification with the private ownership of steel.

How to avoid shipwreck – 11 December 1959

The crisis through which the Labour Party is now passing will undoubtedly provide rich raw material for the political historian of the future. It would be idle to deny there is such a crisis.

Ever since the peak of 1945 Labour's position has declined. The victory of the Tories in the recent election was the third in a series.

In face of this gloomy record, searching questions are bound to be asked as to whether there is not something fundamentally wrong with Labour's policy and organisation. The discussion of these questions inevitably creates the impression that the Labour Party is disunited, torn by dissension and in danger of disintegration.

SUPERFICIAL

Nevertheless, that impression is superficial. It is the fate of Left Parties that they convey, from time to time, an appearance of internecine and, sometimes, even suicidal strife.

Unfortunately, it is also true that quite often the appearance corresponds to the reality, as we have seen in France and Italy. Where the winds of controversy are too strong and the ballast too light there is always the possibility of shipwreck.

In the past the Labour Party has always survived such storms because it is not only a party: it is also a movement.

That is to say, it is not only a voluntary organisation made up of individuals held together by certain ideas embodied in political programmes. It is also composed of institutions which were called into existence to satisfy perennial needs. So long as these needs persist, they form the ballast that serves to steady the Labour Party when ideological storms threaten its stability.

These institutions are the trade unions. They are so deeply embedded in the Labour Party that the whole complex structure, political and industrial, is spoken of not as a party but as a movement.

When the Co-operative movement is added, it is easy to see that it would be wholly wrong to look upon the British Labour Party as in any way comparable with political parties elsewhere, with the exception of the Scandinavian countries where the British model is repeated.

It is, therefore, not an accident that the Socialist parties of Norway, Denmark and Sweden possess the same hardy qualities of survival which have marked the history of British Labour for more than half a century.

But, although you must first survive before you can hope to succeed, survival is not of itself enough to sustain a political party. It must also believe in the possibility of winning a majority of the electorate to its side. It is just because three defeats in a row seem to be ruling out this prospect that the Labour movement has been re-examining some of its basic assumptions.

MORE FRUITFUL

In the few months ahead the examination is likely to be suspended but there can be no doubt of its renewal later on. When it does take place, it is certain to be more fruitful than recent discussions.

In the immediate aftermath of an electoral defeat too much attention is inevitably given to the character of the election campaign. But the lessons learned from one election are scarcely likely to be of much value in preparing for another, not only because of the passage of time but also because a future election is practically certain to be held in widely different conditions, concerned with new issues and in an emotional climate wholly unlike that of the past.

Indeed, it would be most unwise to carry too many conclusions into the future or we should find ourselves in the position of those Generals who begin every war as though it was merely a continuation of the last. If social and political conditions repeated themselves with enough fidelity to enable us to draw valid conclusions from them, politics would not be an art but a science.

LESS TRUE

All this is especially true of modern society where conditions are changing at such a pace that what was true of yesterday is less true of today and is likely to be wholly inapplicable to tomorrow.

All the same it would be a mistake to deduce from this that no guiding principles can claim our allegiance. If this were the case a political party would be like a ship at sea, not only without a compass but with no idea of what port to steer to.

The present controversy in the Labour Party has been described as a division between the pragmatists and the fundamentalists. This is a false description.

Those described as fundamentalists are people who believe that there are certain principles that have held good and are likely to hold good so long as British society is based in the main upon the institutions of private ownership.

They take the view that if the Labour Party was to abandon its main thesis of public ownership it would not differ in any important respect from the Tory Party. The only conflict would be about nuances, about semi-tones and half-tints. Such an attitude would take us back to the situation as it existed when the Liberal party was in its heyday.

In point of fact, if such a pragmatical attitude were to be adopted by the Labour Party there could not be the slightest major objection against a fusion between the Labour Party and the existing remnant of the old Liberal Party.

ARGUMENT

Political controversy would become once more an argument between Tweedledum and Tweedledee. The basic assumptions of the economic system would be accepted.

All that would be left would be an argument about whether the national revenues were being fairly apportioned as between the rewards of property and the claims of the social services.

If the Labour Party decided to adjust its policy in accordance with these ideas, it would be practically certain to wreck itself. The Party has been nurtured in the belief that its *raison d'etre* is a transformation of society.

It seeks, not social justice based upon the vitality of the principle of charity, but the planned organisation of the nation's economic life with priorities determined not by those in possession of supreme economic power but by the public conscience.

In short, the controversy is between those who want the mainsprings of economic power transferred to the community and those who believe that private enterprise should still remain supreme but that its worst characteristics should be modified by liberal ideas of justice and equality.

It is in fact a classic conflict. It has been going on in Western European society right throughout the first half of the twentieth century.

It is hardly likely to be settled in the Labour Party by an absolute victory of one side or the other, but what is quite certain is that the overwhelming majority of the Labour Party will not acquiesce in the jettisoning of the concept of progressive public ownership.

3

IDEAS, VALUES AND SOCIETY

A swastika nailed to England's mast – 24 June 1938

THE OUTSTANDING Parliamentary event of the week was the Debate on the bombing of British ships in the ports of Government Spain.

The Debate had been expected for some time. More than a week before the Leader of the Opposition gave notice to the Prime Minister that he intended to demand a day for the subject, so that the Government had plenty of time to prepare their case.

In the meantime the Government Press did its best to create a psychology favourable to the Prime Minister.

It is indeed a formidable array of newspapers which supports him. At no time in the past twenty years has a British Prime Minister had such powerful backing in the national Press in between elections. The papers, which opposed Stanley Baldwin on personal grounds, supported the new leader of the Conservative Party with feelings of profound relief that now both their personal and political sentiments were reconciled in the same man.

It is this support which has enabled the Prime Minister to survive incidents which might well have broken a man less powerfully entrenched in the organs of public opinion.

WHEN PREMIER LOOKED UNHAPPY

On this occasion the desire to assist their hero overshot the mark. They had seized on two issues on which to nurse public sentiment on behalf of the Prime Minister.

They gave great prominence to his attack on Mr. Geoffrey Mander on Monday night. Mr. Mander asked about a report which appeared in American and Canadian papers, containing statements which a 'high British authority' was alleged to have made to a number of American and Canadian newspapermen on the subject of foreign policy, in particular, regarding Czechoslovakia.

It was freely whispered that the 'high British authority' was the Prime Minister himself, and that the occasion was a lunch given by Lady Astor.

Chamberlain made a splenetic attack on Mander, for what he called 'mischief-making,' but he did not affirm or deny the interview.

On Tuesday, in the debate on the Spanish bombing, Sir Archibald Sinclair took the matter up again and quoted from the papers concerned. The Prime Minister looked obviously unhappy, but again he refused to answer any question about it, taking the view that he could not be expected to deal with every rumour associated with his name.

While this exchange was going on, Lady Astor and her son fluttered about, obviously in a state of nervous excitement, leaving their seats and conferring together outside, and again returning to their seats, alternatively pale with anxiety and red with confusion.

THEY RESTRAINED LADY ASTOR

It was clear that the Prime Minister and Captain Margesson were afraid that Lady Astor's volatile nature would cause her to make a statement, and indeed she half bobbed up to do so, but she was restrained in the end, and the incident passed off leaving many questions unanswered in the minds of the Members of the House.

But the damage is done to the Prime Minister, for his friends of the Press have focused attention on the incident and people will undoubtedly form their own conclusions.

The second nursing of the atmosphere by the Government Press concerned a more important issue.

Articles appeared from inspired sources stating that the Government had taken steps to bring about mediation in Spain between the two sides, and that, in order to enable Britain to approach Italy with prospects of success, France had agreed to close her Spanish frontier against the passage of all means of war.

We all expected the Prime Minister to make some statement on this, but to our astonishment he said nothing beyond a few general phrases, which are common form.

WORST SPEECH ON RECORD

It was far and away the worst speech the Prime Minister has made in his present office. I am not quite sure that it is not the worst speech ever made by a Prime Minister.

It followed upon a first-class effort by Philip Noel Baker. His speech was fully documented throughout, and on this occasion he did what he does not always do: he guarded himself against the obvious reply.

His illustrations were crisp, pertinent and less academic than usual. He was on top of his material, and he marshalled it into a crushing battery of attack.

At the conclusion, David Grenfell drove it home in a speech of sustained reasoning throughout.

In the middle of the debate, Mr Lloyd George intervened and made an attack on the policy of the Government, which was reminiscent of his best days.

Throughout it all the Prime Minister sat flushed and unhappy. In his own speech, he had said that he could do nothing to protect British sailors engaged in their lawful trade, other than send notes of protest to General Franco. He went on to say that the trade was attracting large profits, and that those who make them must do so at their own risk.

If the Prime Minister is prepared to carry this out everywhere he would have a great deal of support. Will he apply it to British oil in Mexico and in Trinidad? Did he do so to Metro-Vickers in Soviet Russia? Of course not. Why then does he apply it to Spain? Because it would be the Spanish Government who would be the sufferers, and that is just what Neville Chamberlain wants.

WHY THEY ARE MURDERED

He has staked his political reputation on the Agreement with Italy, and British seamen are being murdered so that his reputation may not suffer.
It is a condition of the agreement that it cannot come into operation until there is a settlement in Spain. In the minds of the British ruling class that means a victory for Franco. It is this that British diplomacy is out to achieve, and its purpose becomes more naked each day.

They have closed the French frontier to the Spanish Government. They now propose to close the ports, and this at the expense of the lives of British seamen.

UNDERLYING CLASS STRUGGLE

For those who still deny that the class struggle is the underlying motif of politics, I advise the study of two scenes. One, the House of Commons when the Vickers engineers were in prison in Russia, and the other last Tuesday when the House was discussing the deliberate murder of British seamen by Mussolini.

On the first occasion Sir Stafford Cripps was not allowed to speak for about ten minutes because of the howling of the 'Gentlemen of England' packed on the Tory benches. On Tuesday they cheered the Prime Minister when he said that he did not propose to protect the lives of our sailors against murder from the air.

The answer is clear. The Union Jack is regarded by them as a national flag only when their class interests and the nation's coincide. There is no protection for a British subject under the Union Jack unless he is promoting the interests of the British ruling class.

The ruling class of England are ready at any time to exchange the Union Jack for the Swastika should the change over be necessary to preserve their class privileges.

This is How Fascism is Born –
1 July 1938

One more month and Parliament will rise for the summer Recess. For the Government something like an obstacle race has begun. Can they reach the end of the Session without a major disaster?

At the moment three Ministers, including the Prime Minister, are in the dock. One is the subject of a Court action, and when the Court has finished with him the House of Commons will demand satisfaction. Another is in serious trouble for an obvious attempt to bully a Member who has proved embarrassing in his search for knowledge.

As for the Prime Minister himself, he is caught in the toils of his Italian policy, and the daily murder of British sailors punctuates his futile struggles.

HOME TO ROOST

The supporters of the Government are showing less and less enthusiasm for the Prime Minister's policy. The more intelligent and far-seeing of them realise that the prestige of Britain is receiving a hurt from which it will take her a long time to recover. The effect on the psychology of the British people is something that no Tory likes to think about.

After all, it is impossible to be indifferent to the sinking of British ships and the slaughter of British merchant sailors, and still expect the people to be indignant later on when some property interest is affected in other parts of the world. It will be difficult to convince the country that the Anglo-Persian pipe-line is a vital British interest and that British lives are not.

Many Tories fear that their leader is hatching a number of chickens which will come home to roost in a highly unpleasant manner. These are what one may call the enlightened Tories.

The true-blue ones are in hardly better shape. It is gall and wormwood to them to see the Union Jack flutter in the breeze alongside the Red Flag.

Yet this is what is happening more and more, for as the traditional policy of Britain is being sacrificed to the narrow class interests of the Tories, the conjunction of the Union Jack and the Red Flag in the hands of the Labour Party is reaching consummation. No doubt this situation has its dangers for the Labour Party, but for the Tories it is rank poison.

NATIONAL SYMBOLS

A ruling class succeeds by appearing to identify its class interests with the general interest, so that the people are involved in the defence of both at the same time. They are able to represent their sectional interests in terms of the national symbols, and the emotional and traditional associations with which these latter are seeped are an immense source of strength to the ruling class.

One of the main disadvantages besetting the working-class movement is that it appears to be in opposition to these sacred symbols of the State, and class feeling alone provides an insufficient source of emotional drive.

A moment is reached in the life of the ruling class when it can no longer afford the maintenance of the very traditions for which it formerly appeared to stand. These are the conceptions of liberty and progress, which it waved like flags in its own early battles.

The growing economic necessities of the ruling class cause it to attempt to swallow its own social progeny, and to desire those liberal institutions which were its early pride.

At this moment the working class steps forward in the defence of these liberal institutions and conceptions of liberty, for they are necessary to its own progress and ultimate victory.

Then begins the struggle for the symbols. In this struggle the working class reverses the position.

By defending the symbols which are universally revered, it identifies its own class interest with the general interest, and begins to draw strength from both sources.

The interests of the ruling class emerge more and more as a naked opposition to the general or national interest, and members of the ruling class begin to think more and more of their defence in military terms, and less and less in terms of constitutional action.

This is the supreme moment, for it is at this point that Fascism appears, having for its purpose the destruction of the constitution which hampers the maintenance of the ruling class. We saw this happen in Germany and in Spain, and we see the beginnings of it in Britain.

A NUISANCE?

Parliament becomes a nuisance to the ruling class, for it becomes progressively impossible to defend its conduct in accordance with traditional ideas. Thus attempts are made to suppress unpleasant questions in Parliament, and incidents like the Sandys affair occur more and more frequently.

The Government yearns for the Recess, because the arguments it advances in support of its policy are too thin to stand discussion, as in the case of the Prime Minister's defence of his Spanish policy.

The Press which supports the Government demands that Parliament should not discuss foreign policy so often, as we have seen recently, for in these discussions the Government is worsted.

The Ministers, who are called upon to defend in Parliament the policy to which the Government is committed, suffer in their personal prestige and no longer enjoy public confidence.

USED-UP REPUTATIONS

The Government Front Bench grows into a collection of used-up reputations, and the Prime Minister is at his wit's end to find Ministers to fill the more crucial positions. Those Ministers who most closely identified themselves with British policy find it distasteful to take responsibility for the neo-Fascist new line, and either resign, as in the case of Lord Robert Cecil and Anthony Eden, or go into open opposition, as in the cases of Winston Churchill and Sandys and others.

The names of the individuals who will fill the roles change in a bewildering way, but the roles themselves are fixed by the inexorable thrust of historical necessity.

Seen against the background of history the political scene takes on shape and form and meaning. Without it we are in a fumbling fuss of personal intrigue and political adventuring.

Freedom is not enough – 26 July 1940

A short time ago I listened to a broadcast by Attlee. He said one thing that stuck in my mind and I have been thinking about it off and on ever since. He referred to the general use of the term Quisling and told his listeners that for his part he preferred 'the old fashioned word traitor.' I daresay most of those who heard him agreed with him, but I wonder how many of them gave much thought to its significance?

To be quite frank about it I thought that remark of Attlee's revealed profoundly muddled thinking about the present situation.

Why is it that the present war has produced such a crop of Quislings or traitors, whichever you like to call them? Surely the answer is because the war has come to resemble more and more a civil war and not a war between nations. Are the alien anti-fascists in this country who are assisting Britain to defeat Germany traitors? Of course they are not. They are fighting for a set of ideas for which they believe Britain stands, just as in the same way there were men in Denmark, Norway, Belgium, Holland and France who believed in the things for which Hitler stands. And there are men in Britain who want Hitler to win because they believe he is trying to make the kind of world they want to see made.

It would be very foolish to under-estimate the appeal that the Fascism of Hitler and Mussolini makes to many minds in Europe today. It is not enough to dismiss them as gangsters. Of course they are that, but to say so does not answer the question: 'Why is it that the will of the populations they rule was so enfeebled that such abhorrent types came to power?' They won power because enough people wanted them to and because those who did not, did not hate them enough to stop them.

When so many gangsters, in so many nations, win supreme power in so short a time and with such ease, their appearance becomes a social problem of the first magnitude, and we must pass from abuse to an attempt at understanding. For unless we understand and make use of it we shall not win the war. We must find a different and better answer to the kind of problems that Fascism pretends to solve or people will go Fascist. Furthermore, unless our answer probes right down to the unspoken dreads, anxieties, frustrations, broken hopes and dim gropings of the European mind of today we shall fail to generate the temper which alone can oppose and overthrow the challenge of Fascism.

At the moment the spokesmen of this country offer Europe nothing but a return to the state of affairs which existed before the war. If we continue to do so the continent will turn away from us and come to regard us as its enemy.

The promise of Fascism to the tortured soul of Europe today is order, security, and exemption from the pain of personal decision. This generation has been afflicted by two major wars. Before and in between those wars it has been further tormented by the most complicated economic disorders ever known. Actual unemployment, or the fear of it, has oppressed the spirit of Europe during the whole of my life-time and its attendant poisons have infected every class in society and no nation has been immune. The artificial nationalisms of Central Europe made a crazy patchwork-quilt of a land-mass which was intrinsically one, but no peaceful way seemed to offer itself to bring about the necessary political unity.

In short the social machinery which men had been building up since the beginning of the industrial revolution got out of hand and it came to be realised that the most urgent problem of the day was to bring society once more under control. Men therefore longed for order, for only order could bring security; and for security men have always been prepared to give up freedom. It is in this mood and against this background that Fascism makes its fatally seductive appeal. It says to the tortured soul of Europe, 'Give up your freedom and in return we will give you security.' What is the answer Britain is making to that? She is saying, 'Cling to your freedom.' Back comes the question, 'What of security?'

Here is the dilemma. It is no use trying to escape it, for it takes no account of frontiers. It is the root problem today. Men love liberty but to be free they must first live. The old world made the two incompatible with each other in the conditions of the old world. All Fascism does is to make the divorce absolute.

If Great Britain is to oppose successfully the shameful betrayal of man's future that Fascism induces this generation to make it must answer that appeal, which comes from the hearts of all of us. Mankind says 'Give us a future in which we can be both secure and free and we will fight for it and if need be die for it, but don't ask us to fight for the restoration of the old world for it is not worth it and we won't do it.'

It was the merit of democratic socialism that it endeavoured to answer that appeal. It was the hope of all of us – though with much foreboding –

that the inclusion of socialists in the Government would have the effect of changing the major policies of Britain from a negative fight for the old values to a dynamic positive conception of the sort of world we are fighting to create. It is true that socialist ministers have done good work in the provision of labour and materials for the war effort. But in the realms of higher policy they have conspicuously failed.

This is bad enough but what is much worse is the fact that having put its leaders in the Government the whole socialist movement of this country is lying back waiting to see what will happen. Socialist propaganda has practically ceased, socialist organisation is in cold storage – all with the result that never has the intellectual vitality of the country been lower. When I speak to some prominent Labour people about this the reason they give me fills me with alarm. They say it is unwise to press socialist claims just now because it would impair if not rupture the implied bargain made by Labour when it joined the Government.

This means that we must be content to rally our people behind the war effort and at the same time ignore the profound psychological malaise which in so many countries has spewed up Fascism.

Consider how deeply defeatist such a view is. It means in effect that our property-owning partners in the Government will drift into Fascism. Apparently they will not accept such doses of Socialism as are necessary to inspire the people with the knowledge that when we leave the agony of war behind we shall emerge into a new kind of world in which the order and security promised by Fascism will be joined with the decent dignities and personal freedoms of a higher social order. This was the fear that led to the collapse of France and the enthronement of French reaction.

The story of the rise of Fascism in Europe is the story of Socialist or semi-socialist Governments who were too timid to press on with their socialist alternative for the future organisation of society and who were in consequence thrust aside by fascism. Fascism is not in itself a new order of society. It is the future refusing to be born. And it is timid socialism which refuses to give birth to the future. Fascism finds a spiritual, social and political vacuum and rushes in to fill it. There exists in Europe today a nostalgic yearning for security which endangers human liberty. Socialism courageously applied is the proper remedy.

I say to Churchill and Attlee: Take heed of the banners under which you lead us to battle. FREEDOM IS NOT ENOUGH.

Meaning of the Alliance – 18 July 1941

Many interpretations have been placed upon the alliance which has just been signed between the Soviet Union and Great Britain. Whatever may be said about them there is one interpretation which certainly is true. It means that Hitler has played his last card and lost. An attack upon the Soviet Union was the one card that Hitler held up his sleeve, to play against his enemies. He expected that when he marched his armies against the Soviet Union this action would confuse and divide the peoples of the United States of America and Great Britain.

I believe it is a mistake to suppose that the decision to fight the Soviet Union was based primarily upon military considerations. Hitler is in the first place a politician, and only in the second place a general. The world has been dazzled by the military successes of the German war machine. What has not been sufficiently appreciated is the extent to which these military successes were prepared by the most astute political manoeuvring.

The technique of Hitler is to strike only at nations which have either been isolated or weakened first of all by political and diplomatic intrigue. More than any single political leader outside the Soviet Union, he was deeply conscious of the antagonisms which exist in modern democratic capitalist society. He had every reason to suppose that the exploitation of these antagonisms would serve him to the end.

Over and over again he had proved its value. It was by exploiting the deep distrust and hatred of the Soviet Union which existed in France and Britain, that he broke up the combination of Powers which were brought together under the aegis of the League of Nations. Powerful opinion in France and Britain was persuaded that Hitler should be allowed to re-arm Germany, as the only bulwark between western capitalism and the tides of Bolshevism, which were fretfully lapping against the frontiers of the border states of central and eastern Europe.

***

Carefully nursing this hatred and distrust the Nazis were enabled to build the most formidable military machine of all time. Reactionary circles in France and Britain were deluded, cajoled and bemused into believing that this military machine was to be used against the Soviet Union, and Hitler ceaselessly fed this delusion.

The whole diplomacy of the last four or five years can be summed up in one sentence. The France of Daladier, and the England of Chamberlain whispered to Hitler, 'Go East, young man, go East,' and Stalin trumped their ace by signing with Germany the famous pact of 1939, saying in effect to Hitler, 'Go West, young man, go West.'

Having the choice between the solid edifice of the Soviet Union on the one side, and the ramshackle, class-ridden, inhibited structure of France and Britain on the other, Hitler decided to go west. And the result is what we all know. In less than two years, ten nations have fallen before the onslaught of the Nazi panzer divisions.

However, Great Britain summoned from her traditions, from her history, and from her robust fidelity to democratic principles, a resistance which astonished the world, and dumbfounded the Nazis. From the summer of 1940 to the summer of 1941 the common people of Great Britain defended themselves with such vigour and spirit and success against everything that the Nazis could bring to bear against them, that it became clear to Hitler and his advisers that the subjugation of Great Britain was going to be no easy task.

***

It was therefore natural in these circumstances that Hitler should have recourse once more to a device which had served him so well. He decided to return to the original motif of this Nazi movement and to launch an attack upon the Soviet Union.

There can now be no reasonable doubt that he had made diplomatic preparations before he launched the actual military attack. The visit of Hess to Great Britain was undoubtedly inspired by a desire to divide opinion here. There is no doubt also that he hoped, by making himself the great champion against Bolshevism, to whip up enthusiasm for his cause, not only among capitalist elements in Britain and America, but also among Catholics in all countries, taught for so many years to detest the alleged anti-religious policy of Russia.

Whatever may be the result of the titanic military struggle now taking place between the Soviet and Nazi armies, there can be no doubt that substantially Hitler's political move has failed. The alliance between Britain and Russia, if it means nothing else, does mean that the two countries hate the Nazis more than they distrust each other.

Naturally the reaction in America has not been quite so wholesome and there is evidence that American public opinion has been made temporarily less warm towards the Allied cause. But this is almost certainly only temporary, and the avalanche of American opinion towards support for Britain, which was well under way before the attack on the Soviet Union, will soon resume its onward sweep.

***

It is natural that political discussion is now largely centring around the significance of the Anglo-Soviet alliance. People are now discussing not only its effect on immediate military events, but its bearing on the Peace Treaty, and the kind of society which will emerge from it. One thing is already clear. The Soviet Union has been brought into the main stream of western democratic history. She will inevitably make her contribution towards the shape of future society. Her experience of economic planning, the conscious organisation of her productive life, the subordination of economic activity to wider social purposes, which have been essential characteristics of her economy, all are bound to have the most profound repercussions upon western thinking.

At the same time, the way in which the ordinary people of Great Britain and America have clung fiercely to traditional liberal conceptions of personal liberty, to the more spontaneous characteristics of social organisation, will bring to the world conference of the future those urbane, and I trust somewhat more civilised conceptions, which will help to modify the more austere contributions of the Soviet Union.

For here it must now be borne in upon the mind of our generation that the great task that faces us is, how can we reconcile the subordination of economic activities, to central state direction, without at the same time sacrificing those principles of personal choice, of personal liberty, and sanctities of private judgment, which are the most cherished contributions of the last 200 years of progress? Without planned economic organisation liberty cannot live. But planned economic organisation alone does not preserve liberty. The society of the future must bring forth both conceptions.

It is because the Soviet Union has made such massive contributions towards the one, and democratic society towards the other, that in their common co-operation, as much as in their immediate common sacrifice, lies the possibility of constructing a society in which it is safe to be free.

Wales – 20 October 1944

For many years Welsh Members of Parliament have clamoured for special consideration to be given to the claim of Wales. It was natural and inevitable that they should do so, for Welsh national sentiment is very strong, and so far from declining there is plenty of evidence of an upsurge of national self-consciousness even in those parts of Wales where Welsh is not the language of the home. People from other parts of the country are surprised when they visit Wales to find how many Welsh people still speak Welsh, and how strong and even passionate, is the love of the Welsh for their country, their culture, and their unique institutions.

In all this there is nothing to deplore. On the contrary, it is very much to the good that distinctive cultures, values, and institutions should flourish so as to counteract the appalling tendency of the times towards standardisation, regimentation and universal greyness. Furthermore, a wholesome patriotism should be cherished when it is the only custodian of these precious verisimilitudes, and multi-coloured flowerings of human experience. A passionate dedication to, and jealousy of, national cultures have inspired some of the noblest achievements of mankind, and we should lose touch with much that helps now to adorn our world if the super-state were allowed to obliterate all the differences which people have from each other.

There was therefore plenty of sympathy for Welsh M.P.s when they insisted on their right to have a Parliamentary Day set aside for the exclusive discussion of Wales and Welsh subjects. But we doubt whether the experiment should be repeated. Consideration for specific Welsh questions was inevitably overlaid by the intrusion of subjects which are common to England and Scotland. Coal and steel, agriculture and the location of industry, along with the fate of State factories are questions of national policy affecting the rest of the country as well as Wales and can be settled only by decisions which embrace all. To try and discuss them within the narrow limits of Wales or Scotland is an artificial framework.

In our opinion, therefore, Wales should hit on a more effective constitutional device for enabling Welsh life to be articulated on a national level. Nor do we believe this would be achieved by the appointment of a Secretary for Wales. Scotland possesses one already, but there are few Scottish Members of Parliament who will claim that Scotland benefits much thereby. Scotland has been partly denuded of her population whilst enjoying a Scottish Minister, equally with Wales, which does not possess one. The same is true of housing. Scotland suffers more than Wales in that respect.

In so far as Wales is different from England, it is the difference, and not the similarity, which requires special recognition and a special constitutional medium of expression. Wales is different, not in the fact that she possesses coal and steel, docks and harbours, factories and an intricate web of economic activities. These are part of the common life of the United Kingdom. She is different in that she has a language of her own, and an art and a culture, and an educational system and an excitement for things of the mind and spirit, which are wholly different from England and English ways. It is in the commonality of this difference that Wales has a claim for special recognition and where she should seek new forms of national life.

It would be a thousand pities if she allowed this uniqueness to be smothered in the bleak unsatisfactoriness of a Special Parliament Day.

The Parties' Line-up in Parliament – 1 December 1944

What will almost certainly prove the last Session of this Parliament has begun. Public attention will be focused on the programme of legislation outlined for it in the King's Speech. Some ingenuous souls may imagine that this is the programme Parliament will pass into law before the Election is held. That would be a mistake. The Election will be held when the Tories want it to be. If the programme is unfinished, or even not started, the Election will take place exactly at the time and in the circumstances the Tories decide will best serve their chances of success at the polls. Every other consideration will be subordinated to that. It is idle, therefore, to pay too much attention to the words Churchill will put in the King's mouth. At the best it is window dressing; at the worst it may prove a trap for the politically naïve.

It is more to the point to examine the relative positions of the Tory and Labour Parties as they near the end of their wartime collaboration. What is the mood in which both are preparing for the struggle for power? What is the respective armament each brings to the battle and how do they intend to deploy it?

THE CRUCIAL ELECTION

Some shallow critics pretend that both Parties will try to avoid power whilst appearing to try to get it. They base this silly reasoning on the ground that the immediate post-war situation will prove so difficult and intractable that the Party which gets a majority at the next Election is bound to lose it in the one following. Therefore, they say, the Election that matters is the one after this.

That argument conceals a secret desire to avoid power altogether. It expresses a profound debility of the political will, and where you find it among Labour people, it is the principle of democracy turned sour and become decadent. Furthermore, it is cynically immoral for it offers a pretence of choice to the people, and seeks then to cheat them of the reality whilst offering them the outward forms.

> *The crucial Election is the one immediately ahead of us, for upon it turns not only the future of this country but the fate of other countries as well, in so far as they are influenced by our decisions.*

The chief weapon in the arsenal of the Tory Party is the personality and alleged war record of the Prime Minister. *They hope the British people will accord Winston Churchill a vote of thanks and gratitude by putting the Tories back in power.* To this end every trick of publicity and every means of mass suggestion are devoted to presenting him to the people as the War Winner, the Master Strategist, the Greatest Parliamentary Orator, and the Architect of Allied Unity. *In this they are backed by a national Press more servile than we have ever been cursed with in our history. In this I make no exception. There is not a single national newspaper which emerges from the war with a clean record in this respect.*

For more than four years the British people have been denied objective criticism of Government policy. If a newspaper ventured to produce a discordant note in the universal symphony of adulation, it was either threatened with suppression or suborned by making its proprietor, or its managing director, a temporary Civil Servant. Where it could not be bullied it was bought by office. It is the pride of British journalism that neither proved necessary on many occasions.

It is difficult to call attention to these facts without exposing oneself to the charge of extreme personal bias. Nevertheless, it is essential to do so, because, when the Election comes, the British governing class will seek to perpetuate its power exploiting the Churchill myth so carefully and so unscrupulously built up. Mr. Ralph Assheton, the newly appointed Chairman of the Tory Party, has already given us a preview of what we can expect. On Saturday he ended his speech with these words:

> 'But what I believe we want above all in the years after the war is a strong Government, led by the great leader who has brought us through the storms and perils of war, and on whom we can rely to bring us back into the calmer waters of peace.'

The fidelity of the people in the years of war is to be rewarded by putting the whip back in the hands of their masters. It is the virtues of the people that ensnare them; not their vices.

SECOND TORY ASSET

The second asset of the Tory Party at the Election will be a universal desire for privacy and freedom of personal choice. This is the normal result of war and of any sustained collective effort. Human beings possess the attributes of the cat and the dog. They want to hunt in packs at one time, and to hunt alone at others. They are both gregarious and self-sufficient. They need the warmth of association and the withdrawals of private sanctity. They are capable of self-sacrifice for group needs, and of sacrificing the group interests for their own immediate desires. War insists from its onset on the nature of the dog, and the cat qualities are held in abeyance. When the war is over the cat nature demands satisfaction, and this takes the form of a romantic nostalgia for a life of freedom from the disciplines of State interference.

A return to normal conditions represents itself to the individual as a rejection of the restraints, controls and restrictions of war economy. The soldier wants off with his uniform, the housewife with coupons, the worker with Labour Exchange 'Directions,' and the small employer and the farmer with filling up forms and asking permissions from Government departments.

All this results in a general lethargy of the collective will. A call to continued State action is irrationally resented, and anyone who resists it easily becomes a champion of personal liberty.

Such a state of mind fits in ideally with Tory propaganda because the employer wants to regain control over his own property, and through it over his employees. The worker, engulfed in the full spate of his revulsion against hateful disciplines, mistakes the demands of the ruling class for what he himself feels he needs, and so he falls a ready victim to the carefully prepared propaganda of newspapers like the Beaverbrook Press.

I emphasise this matter of the mood of people because the Tory never addresses himself to the merits of political issues, but rather to the subjective attitudes and moods of the electorate. Let me quote again the Chairman of the Tory Party. He said:

> 'There is one control which is the most irksome of all, and that is the control of men and women, and whatever we may have to put up with during the war the one thing which all of us are anxious to regain is our right to work where we want, for whom we want, and at the job we want.'

What he really means is that the employer wants to employ who he wants, when he wants and at what pay he wants. Of course, this was a freedom which never really existed for millions of workers before the war, but the Tory Assheton is not concerned with the sociological fact, but rather with the pervasive public mood. The Tory fights with emotions not with facts, and if Labour is to win it must evoke an emotion superior to the one the Tory seeks to exploit.

What is that emotion? I will put it in a sentence, a colloquial sentence. It is the suspicion of being had. In a recent speech Sir Stafford Cripps used a form of words which were, on the face of it, obscure, and yet they were immediately understood by millions. He talked of 'They' and 'We.' Ordinary people are always suspicious of being 'Had.' Heaven knows they are completely justified. This is especially so just now in politics. What the Labour Party needs to do is to mobilise the 'We' against the 'They.' The first necessity is to inoculate the people against the Tory attack on their emotions, and this can be done by rousing their suspicions. We are still near enough to the last war to recall how 'They' had us then, and Winston Churchill was one of the 'They.' Old dogs don't learn new tricks, and Churchill remembers well enough how effective the trick was then not to try any other this time.

LABOUR NEEDS AN EMOTIONAL DRIVE

Labour, however, must realise that if the 'We' are to be mobilised against the 'They,' all the members of the 'We' must be in the same camp. This means that the Labour Party should be ready to come to terms with all those sections and Parties that can be properly described as belonging to the 'We.' The details of their respective programmes are less important than the fact that, in the mind of the mass of people, they belong to the same emotional grouping. We must never lose sight of the over-riding fact that what Labour needs is an emotional drive that swamps the insidious and dangerous propaganda of the Tories.

The next thing Labour needs is an attitude of self-confidence. At the moment this is completely lacking at the higher levels of Party leadership. Take, for example, the approach to suggested legislation. On behalf of the Parliamentary Party, Arthur Greenwood has demanded that the Coalition Government should implement its White Paper on Social Insurance before the dissolution of Parliament. That is a most defeatist attitude.

As I have already pointed out, it will have no effect on the date of the Election, because that will be held when the Tories want, notwithstanding the state of the Parliamentary timetable. As soon as Churchill is able to parade as the victor of the European War the Election will take place, and the merits of this or that scheme will be swamped in the emotions of the time. Furthermore, the passage of the necessary Bills will be punctuated by a series of crises within the Parliamentary Labour Party, because a number of us are not prepared to perpetrate the fraud of the White Paper as though it is a piece of Socialist legislation.

There are three aspects in which the White Paper is bound to produce dissension in Labour ranks: the distribution of the financial burden between rich and poor, the children's allowances, and the refusal of the Government to take into consideration the cost of living in its bearing on the level of benefits. That would mean protracted debates, bitter friction, and the postponement of the Election until the autumn of 1945. Even if it were practicable it would injure the unity of Labour.

A self-confident Labour Party would not bother at this late hour about begging the Tories to pass this or that bit of ameliorative legislation. All that would flow from a Labour victory at the Election, and that should be our sole target.

The Labour Party has decided to break with the Coalition. That puts us in the position of challenger, and it is not consistent with such a role to appear shy of hastening the battle.

The time has, therefore, come for Labour to take up a positive attitude. The compromises, shifts, and half-meanings into which it has been led by four and a half years of collaboration with the Tories should be ruthlessly sloughed like an old and dirty skin. Or, to change the metaphor, they should be cast aside like a soiled glove, as the Tories will cast aside any Labour Minister, when they have finished with him, who is foolish enough to want to continue in their company.

When the Labour Party Conference meets in December the Labour delegates will want to be assured that we are not going into a mock fight on our side. The first guarantee of that is a clear pledge that whatever the result of the Election the days of Coalition are over. There are sinister rumours to the effect that it will be re-formed after the Election; rumours fed by the equivocal speech of Shinwell's about retaining Churchill as Defence Minister for the war with Japan. We shall require the guarantee not only from the leadership collectively, but from the leaders individually. We don't want to be led by men who might be suspected – however unjustifiably – of having one foot in the other camp.

Led by a resolute leadership, inspired by the knowledge of what can be accomplished, and conscious of all that depends on our efforts, we should now prepare for the struggle for power. What we want, if we but want it enough, we can win.

July 5th and the Socialist Advance – 2 July 1948

WHAT RELATIONSHIP DO YOU SEE BETWEEN THE SOCIAL REFORMS TO BE INTRODUCED ON JULY 5TH AND THE GENERAL PROGRAMME OF SOCIALIST ADVANCE?

The Socialist Movement has advanced on three fronts. Each advance has been based upon a philosophical appreciation of the relationship of the working-class in the modern world towards modern society.

In the first case, the aim has been to increase the share of the available social product by way of higher wages and salaries. In that activity the trade union movement has been the spearhead. During the past century very considerable progress has been made, and the trade union movement has now an established position in society. This part of the front was obviously limited, because the assault was directed not to bringing about a transformation in the structure of society, but to winning a more agreeable place for the workers in the existing structure.

On the second front we aimed at the transference of power by the transition from private to public ownership of the forces of production. Here we have made some headway in Great Britain in the last three years, but, of course, there is still a long way to go. We have transferred coal, transport, electricity, and gas. We are about to transfer steel. This is a fundamental change, because it is a transference of power.

The third front – and the one which has its roots more deeply in Socialist philosophy than any other – is what we might call the distributivist front, that is, the slow destruction of the inequalities and disadvantages arising from the unequal possession of property and the unequal possession of individual strengths and opportunities.

HOW MUCH DO YOU THINK THE NEW SCHEMES SATISFY THE SOCIALIST IDEAL OF AN ADVANCE TOWARDS EQUALITY?

The most important feature of the social services of Great Britain is the advance which they make possible on the distributivist front – what Marx called the 'withering away' of wages by the reward according to people's needs. This is done partly by the development of the environmental services, with which we are so familiar in this country that we do not realise the impact they have on the life of the community – sewage, modern water supplies, sanitation, scavenging, proper roadways, and all the other governmental services of that sort which are mainly responsible for the great improvements made in public health.

Another category is provided by the direct social services like old age pensions, housing, widows' pensions, family allowances, school feeding, national insurance from July 5th, assistance of various kinds under the National Assistance Bill, the Children's Bill, and now the Health Act.

The effect of all these measures, taken in totality, is to iron out the differences between one citizen and another which arise as a consequence of the anomalies of the wages system. If the wages system alone was the sole means – as, to a great degree, in America – whereby the social product reached the individual citizen, it would reach him as unequally as the wages are unequal. But social services give people a share of the national product in accordance with their need, and thus emphasise the distributivist aspect of the Socialist advance. This advance is, in fact, undermining the wages system. The wages system is maintained as a stimulus to production, a traditional relationship between the worker and his industry; but distributivist activities undermine the worst consequences of the inequality.

*

The National Health Act does this much more effectively than any other part of the social service system, because it is not based on contributions. It is on the financial side a vast redistribution of national income. On the active and administrative side, it brings to the individual citizen all the battery of modern medicine, irrespective of the individual's means. Furthermore, it is not only distributivist, but it is perfectly democratic, because it democratises the social consumption of the recent advances in medicine, and it destroys the money barrier which inevitably existed in orthodox capitalist society between the doctor and his patient.

The insistence which Socialists lay upon the development of this distributivist service sharply distinguishes the Labour Movement from the Tories. The Tories are laying increasing emphasis upon what they call 'property-owning democracy.' They want the consumption of the individual citizen always to be governed by the amount of property he possesses. The more property he has got, the higher his consumption. The extension of the social services ignores that property qualification, and insists on the equality of the individual citizen as such.

Here, then, is the main line of advance, whereby we are withering away the disabilities of the wages system, and it can be regarded in any respects as the most revolutionary feature of the British Socialist programme.

Where you speak of national insurance, the element of distributivism is not so marked. The element of equality is still there, of course, because the benefits are equal; but as a very large proportion of the financing of the scheme is provided by the workers themselves, the distributivist element is to some extent modified. In all the other social services, however, which are financed by taxation and by local rates, the central money pool from which they are financed is strictly related to the earnings of the taxed individuals. The distributivist element is most marked.

It is not yet possible to express in arithmetical terms the value in weekly wages of the totality of social services in this country, but it must now be very considerable. Moreover, the economies of distributing social services, instead of selling them, are enormous. Think what an army of persons would have been required if all these needs that we are now becoming accustomed to see supplied as social services were sold as commodities. You see the economic utility, as well as the social justice, of this expanding programme.

HAVE YOU ANY COMMENT ON THE DIFFICULTIES WHICH MAY BE ENCOUNTERED IN PUTTING THE NEW SCHEMES INTO PRACTICE?

I would like to make one reference to some of the difficulties that I have encountered in launching the National Health Service. It is an attempt at the introduction of egalitarianism through the medium of a society which is certainly not egalitarian, either in its structure or in its inspiration, and further, through the medium of a profession, highly conservative, deeply traditional, and in many sections of it, hostile.

Further, it had to be introduced at a time of sharp inflation. This made the professions concerned even more resistant than they would have been in normal times. Were it not for the powerful authority of the Labour Government, and its massive support amongst the people as a whole, it is fairly certain that professional resistance would have been too difficult to overcome.

However, the Act will now be launched on July 5th, and it is to be hoped that the momentum of this vast machine will begin to develop a tradition of its own, and extinguish the evil inheritances which tended to threaten it at its birth. It must be clear, however, to everybody in the Labour Movement that we are not going to obtain from the National Health Service the best results possible, except by the utmost vigilance on the part of the whole Socialist, Co-operative and trade union movement.

The People's Coming of Age – 3 February 1950

Judged by long term values the chief danger in a general election lies in the loss of perspective. The foreground of the political stage is too crowded by personalities, colourful and otherwise, the air is thick with incidental noises, and subordinate themes obtrude themselves to the exhaustion of the grand motif that historical reflection will eventually winnow from the ruck of contemporary irrelevances. Of course major themes are always implicit in any political situation. It is the task of political philosophy to make them explicit in the minds of the actors so that a knowledge of what happened yesterday and what may happen tomorrow shall inform the conduct of today. It has been sometimes said that this revelation of the undertows of history does nothing more than to make us passive if conscious spectators on an ever-moving escalator of inescapable events. This, of course, is nonsense. The course of the ship can be changed if the tug of the currents is known. Awareness of possible destinations is a pre-requisite for changing them.

This may appear to be a very distant approach to the urgencies of the General Election in which we are engaged. Yet I don't think so. If the Grand Design in which we are involved is hidden from us or even blurred we shall falter, hesitate, and perhaps even lose our way. This is all the more possible because Socialists, in the past few years, have been so absorbed in busy every-day affairs that theoretical thinking has been neglected. More than ever we need lamps for our feet or we shall stumble in the way.

It is certainly true that what I have called subordinate themes are, in themselves, immensely important. Full employment, the social services, the more rational distribution of industry, greater equality in personal spending; all these and many more most properly occupy our minds and move our hearts. Yet even in their totality they do not sum up to a statement of the issue before mankind. They are steps on the way, ingredients in the solution, but they are not the solution itself. That demands a restatement of the relations between the individual and society.

*

The need for this is already vaguely recognised in the current controversy. Arguments about specific economic questions are frequently interlarded by references to individual liberty and the danger of losing it. In the U.S.A. the bogey of Statism is invoked in every argument about the social services. Any intervention by the government of the day to protect the mass of the citizens against the rapacity of a few invariably raises a storm of abuse ranging from accusations of totalitarianism to the creation of hordes of bureaucrats occupied in invading the privacy of peaceful individuals who apparently only want to be left alone, in the enjoyment of unbounded opportunities. The specific merits of any particular issue are never discussed, even by specialists in the given field, expect by invoking imponderabilia, and even quasi-philosophic allusions far removed from the immediate facts. All this is conclusive evidence that re-adaptations of fundamental relations are called for. In the language of the late H.G. Wells 'the framework of the past has been broken' and the individual is adrift on endless and turbulent seas without compass and without chart.

What is the new fact that is mainly responsible for this situation? It is so simple, so obvious and yet at the same time so germinal that it is usually overlooked. It is that the technics of modern industrial civilisation call for an educated, trained population, which in its turn demands full political status. Thus stated the conclusion is so trite that it is in danger of being dismissed as being the parent of such widespread effects. Nevertheless without keeping it in mind we shall completely fail to understand what is happening in the world today. I venture to say that it is nowhere understood more clearly at the present time than in the Kremlin. It is the yeast that is fermenting internal relations in the Soviet Union. You cannot educate a man to be a trained technician inside the factory and ask him to accept the status of a political robot outside. To read blue prints, to make and repair modern complicated machines, to perform the hundred and one activities inseparable from a modern complex civilisation is consistent with only one form of government – a complete political and industrial democracy. A totalitarian state or a one-party state is a persistent contradiction with the needs of a thriving industrial community.

*

It is no answer to point to Nazi Germany. In fact Nazi Germany is a blazing illustration of the truth of what I am saying. For ten short years it tried to violate the laws of modern society. It produced a society, barbarous, perverted and bloody, and it ended, in a collapse more complete than any in recorded history. Hitler could make his dictatorship of a technically highly trained people near-tolerable only by a social extroversion so monstrous that it produced a national psychology of a morbidity that still fascinates students of social psychology.

Where special conditions favour a dictatorship as in Spain, the consequence is a languishing industrial technique. If ever or when the tempo of industrial techniques quicken there, then the days of the dictatorship will be numbered. The machine educates the man and the educated man demands political enfranchisement. This is a law of modern society.

When a dictatorship, dedicated to industrialisation, fastens on a backward and illiterate community it appears, for a time, to cheat this law, but the cheat lasts only for a short time. The law invariably asserts itself. The reason for the pause is obvious. With the beginnings of industrialisation, and the accompanying literacy, the people are at first conscious only of enlargement and liberation. The social climate is one of hope and the conditions of life become more urbane. This is one of the causes of the strength of the Soviet Union and is not understood by those who believe that ideas are capable of universal application regardless of geographical and historical limitations. They would be more humble if they reflected that the industrialisation of Great Britain was accomplished under a Constitution which denied political liberty to the masses of the population and inflicted privations so monstrous that we are all hurrying to forget them. Many of the practices and social habits with which we reproach some of the new nations were a commonplace here in this country when we were at the same level of industrial advancement. In saying this I must not be thought to attempt, even by inference, to justify the shocking behaviour of the monolithic societies of Eastern Europe. Indeed this behaviour arises directly from their refusal to acknowledge that education and political emancipation must proceed together. Indeed they have less excuse, for history shouts louder in their ears than it did in ours. It is profoundly significant, in this connection, that the political behaviour of the Western satellites of the Soviet Union is the more oppressive the more they find they have to deal with people already considerably advanced in industrial technique. The richer the furniture of civilisation the more incompatible with it is the armament of dictatorship.

But if political dictatorship is uncongenial to a community trained and educated by the techniques of modern civilisation so equally is economic anarchy.

To a worker, accustomed to the smooth coordination of the different parts of a modern factory, mine, shipyard or up-to-date farm, the hit and miss methods of the market place, with its inexcusable fluctuations in the price of the products made by him and the arbitrary decisions made over his head, which intimately affect his industrial and domestic life, are as senseless and oppressive as the edicts of a political dictator. He cannot understand why there should be plan inside the factory and planlessness outside. It does not make sense to him that planned operations in his work should be described as efficiency while chaos everywhere else should be called freedom. This is not merely a question of the Welfare State and the just apportionment of the fruits of industry. It is a question which goes to the roots of his psychology – a psychology which is itself a part by-product of his daily experience. It seems to him that if men are made to fit inside the factory so should factories be made to fit each other. Unemployment is merely a special instance of a general case. Resentment against unemployment is not only so because of the appalling consequences to the worker. It is made more so because it seems to him to be quite senseless. Privation can be borne if it flows from physical limitations or if it is the burden of a common calamity. He will not tolerate it if it appears to him to flow from the privileges of those who have a vested interest in uncertainty – or what is worse, scarcity. It is here that the concept of the common ownership of the basic instrument of production fits into his outlook. It means for him not only the removal of the private owner but also a way of rationalising the relation between industry and industry. The owners fight each other. Industries belong to each other. They are not hostile. They are complementary. They should be made to fit together and their separate ownership by predatory interests is seen as a barrier to their efficient co-ordination.

*

Private economic adventure in the disposal of the products of industry, uncertainty concerning the location of employment, along with violent changes in the rate of capital investment, are all in such gross contradiction to the harmonious dove-tailing of the production-line that the individual citizen is almost a split personality. When the demand is made for an assurance of full employment it does not only mean a rational integration of the process of production and distribution. It means more profoundly that the citizen insists in the depth of his personality that he shall be reunited with his work and with the tools of his work, from which he was forcibly separated by the Industrial Revolution. Only those who have passed through the experience of idle hands surrounded by idle tools can begin to appreciate the deep serenity which will flow in time from the reuniting of man with the tools of his craft and the sources of his wealth. A denial of the right to useful employment is such a mutilation of the primitive psychology of mankind that society perpetrates it at the price of constant instability and intermittent convulsions.

This truth is now beginning to win general recognition, for even the political parties on which the guilt lies are compelled to pay reluctant lip service to it. What they have not begun to see are the implications of their admission. An insistence on the maintenance of full employment means constant intervention by government in the main agencies and streams of industrial and financial activity. Those who believe that the end can be achieved by injecting, or withdrawing, purchasing power from the financial system from time to time are pipe-dreaming. Such nervous methods are short lived and superficial. At best they influence the buying of consumer goods, but before the effects of this are passed on to the capital goods industries, other influences step in. The truth is that such large sums are involved in the heavy long-term investments of the basic industries that the saliva of private greed does not flow long enough to digest them into the economic system. The story of transport, coal, steel, textiles and electricity has been dinning this in our ears for more than a generation. They are on such a scale that they cannot be called private, and certainly enterprising is the last word to apply to their pre-war record. By their own behaviour private enterprise is confining itself to the industries of quick returns. When distant vistas are envisaged public agencies have already had to intervene. Labour has not snatched the crown of economic sovereignty from the head of private ownership. When steel admitted the right of public control over its operations it put its crown in pawn. And, as we all know, the pawnshops are being closed everywhere.

We are now beginning to see the pattern of individual relationship as it is emerging in those nations which are coming under the influence of

Socialist principles. In the first place there is an insistence on full political and industrial democracy as the only condition consistent with the manifold and subtle requirements of modern industrial and social techniques. The background and pre-requisite of this personal liberty implies that the serenities of private life shall not be invaded and disturbed by disharmonies arising from maladjustments in the economic machine. In short the main economic structure must be planned, purposive and reasonably predictable.

*

The third principle in this trinity arises from the first two. The full impact of it is only just beginning to be dimly recognised. It follows that if all the factors of production, both human and material, are fully deployed, then any addition to the total of production or change in its direction immediately gives rise to the question, What goes Where? Who is to be the beneficiary or the loser by the change? This was a question that *laissez-faire* Liberalism never had to answer – except in a narrow budgetary sense – for it allowed human values to emerge from the sum total of individual scramblings. The Liberal never knew what kind of society he intended until he had, in fact, made it. If we, on the other hand, accept the obligation of planning the direction of economic activity, then we accept with it the burden of deciding who and what must first be served. In short we determine the order of priorities. It would be fatal for a Socialist to underestimate the importance of this. Before the Industrial Revolution the burden of deciding was abandoned to the higgling of the market and the compulsions of greed. Now the people, through their representative institutions, must choose between a number of competing claims, and when that happens we have left the lower levels of economic planning and are treading the uplands of moral decision. This is the complete answer to those who think Socialism is merely a matter of appetite. On the contrary, it is the first time in human history that mankind will have accepted the obligation of free collective moral choice as the ultimate arbiter in social affairs. This, in truth, is the People's Coming of Age.

Do not dismiss our ideas of freedom – 3 September 1954

The following is the text of a speech made by Aneurin Bevan at a reception organised by the Chinese People's Consultative Conference on 18th August 1954 in honour of a British Labour Party delegation.

It is not necessary to spend time in formal greetings. Our presence is itself sufficient to show our support for the Chinese people's revolution.

As Mr. Attlee has already said, the Labour movement's reaction to the Chinese Revolution followed the example it set after the first world war when it rallied to the support of the Russian Revolution.

It follows naturally that the struggle of the British workers in their own country against the forces of capitalism causes them to sympathise immediately with the struggles of the workers in other countries.

***

That struggle takes various forms because it is fought under different historical conditions. These conditions do not determine the ultimate objectives of Socialism but they do influence the ways in which they are achieved and also the pace of change.

There is no universal recipe for social progress. If there were, our task would be easy. There are two elements always present in every political situation, the character of the goals we set ourselves and the framework of tradition inside which they must be pursued.

If we fight for our objectives without regard to the national and traditional inheritance then we are in danger of cutting ourselves off from the attitude of the masses whose representatives we are.

Socialism is, therefore, never solely a statement of abstract principles but a living reality which seeks to find its vitality in the actual conditions of struggle.

I say this because there is a disposition in some quarters to judge the European situation by Asian standards, as there is also a tendency for Europeans to be judged by the circumstances which prevail in Asia and elsewhere. Only by the study of the concrete circumstances in each case can we form a reliable opinion.

If the formation of Socialist strategy is allowed to freeze into a rigid dogma then it will lack relevance to immediate and local necessities.

***

For instance, the conditions of many European countries differ in two important respects from those which have prevailed and which still prevail in Asia.

In the first place most European societies possess fully developed democratic constitutions. These offer the possibility of a more peaceful and orderly transformation of society.

The diffusion of political power among the masses and the habit of accepting majority decisions through the medium of parliaments converts the political franchise into a revolutionary instrument if it is used with vigour and determination.

We are under no delusion about the resistance which will be offered by the forces of reaction when the people employ their political power for the attainment of Socialism. But we regard it as infantile and sterile to dismiss political democracy as though it is not a political force in its own right.

In the opinion of British Socialists it is this failure to recognise the challenging character of representative parliamentary institutions which has been responsible for much of the political sterility of people who regard themselves as revolutionary.

***

The second respect in which we differ from you and from many nations in your part of the world is that the struggles which you have waged are at the same time a struggle for national independence against imperialism.

This has the effect of supercharging the social struggle with the emotions derived from national self-consciousness and the yearning for liberation. You are, therefore, possessed of an emotional dynamic which is not present with us.

It brings to the fight for Socialism elements of the population which we cannot mobilise to the same degree. People who differ from you in many of your economic and social objectives are still prepared to work with you because you have offered and still offer the only means of liberating your country from foreign domination.

This mobilises behind your struggle a sustained emotion which sharpens it, gives it a keener fighting edge and which therefore enables you to cut deeper and more quickly into the traditional forms of resistance.

***

It is this combination of national and social struggle which is the main source of the difference between us. If it is not understood then neither of us will be able to grasp the position of the other.

It is responsible for the slower pace of our movement. At the same time it explains why we are exempt from many of the sacrifices which you have had to make. We hope that our visit and this discussion will enable us to understand each other's position better.

There is a possibility that one factor will arise with us which would immediately raise the political temperature in Europe, and that is the threat of war. The consequences of war fought with modern weapons are so sinister that its prevention has now become the principal preoccupation of peoples.

How to make progress and still keep the peace – this is the task of our generation. Peace cannot be based on stagnation. This is what the defenders of the old order cannot be brought to see.

Collective security cannot be based on the social status quo. It must be possible for people to improve their lot without their efforts to do so being condemned as part of a plot to fasten a particular ideology on others.

At the same time it must be recognised that modern war is no longer an opportunity for the emergence of successful social revolution.

***

Just as the industrial techniques of modern science make political helotry impracticable, so the techniques of modern war might condemn all of us to destruction. It must therefore be made possible for people to attain their legitimate national and social aspirations without war or the threat of war.

The acceptance of peaceful co-existence is, therefore, not only the condition for man's survival; it must also have a positive quality. To co-existence we must add co-operation including cultural, commercial and economic intercourse.

We must base our policies not on the leadership of this or that nation, however powerful, but on the equality of all nations, great or small. Not on blocs of nations seeking to establish uniformity amongst themselves, but on diversity and mutual interplay of natural differences.

Each national revolution stands on the shoulders of the previous one, learning from it but not necessarily imitating it in every respect. It is in that spirit we have visited your country. I am sure that it is in that spirit we shall leave it.

We trust that the prospect before you is fairer than the one through which you have fought so long and so courageously, and that the people of China will harvest in peace the fruit of their sacrifices.

Freedom and Socialism – 5 November 1954

READER'S QUESTION: 'SHOULD THERE BE POLITICAL PARTIES IN A SOCIALIST SOCIETY, AND IF SO, WHEN AND WHAT WOULD THEY REPRESENT?'

We are always more sure of what we are against than of what we are for. We fight to redress grievances. What new ones will arise when we have won, we can only dimly perceive.

It is therefore easier for us to see the need for existing political parties than it is to visualise the conflicts of the future.

But that there will be conflicts is as sure as it is that men and women will develop new needs, have other standards of values than we have, and reach for different goals.

In the pursuit of these, men will search out those with similar views, band themselves together with them, and if necessary form parties to give effect to them. What the issues will be we cannot tell because the existing polarisation of political parties fixes our horizon.

It is true that in the past parties have been the expression of economic classes. From this it is deduced that a classless society will not need parties. To my mind this confuses form with content.

Progress is not the elimination of struggle but a change in its objectives and we all hope a more civilised way of carrying it on.

What a democratic Socialist cannot do is conclude that with the accomplishment of a Socialist society the organisation of political parties should be forbidden.

It is not enough to say that with the end of economic classes most issues will be too trivial to justify the creation of conflicting political organisations. That will be for the contestants to decide.

If a Socialist society proves to be so satisfactory that only unimportant differences survive, then people should still be free to express them after their own fashion.

It is essentially an arrogant, authoritarian, and aristocratic attitude to hold that when we have won all winning is ended.

There is no last question so there is no last answer. If this is dismissed as mere liberalism then I must confess to be an unrepentant liberal, at least on such an issue.

We have two duties: to win our own battles and to keep the arena open for others. A closed arena is a closed mind. It is not by accident that these arise together.

Why Winston Churchill has been gagged – 20 May 1955

The General Election in Britain continues its puzzling course; puzzling, because there is, as yet, little to show how the electorate is reacting. Meetings of all parties are poorly attended, with the exception of those addressed by the most publicised speakers. Even the Chancellor of the Exchequer was recently reported to have attracted an audience of only about 22.

The various 'straw ballots' give the Tory Party a slight lead over Labour, but the percentage of uncommitted electors is so substantial that there is still plenty of time for a marked change to show itself.

One surprising feature of the election campaign is the failure of radio and television to stimulate interest. It appears that there is a law of diminishing returns at work here as in many other things. A point is reached at which further bombardment of mind and emotions deadens rather than engages attention. If everyone shouts, nothing is emphasised.

It may be that election techniques are not yet able to perfect the use of television and that the full use of this comparatively new medium is yet to come. If so, it will scarcely arrive during this election. There is hardly time for it now and most of the 'political stars' have already shone if that is the term that should be applied to their performance.

ANTI-CLIMAX

One cause of the tepid climate of opinion is the fact that the election date was announced so long beforehand and that it did not arise over a clash of opinion on an issue of major importance. The immediate occasion for the election was the resignation of Sir Winston Churchill and the elevation of Sir Anthony Eden in his place. This had been so long expected as to be something in the nature of an anti-climax.

Nor is Sir Anthony a personality likely to rouse feelings, either for or against him. He does not so much rise to an occasion as reduce the occasion to his own stature; and that is by no means considerable. Probably this makes him a dangerous opponent in the sort of election we are having. It is for the Opposition to make the running. The Government wants the running to be slow and easy, to keep tempers down and issues blurred. So far they have succeeded.

It is difficult to pick out any one issue on which the electors feel deeply. The Labour Opposition is making much of the cost of living and this may be having more influence than appears on the surface. If so, then we can take it for granted that its influence was at work long before the campaign started.

EXHAUSTION

It is not the sort of question on which the people need enlightenment. The housewife knows all about it and it has probably already affected the vote one way or the other.

There is another influence working against the Labour attack. This is a sort of spiritual exhaustion, a lethargy of the collective will. After all, it must be kept in mind that the British people have been kept on their toes for more than 16 years; more than six of them in the supreme effort of the war. The world has been very much with them all that time. There is now a natural disposition to lie back and enjoy whatever fruits there are for the picking.

This is a tremendous handicap to a party committed to further social and political change. The need for further social experiment is certainly present in Britain. Although she has recovered from the worst consequences of the war there is yet a long way to go before she can afford to relax. But, though the need is there, the mood is not.

Perhaps the greatest indictment that can be levelled against the Tories is the way they are pandering to this mood. It may suit them as an election asset, but the price will have to be paid when the election is over. They won't like paying it.

The bill is likely to be high, as is to be seen in the unusually large number of strikes that have occurred recently. The trade union membership is showing resentment against the inflated profits that are announced every day and the workers are demanding their share.

If the Tories win the election we can expect a fresh crop of industrial disputes. This is by no means inconsistent with the political lethargy I have described. I have seen it at work often before.

The pendulum swings from political apathy to industrial militancy and the two movements appear to be in direct relationship to each other.

What law of social psychology is at work it is difficult to discern. But there can be no doubting its existence.

It may be that organised workers [are] weary of the long term and often remote rewards of political activity. They decide in favour of short cuts, and these lie to their hand in demands for higher wages and improved industrial conditions.

FOREIGN AFFAIRS

Direct action has its appeal in the complicated societies of today. The political franchise alone appears to be inadequate to satisfy. Elections to parliament occur too infrequently, and are mixed up with all kinds of questions, difficult to sort out. These often lie beyond the boundaries of the imagination of men and women, immersed in everyday affairs. It becomes easy to grasp the 'cash in hand and waive the rest,' and to 'listen to the brave music of a distant drum.'

Foreign affairs are not having the influence on the election that might have been expected. This is probably due to the fact that the international situation shows signs of easing. This may be entirely superficial. No doubt a great deal of it is due to the election.

The United States Government is clearly anxious to do all it can to help Sir Anthony Eden during his election campaign. What will happen when it is over is another matter. In the meantime everything is kept vague and obscure.

No clear picture emerges of what the Western Allies intend to propose about the future of Germany. The Austrian Treaty is welcomed, but 'official' comments are careful to point out that it cannot possibly be a model for Germany. 'Austria is too small and militarily unimportant for her neutrality to weigh one way or the other.' Thus the neutralisation of Germany, as one possible solution, is being ruled out from the start.

Nevertheless, no one in the West is under any delusion about the delicacy of Dr. Adenauer's position, should Russia propose the neutralisation of Germany, as the price of unification; especially if this is accompanied by the contingent proposal that Russia and the West should guarantee her frontiers. In order to counter the attractiveness of this, feelers are already being put out that Russia should proffer the neutrality of her satellite, border states.

But it can be taken for granted that nothing definite will be said by the Western Powers while the British election is in doubt. Sir Anthony will get all the credit he can out of the fact that the Four Powers are about to meet. It was the one issue on which he was electorally weak.

It was also the reason why the Tory managers kept Sir Winston 'off the air.' His name was too embarrassingly associated with the notion of 'talks at the highest level' more than two years ago. He would find it difficult to explain why it has taken so long to bring them about.

Now the United States has written him off and their new champion is Sir Anthony. Once they have safely got him re-established in Downing Street it will be interesting to see how far they will let him off the leash. Or has Washington also come to realise at last that peace is obtainable, if the will to ensure it is there?

One thing is certain. If the negotiations with Russia reveal that it will be the West that stands in the way of a reasonable settlement, then the reaction in Britain will be profound.

It will not be less so should it turn out that the Tories will have won yet another period of power by a gross deception of the British people.

Russia must take her share of the blame – 25 November 1955

Even the most gloomy prophet did not expect the meeting of the Four Powers to turn out quite so barren. Having failed to reach agreement on the other issues, there was for a time still some hope that progress might be made on freer communication between Russia and the rest of the world.

The cordial atmosphere that prevailed at the 'summit' conference led many to anticipate that where other avenues to agreement might prove to be blocked, at least the barriers against intellectual intercourse would be reduced if not altogether dismantled.

In dashing such hopes Mr. Molotov used the harshest language yet employed in the recent exchanges. His words have already been fully reported and there can be no doubt that they will be repeated often enough to do damage to the better spirit that had seemed to emerge from previous meetings with Soviet representatives.

Apart from the classic arguments for mental isolation, it is difficult to explain this new shift in Russian policy. For if it is not a new shift, Russian propaganda has seriously misfired.

After the death of Stalin and the removal of Beria it was thought that significant changes were taking place inside Russia itself and that these would lead to an easier relationship with the rest of the world. Mr. Khrushchev especially appeared to go out of his way to achieve the utmost informality in his personal dealings with all sorts of people from the Western countries.

We seemed to be reaching the point where Russia was sufficiently self-confident to engage in the challenge that must arise from the free exchange of ideas. Indeed, Mr. Khrushchev went so far as to invite comparisons between the Eastern and Western types of society.

What has caused the Russian leaders to draw back at this moment?

One explanation now being freely canvassed is that the Soviet leaders have been engaging in a re-assessment of the probable lines of economic development in the West and have concluded that a further period of expansion can be looked for, particularly in the United States. This coincides with a resumption of economic strain in the Soviet Union and China, especially in the agriculture of both countries.

DISCARDED THESIS

The thesis of the inevitable collapse of the capitalist systems of the West has been discarded – at least for the time being – and therefore the Communist nations may expect to be confronted by the spectacle of capitalistic countries glowing with economic health and reaching levels of material well-being never before dreamed of.

In these circumstances – so it is argued – it would be foolish for the Soviet Union to invite the challenge of comparison. She must therefore re-adopt her previous exclusiveness and hope to emerge from it later on, in more propitious times.

If there is any truth in all this, it only serves to underline the dangers of the sort of isolation in which the two parts of the world have lived for so long. Neither has any real conception of the life of the other. This is more true of the people of China and Russia than it is of the Western countries. The cultural gap is wider still, as is frighteningly obvious to those who have visited China and Russia.

The longer the isolation continues the more difficult it is to end it, for the mutual revelation would result in deep shock.

A gradual coming together, growing ever broader and more intimate, would enable each to adjust itself to the other and come to appreciate that differences of mental outlook and ways of life do not necessarily express levels of inferiority or superiority.

It is possible to sympathise with the fears of China and of Russia. The first is just emerging from a prolonged civil war and the dislocations inevitable on revolution. The second has been the victim of military invasion and material destruction on a vast scale. They may not feel it is feasible to let down all barriers in one sweeping operation and so expose themselves to unfair comparisons and vicious misrepresentation.

But to continue the previous isolation would be even more disastrous, for the point might never be reached when they felt it safe to invite comparison.

Another explanation which one hears frequently is more alarming still. It is that the friendlier Soviet tone has achieved its intended objective in causing the West to relax its tense poise and military preparedness.

The character of Western society – so it is argued – makes it impossible to rectify this without a tremendous political effort, accompanied by the artificial stimulation of fresh fears of war and all the apparatus of hate with which we are so sickeningly familiar. This is a danger to which the tighter social disciplines of the Communist countries are not exposed, for they can change their diplomatic tone without paying any price either in reduced arms production or reduced vigilance.

If there is the slightest truth in this, then it discloses a frivolity gravely at variance with the sombre issues involved. It is an argument the Soviet leaders should take the earliest opportunity of answering, for it will bear closely on any future overture they might wish to make. The meeting at the 'summit' was a major Soviet objective. It was arranged after a prolonged diplomatic campaign. Throughout the world people were led to believe that their statesmen had serious intentions which presaged a genuine attempt to face the challenge of the atom age.

If nothing is now accomplished, it will be cynically assumed that nothing was intended, except the fruits of deception.

Perhaps it was too much to hope that the parties to the negotiations could agree about Germany or about disarmament. These are questions as stubborn as they are delicate and greater efforts will be needed for their solution. But above all what is required is evidence that statesmen are anxious for a deeper understanding, following a closer communication between their peoples, in order to prepare for a more hopeful approach to the greater difficulties.

It is in this respect that Geneva is so disappointing, and the Soviet Union must accept its share of the blame. It would be a disservice to leave her under any illusions about that.

She should not have encouraged so many expectations, if all along she did not intend them to be taken seriously.

This famous victory – 3 February 1956

The report of the Committee of Inquiry into the British National Health Service is undoubtedly a triumph for the principles that inspired its conception.

In its general conclusions the committee states: 'We believe that the structure of the National Health Service laid down in the Acts of 1946 and 1947 was framed broadly on sound lines, having regard to the historical pattern of the Medical and social services of this country'.

The Committee then examines each section of the Service in turn and finds, with comparatively unimportant exceptions, that no case can be made out for substantial alteration.

Naturally these conclusions are a source of great pride and satisfaction to me, not only in a personal sense, but also because they are a vindication of the Socialist principles on which the Service was based.

It must be kept in mind that there were no precedents to be followed in any part of the world. It is true there existed in many countries schemes of medical care, usually based on insurance premiums and sometimes accompanied by elements of free service. But nowhere was there a comprehensive service, providing freely, at time of need, all the forms of medical care, treatment and aid, at the disposal of the medical arts and sciences.

It was therefore not possible to predict, from past experience, how the people would use such a service, to what extent it would be open to abuse, and how the administrative machinery would stand up to so many novel problems.

After seven years' experience of the working of the scheme it is remarkable that so little fault can be found with its operation.

It is equally remarkable that the degree to which the Service is abused is so small as to call for no radical modification.

The problem of providing a universal free health service has been summed up by an American economist in the following sentence: 'How can a nation make the most efficient use of scarce resources?'

The conclusion reached by the economist is that by virtue of their scarcity they cannot be made universally free, because there would not be enough to go round; they would be spread so thinly, at every point, that nowhere would the resources be efficiently employed.

This was the argument I had to meet back in 1945 when I was faced with the task of creating the Service. It had to be answered, because until it was the way ahead was not clear.

MOST IN NEED

What is meant by the phrase 'scarce resources'? It means in practice, that in the nature of things, there never could be sufficient resources available for an ideal free health service; the point was bound to be reached when the claims of the service would come up against other claims upon the nation's resources, such as the armed services, education, etc. Put like that the problem seemed insoluble.

But suppose, I said to myself, I phrase the question differently? Suppose I asked, 'Having regard to the medical resources available to the community how can they be so organised as to be made freely available to *those most in need*?'

The American economist answered the problem by saying: 'Medical resources being scarce they can be efficiently used only if they are confined to those who can afford to pay for them'.

My answer was different. I said, 'Medical resources being scarce, their most efficient use depends upon their being concentrated, in the first place, upon those who have the greatest medical need'.

A doctor's skill would be more efficiently employed if he attended a patient really ill who could not afford to pay him rather than in holding the hand of some rich hypochondriac.

I am glad to say that this was also the attitude of most enlightened members of the medical profession and many more have now come round to the same view.

I have deliberately not mentioned all the ethical considerations, which are of course paramount to any civilised mind. It is more effective to meet the economists on their own ground and so avoid the charge of 'maudlin sentimentality'.

The same arguments apply to the proposal that I should have introduced the Health Service in stages. This was, in some ways, the most dangerous of all the objections I had to contend with. It appeared so plausible and sensible and made my own proposals seem wildly reckless and ambitious. I am therefore delighted to see that the Committee of Inquiry comes down firmly against the idea of the 'stage by stage' suggestion.

I am convinced that, had I accepted it at the time, the National Health Service would never have been established.

And this, for the reason that there was no section of the medical world where it could be said that the resources available were adequate in every sense of the term. Consequently if I had yielded to bringing in the Service piecemeal, I would have been driven from one weak position to a weaker one in the endeavour to prove that resources were the test and not personal medical need.

What of the politically delicate and vexed question of charges on the Service? This has caused more bitterness than almost any political issue of recent years.

In the light of subsequent events it is now possible to assess the wisdom of those who pressed for the charges in the first place. Were they made necessary by the mounting cost of the Service? Here is the answer.

As a proportion of the gross national product the Health Service cost 3.57 per cent. in 1948–49; 3.80 per cent. in 1949–50; 3.75 per cent. in 1950–51; 3.56 in 1951–52; 3.50 in 1952–53; 3.42 in 1953–54.

The Committee remarks: 'It may come as a surprise to many to find that the National Health Service has absorbed a decreasing proportion of the country's resources since the year 1949–50 i.e. the first full year of the Service'.

'Ah', you may say, 'but this was because the charges reduced the cost'.

This is what the Report says in reply: 'The indirect effect of the new charges in cutting down demand (estimated at £14 million) can account for less than one-third of the decline in the proportion of the national income devoted to the National Health Service'.

In order to maintain a sense of comparative values it is only necessary to recall that in the past four years, income tax has been reduced by hundreds of millions of pounds. Thus, in the apportioning of available national resources, the National Health Service has received not an increasing but a declining amount.

I quote just one more figure so as to put everything in proper perspective. In the first full year of the Service the cost per head per annum of the whole British population was £7 13s. In 1953–54 it was £8 15s. (at 1948–49 prices).

A great deal of the increase was of course due to improvements in wages and salaries of those engaged in the Service.

The conclusion to be drawn from all this is that one of the greatest social experiments of the twentieth century is an outstanding success.

Now that the verdict has been pronounced it is to be hoped that other nations will have the courage to follow in the same path.

At last the Socialist International wakes up! – 12 July 1957

Immediately following the conclusion of the Socialist International in Vienna comes the news of the latest political crisis in Moscow. Of course, these two have no connection with each other. Nevertheless, they are not strictly unrelated in their historical import.

Manifestly, the Communist International is in process of rapidly increasing disintegration. The Socialist International, on the other hand, shows every sign of re-awakening.

In recent years, ever since the war in fact, the Socialist International has been sunk in a kind of twilight sleep. This was largely due to the fact that in France, Italy and Britain, the Socialist parties either had complete governmental responsibility, or shared this with other parties.

CAUTIOUS

The effect on the Socialist International was to make it cautious and pragmatic. It was unwilling to lay down principles and to make criticisms which might appear to reflect on the conduct in government of certain of their members.

In these circumstances, the development of a coherent International Socialist strategy was rendered impossible or at least undesirable. Another factor which contributed to the sterility of this era was the anti-Communist posture that the members of the International took up by instinct, later becoming a fixed habit.

EXILED PARTIES

This attitude was reinforced by the presence of representatives of the exiled Socialist parties from the Baltic states and from Eastern Europe. It was altogether natural that these looked upon everything that came from Russia with unrelieved hostility.

The prevailing mood of the representatives of exiled parties is, inevitably, one of bitterness, shot through with nostalgia. As the years pass, and they get increasingly out of touch with the countries of their origin, their advice and policies are bound to lose any sense of contemporary values.

In contrast with these experiences, it was refreshing to observe a new vigour displayed in Vienna. The Conference was not afraid to express itself on French policy in Algeria, Disarmament, the Middle East, Germany and Central Europe, and a policy for peace.

The resolutions necessarily made allowances for the feelings of certain delegations, and therefore fell short of outright condemnation; but what made one feel more buoyant than before was the fact that self-criticism and criticism of each other were no longer looked upon as fatal to the continuation of the International.

CUSTODIAN

It is now necessary to formulate the outlines of a Socialist International policy and to get it understood as such among the rank and file of all the member parties. Such a policy cannot be imposed against the will of Socialists of any particular country. The International possesses no disciplinary powers short of outright expulsion, nor indeed will it seek to obtain them.

But what the International does possess, and it had it even in its less robust years, is the status of the custodian of Socialist principles. The influence of this authority is seen at work in the strong resistance which is offered up when any resolution is put forward which appears to condemn or rebuke the policy pursued by one of its member parties.

We have already observed this in the case of France and Italy. There can be no doubt that the recent news from Russia will feed the desire existing among tens of thousands of working class people for a statement of international Socialist aims to take the place of the intellectual vacuum left by the disintegration of the Communist International.

It is not possible to pronounce with confidence on the internal struggle within the Communist Party in Russia. The elements are too confused in themselves, as well as being obscured by the bewildering procession of rising and falling prominent personalities.

PARTY GRIP

In so far as policies can be disentangled from the individuals advocating them, it would seem that de-Stalinisation is proceeding. On the other hand, it would be wrong to conclude from this that the cult of personality is either dead or dying.

The growing stature of Khrushchev, and his obvious grip on the party machinery, hardly seem to be manifestations of an increasing democratisation in Russia or inside the Party machine itself.

I am concerned here, however, not so much with Russia's domestic situation, as with the effects on international Socialist organisation and doctrine.

It is no longer possible to speak of a Communist International, except as an historical reminiscence. Communist leaders in various parts of the world cling to their official positions, at the same time that the tide of current developments sucks reality from under them.

CANNOT ESCAPE

Their complete identification with the Communist Party of the Soviet Union makes it impossible for them to extricate themselves from the consequences of their affiliation.

So long as Russia was dangerously weak and exposed to constant attacks from the capitalist world, the Communist Parties could justify their intellectual subservience to the Communist International. Those days are gone. Russia is not only strong in the material and military sense of the word, but she has now alongside her triumphant Communist Parties in China and elsewhere.

REMARKABLE

Communism is not being judged today by whether it can succeed, but by a second and much more important question – what sort of a success is it? Is it the sort of success that the rest of mankind would like to imitate?

Capitalism has proved that it is capable of harnessing the productive energies of mankind in the creation of material wealth. The Communists have proved that they can do the same thing.

The economic achievements of the Soviet Union, especially when considered against the horrors of two world wars, foreign intervention and civil wars, are remarkable.

FALLING IDOLS

But have either Communism or capitalism brought into being the sort of society upon which other peoples will want to model themselves, and live their lives? Are they the designs for living which are likely to inspire the young men and women in the second half of the twentieth century?

It is here, in the most sensitive aspect of the question, that the news from Moscow makes the most impact. On the quarrel between Malenkov and Khrushchev, the outside world can make little informed judgment. But it cannot be said that a social system is either stable or worthy of imitation when leaders, so recently venerated, are one after the other cast down from their high places amidst a cacophony of execration.

If so much that rises to the surface in Communist countries commands so little respect what are we to guess at about what lies behind and below?

We can only conjecture, try to find out the truth, and hope that what is about to emerge is better than what we have already experienced.

Whatever the answer may be, democratic Socialists have every reason to be proud of the values of which they are the exponents.

The cautious, hesitant and timid years of the Socialist International are over. The Vienna Congress began to show the way, but only began.

When so many millions are turning their faces towards Socialism, it is the duty of the International to make clear its distinctive contribution to the solutions of the problems facing mankind.

It is even more its duty to delineate its own design for living, so that it may be fairly and thoroughly compared with what is offered by others.

Spectre over Europe – 19 July 1957

A new spectre is haunting Europe. It is no longer Communism. At least, this spectre has temporarily receded into the background. Inflation has taken its place and has become the well-nigh universal topic of conversation.

Ordinary men and women speak of it as the high cost of living. Economists speak of it as inflation. Others talk of too much money chasing too few goods.

Last year, the British people's buying power in the domestic market rose by 7 per cent; production increased not at all.

Government policy directly aimed at defeating inflation turned out to have the opposite effect. It decreased the amount of goods and increased the amount of money.

As a general rule, inflation – although by definition it marches ahead of production – does serve as a stimulus to industrial activity. This for the simple reason that industry attempts to increase its products in order to take advantage of the rising prices.

NEW CAPITAL

The Government sought to reduce the quantity of purchasing power injected into the system by restrictions on credit, by increasing the price of money, by limiting new capital issues, and by curtailing local government expenditure. These measures, although unusually slow to take effect, did put a check on production, but they did not stop the flow of purchasing power to anything like the necessary extent.

So we were presented with the spectacle of more money chasing even fewer goods.

The position in this country is much more clearly seen if it is realised that in 1957 the value of the 1938 pound, in terms of purchasing power, as expressed in the Retail Price Index, is only 7s. 5d.

HOPELESS PLIGHT

The effects of this catastrophic decline are not, of course, spread evenly over all the members of the community. Those whose incomes are fixed in inelastic money terms are unable to protect themselves, whilst those who deal in commodities or are able to negotiate their wage and salary contracts can recoup themselves.

Old age pensioners, for example, find themselves in a hopeless plight. The value of their pensions is eaten away by the fall in the value of money, and then the Government defends itself against the proposal to increase pensions by the argument that it would have further inflationary consequences.

This is, of course, nonsense, provided that pensions are increased at the expense of the incomes of richer members of the community, for in that case no increase in total purchasing power results.

THEIR DILEMMA

The answer to this has always been that such a transaction would transfer purchasing power from the investing classes to the spending classes, and so retard production. This answer should not come from the mouths of those who directed their plans last year to curbing indiscriminately the capital expenditure of the investing classes.

Here then is the dilemma of the capitalist system in the more economically advanced countries. In a desperate attempt to arrest inflation, efforts are made to plan the use of credit and the activities of the monetary system while leaving production to the impulses of private initiative.

The result, if such a situation could be conceived, is like a ship only a half of which obeys the steering wheel.

By refusing to undertake the task of planning production, the British Government is able to think only in terms of the totality of production set against the totality of purchasing power.

It is thus able to make no kind of discrimination between one form of production and another, or between one type of purchasing power and another. Its attempts at remote control produce the situation I have already described; stagnant production accompanied by continued inflation.

A remedy can be found only by discriminating between different types of production and, therefore, different classes of investment. Investment in industries producing consumer goods cannot go beyond the point where they can be served by the primary industries.

BLIND TORIES

For instance, the *Financial Times* has admitted that the end of the boom in 1954/55, and the slump which resulted in widespread dismissals, was partly due to the grave shortage of steel. This was the situation even after the British Foreign Exchange account was put in peril by heavy purchases of steel from abroad to the extent of £80,000,000 per year.

So blind and doctrinaire are our Tories that they are handing steel back to private ownership, where it is less amenable to public direction and control.

If primary industries like steel, coal, electricity, expand too slowly, the whole system gradually takes on the shape of a pyramid attempting to rest upon its apex. Or, to change the metaphor, the whole economy is like an athlete trying to win a race with a weight around one foot.

If investment is to be injected as it should be into the expansion of the primary industries, it must be held back in the meantime from industries making demands upon steel and coal and electricity which are not there.

By 1962, we shall require production of at least 28 million tons of steel per year. To achieve this, it will be necessary to invest a sum of the order of £700,000,000. Lord Bruce, Chairman of the Finance Corporation of Industry, stated the other day that 'Its provision has been the subject of prolonged discussion by the Treasury, the Bank of England, the Banks, the Issuing Houses, ISHRA, and the insurance companies, but so far without finding the answer.'

WRONG GOODS

The dilemma for the Government is not really how to find the £700,000,000. That can be done. Its real dilemma is to decide what concerns are not going to get any part of the £700,000,000 for their particular purposes, so that the money can be made available for steel.

The definition of inflation should, consequently, be restated. It is not too much money chasing too few goods. It is money chasing the wrong sort of goods.

Discrimination and planning in the productive process, with their necessary corollaries in the financial field and in politics, are the only ways in which the problems of inflation can be satisfactorily solved.

But these are just the remedies, tinged as they are with Socialist hues, that the defenders of Western capitalism cannot abide.

Like witch doctors, confronted with forces they either do not or will not understand, they confine themselves to exhortations, pleadings and lamentations – to be followed soon, very likely, by incantations from all the High Priests of what has come to be called the 'Establishment.'

Why Russia wins the space race – 11 October 1957

One swallow does not make a summer, nor one manmade satellite a firmament. Nevertheless, it would be churlish not to accord to the Russians their moment of triumph.

Some of the reactions to this illustration of Russian technical progress have been absurd, indeed childish.

It has been suggested, for example, that this is yet one more, and so far the most significant, step towards their domination of the world. Mr. Khrushchev himself has put the whole thing in proper perspective.

BIG LEAD

He is reported to have said that 'he did not want to say that the Soviet Union was ahead in the development of all weapons. The Soviet Union might be ahead on one thing today, but the United States would have it tomorrow, and vice versa.'

That appears to be the common sense of the matter.

He did, however, draw one deduction which has a direct bearing on proposals for disarmament and inspection. He pointed out that all arrangements for the inspection of airfields were now out of date.

It was the launching sites that would have to be identified and controlled in any future proposal for inspection.

It is not yet known to what extent the Russian satellite can provide the Russians with eyes and ears, enabling them to find out what is happening in other countries.

I am told it is extremely improbable that this is the case, at least in respect of this first satellite.

We can now expect that the scientists of other countries, especially those of the United States and Britain, will strain every nerve to catch up and to pass the Russian achievement. All this is very exciting and harmless, provided it is not done as part of a race for military domination.

HIS WORLD

It might be better if man first behaved intelligently about his own world before he set out to discover others. But at no time in history has it been the case that achievements in one part of the world were first made generally available before further advances were made.

On the contrary, many people, even in the country where the particular discovery was made, are often unable to have access to it for centuries, only a few enjoying its benefits.

The technical achievement of science is one thing. The social assimilation and universal enjoyment of its benefits another.

Progress, we are often told, is not a spiral, but a zig-zag. Some are on the zig, while others stay on the zag.

One of the most illuminating aspects of Russia's present feat is what it tells us about the structure of Soviet society. This subject has fascinated me for a number of years.

Here we have a society which is technically dynamic, and yet has political institutions which, by Western standards, impose intolerable restrictions on individual liberty, especially freedom of expression and of organisation.

The attention of the world has tended to concentrate on the latter and to ignore the significance of the former. Many, if not most, of the mistakes we have made about Russia have followed from this squint-eyed way of looking at Soviet society.

FINE POINT

We have confused freedom of expression with freedom of self-expression. This may, at first, seem too fine a point. But if you look at it more closely, it will be apparent that there is a profound difference between the two.

In this difference the secret of recent Russian history can be found.

Very large sections of the Russian people are conscious of enjoying great freedom of self-expression compared with the illiteracy and repression of their forbears in pre-revolutionary Russia.

A technically dynamic society creates conditions for increasing self-expression. More and more people are drawn into the diversified activities that follow the development of the physical sciences and the arts.

LIBERATION

The framework of the past having been broken, millions of workers have a feeling of liberation. Their personal lives had not sufficiently expanded before the revolution for them to resent the constrictions of the new political and social framework imposed by the revolution.

This emphatically does not deny that there are many people in Russia who feel today, and have felt in the last few decades, that the political institutions of their country are repressive.

All I am stating is that it would be folly to deny that the dynamism of Russian society has opened up for Soviet youth horizons of which their parents, and certainly their grandparents, could not catch even a glimpse.

It is fascinating to watch how the political institutions of Russia begin to adapt and adjust themselves to this ferment of technical and social change.

In the period that follows great political changes, the political pioneer and the idealist have usually spent themselves. The 'practical man' and the empiricist take the centre of the stage. They have plenty of scope.

Until they catch up with their new opportunities, they are apt to be impatient with those who say that they have not enough liberty.

Such an empiricist is Mr. Khrushchev. He is preoccupied with the administrative adaptations which have to be made as Russian society advances.

An ever-moving conveyor belt, carrying ever-increasing numbers of artisans, doctors, lawyers, professors, technicians, scientists, artists, the whole kaleidoscope which make up a modern society, keeps surging forward.

The administrative revolution now taking place in Russia is as significant an event as anything that has happened there since the war.

Only those who have had experience of the inertia of established bureaucracy, both in public and private enterprise, can have any idea of the task the Russian leaders are now facing. Such ruthless switchings of policy as go on in Russia could not be accomplished except under a political dictatorship.

Nevertheless, it must be credited to the Russian system, that like the rocket mechanism itself, it retains the capacity for successive explosions, proving that the original thrust of the October 1917 revolution is by no means exhausted.

Now that Russian advances in the physical sciences can no longer be denied, perhaps the attention of the outside world will focus itself more and more on the Russian educational system, the system as it is today, and as it is likely to be tomorrow. Here also great changes are under way.

The essential character of Russian education is its integration. In a society where public ownership of the means of production is the prevailing mode, working and teaching are reciprocal activities.

STATE JOB

In societies based upon private ownership, there is a duality. Work is the function of private enterprise, teaching the function of the state.

To this duality, many of our shortcomings can be traced. A 'pure' scholasticism on the one hand, and 'practical' learning on the other.

In Russia, the danger of this kind of duality is recognised, even though it has not been permitted to reach the lengths it has gone to in other countries.

The new changes contemplated in the educational system are directed to correcting it.

It might be that here we have the secret of the tremendous progress the physical sciences have made in the Soviet Union after so late a start.

Communism or suicide? That's not the real choice – 14 March 1958

A friend of mine, just returned from Paris, met a Russian lady who came to visit a relative of hers whom she had not seen for 25 years. When asked whether she intended to return to Russia, she said: 'Of course. I have enjoyed my visit but I find Paris very dirty and far less attractive than Moscow.'

I am not claiming that this incident is at all representative. Nevertheless, it is one that could not conceivably have occurred even a few years ago.

Whatever else might have been claimed by the Communists, they were always prepared to admit that in comparison with life in the Soviet Union, the material standards of the West were superior.

SHORT PERIOD

Of course they went on to declare hurriedly that the ravages of a civil war and of two world wars, in addition to the economic backwardness of Czarist Russia made it impossible for the Russians to compete with the West in material progress over so short a period.

When my wife and I were in Russia last September, we were impressed by the spaciousness and general attractiveness of the streets of Moscow. There can be no doubt that, all too slowly for the Russian people themselves, the standard of living is rising, and this is reflected in the appearance of the buildings.

Much of the new architecture is altogether too stodgy and heavy, reminiscent in many respects of the worst features of the Victorian period. Even the Russian showpieces such as Stalin Allee in East Berlin compare unfavourably with the newest specimens of Western architecture.

After a visit to East Berlin I remarked that I was intrigued to find conservative architecture in the revolutionary sector, and revolutionary architecture in the 'reactionary' west.

Under the prodding of the formidable Mr. Khrushchev, Soviet architects are beginning to get away from the portentous heavy-handedness of the Stalin period.

I call attention to these facts because, if time is permitted us, they will have an increasingly important bearing on the great argument now taking place in Great Britain and on the Continent of Europe, especially in the German Republic.

GAP NARROWS

The gap between the material standards of the West and those of the Soviet Union is being narrowed.

It is still considerable, especially for large numbers of poorer Russians, but it is significant that the Soviet leaders now feel it safe to permit at least the most favoured of their people to pay private visits abroad, not only knowing that they will return, but that they will make comparisons not always unfavourable to the Soviet way of life.

I believe it can be taken for granted that as the pressure of material privations is lightened, some benign consequences will be felt right throughout the Soviet system.

In the course of time, perhaps shorter than many imagine, even those political institutions so much disliked by the Western mind will undergo such modifications that they will be stripped of their more repulsive features.

It is no doubt these developments that Khrushchev has in mind when he talks about 'peaceful competition with the West.' The great argument to which I have referred relates to the character of the military defences now being built up by the NATO powers, and particularly to the objective of those defences.

Up until the time when Mr. Foster Dulles and those who think like him began to muddy the waters, the people of Europe were fairly clear about the purposes of their expenditure upon arms.

They thought they were intended for defence against military aggression. As such, they formed part of the purposes set out in the Charter of the United Nations. What they had in mind was aggression, pure and simple.

Gradually, however, this concept has tended to be overlaid by another, which is, that the West was concerned to defend itself against the encroachment of Communism.

The correspondence columns in *The Times* of March 11 gave several classic illustrations of the sort of confused thinking now existing.

A lady wrote passionately: 'No one wants to be atomised, but to the Christian the choice between extinction and subjection to atheistic Communism is surely automatic.'

On the other hand, Professor A. J. P. Taylor, writing immediately above, said: 'A number of your correspondents announce that they would prefer suicide to life under Communism. So would I. Our wish can be met simply and cheaply by issuing a phial of poison to every registered anti-Communist.

'But why should we insist that the rest of the population accompany us on this death-ride; that many millions of Russians also be obliterated; and that the atmosphere be polluted so that future generations will be maimed or monsters?'

THE CHOICE

Those who have distorted the purposes of military expenditure to ideological ends, do not seem to realise that by doing so they are losing scores of millions of men and women to the Communist side of the argument.

If the choice is put thus starkly – the extinction of mankind by hydrogen bombs or the spread of Communism – how many people would really choose the former? After all, mankind has lived for most of its existence under authoritarian regimes of one kind or another – and survived them.

If Mr. Foster Dulles and his friends insist that this is really the choice, they have lost the argument before it starts. If, on the other hand, they would only rest their case where it originally belonged, which is that civilisation can survive only by the establishment and maintenance of the rule of law among the nations, they would never have been caught in this impossible dilemma.

It is their apocalyptical way of presenting their case which is depriving them of the support of ordinary people everywhere.

Furthermore, there is really no evidence that the Communist leaders nurture plans of extending the frontiers of Communism by naked physical force. Instead, evidence is accumulating to the contrary.

It is true that immediately following the end of the war there was Czechoslovakia and Berlin, and, more recently, Hungary. Russian conduct in Hungary was abominable, but it was not an attempt to extend the frontiers of Communism, but rather to hold them.

Even in the case of Czechoslovakia it was a political coup d'état – wholly wrong in my opinion – carried out under the shadow of the Red Army stationed on the frontiers. As for Berlin, the situation speaks for itself.

It appears that now that the Russians are embarking on a new phase, certain people in the West insist on basing their strategy on the old one.

The economic exploitation of a modern advanced industrial community by military garrisons imposing an alien ideology is wholly impracticable. The Russians are beginning to learn this at the very time when the West is beginning to forget it.

Unless many of the leaders of Western opinion can disentangle themselves from this ideological cats' cradle, they will never be able to think clearly about the inner nature of the problem facing the world today.

Private enterprise v. public ownership: The moon and the £ – 9 January 1959

The latest Russian achievement in putting a rocket in orbit round the sun is bound to give rise to a furious argument. This is likely to take many forms. Inevitably comparisons will be drawn between the relative merits of the Communist and other systems of government.

For the first time for many millions of people among the Western nations, the balance of the argument is beginning to shift. This is not to say that people are less inclined to support the institutions of political democracy. But more and more people are beginning to ask themselves whether it is possible for these institutions either to flourish or to achieve their full potentialities when linked with the capitalist economy.

The old Marxist argument that the relations of private property and the social stratifications that come within them tend to stultify and even inhibit technical progress and maximum production of wealth, is receiving fresh reinforcement.

It is not as though the Soviet achievement is confined to one narrow and highly specialised field. On the contrary, their seven-year plan shows that the advance is on the broadest possible front. Even the reform of judicial procedure has not been neglected.

BORNE IN MIND

All this does not prove that the principles of Communism, as practised in the Soviet Union and in China, have disclosed a higher type of civilisation than any we have yet known. Socialists have never needed to have it proved to them that most people are capable of the same technical accomplishment if given favouring conditions.

What remains to be proved is not the capacity to produce this or that, or even a whole series of clever gimmicks and gadgets, but whether a better type of society with a higher species of human being is in fact being evolved.

Speaking for myself, I think the weight of the argument still lies with the defenders of Western democracy. But it is inevitable for doubts to arise about the possible lines of future advance.

It must be borne in mind that these evidences of Russian scientific and technical achievement are taking place against a background of industrial stagnation and even of economic recession among the capitalist nations of the West.

In short, as an instrument for expanding production and stimulating the industrial arts with apparently a rising momentum, then the Soviet leaders have thrown down the gauntlet.

On several occasions recently, Mr. Khrushchev has expressed himself as being happy about this. He declares that there is nothing he wants more than the opportunity of peacefully proving the growing ascendancy of Communism as practised in the Soviet Union.

One of the rejoinders to Soviet claims with which we are made familiar is that in a police state where freedom of choice is not generated spontaneously, those in power are able to direct the energies of the people to whatever project or projects they consider to be worthwhile at the time.

They are able to impose upon the economy their own order of priorities and to insist upon it being obeyed by coercive disciplines.

These issues of fundamental importance are raised by this contention. First, should there be priorities? Second, how should they be arrived at? And, third, what measures are essential for their attainment?

Let us take the last first. Does anyone really believe that the extraordinary accomplishments of Soviet science are produced by fear? Since when did fear cause people to think more intelligently?

ECONOMIC PRIORITIES

Think more rapidly and even feverishly, yes. But think more intelligently and purposefully, no.

It must be accepted that whatever rewards and opportunities are available in the Soviet Union, they are adequate to create a climate of opinion in which science and scientists can flourish.

Should there be economic priorities? Here we are at the heart of the matter. If there are not priorities, then there is no touchstone by which the economic activities of a nation can be judged. There is no chart from which the course can be mapped.

The destination is what it turns out to be and not what is intended, because all pretence at intention is discarded at the very outset of the voyage.

This is the situation in which Western Europe and the United States find themselves. They are floundering about, forced to make purely empirical choices among a number of alternatives at a very low common pattern, except a pattern that can be said to emerge from a myriad of unrelated decisions. The total result is a total absence of design, and without design the human soul feels itself adrift.

Of course it would be untrue to say that Western society admits no prior claims upon its resources. But these have been built up and inherited by tradition and by a number of political and social compulsions that were never planned in any hierarchical order.

Nobody doubts, for example, the priorities given to defence both in Britain and America, and no one can doubt but that these claims have thrust aside what most people would consider to be those of higher values. Only quite recently, the British Government agreed to admit the prior claims of international moneylenders, although we know that on many occasions these have come into successful conflict with the needs of the poor and of the sick and even of national security.

These are some of the priorities that are imminent in capitalist society, but they are never stated overtly, otherwise their essential unworthiness would become too obvious.

It is the Socialist case that a certain order of priorities should be voluntarily accepted by a democratic nation. Having been accepted it should then be driven through against all opposition and private vested interest.

THE BACKGROUND

There must be argument and even hot controversy about the order of priorities, and in what relation to each other the priorities should be arranged, but once the conclusion is reached it would be manifestly absurd to allow other claims to successfully oppose it, for it must be assumed that the latter will already have been set aside in the preliminary examination.

This is the background against which a Socialist must judge the position of private ownership, because if the private ownership in the means of production and exchange is seen to be in opposition to the pattern of priorities, then it must be the latter that should always prevail.

4
WAR
Inside Teruel – 21 January 1938

THE MOTOR journey from France into Spain along the Mediterranean coast-road is a delightful experience. The place names read like chapter headings in a book of old romance. Gerona, Barcelona, Tarragona, Castellon, Valencia. To our northern ears these names have a gracious sound, and an association redolent of sunshine.

Above, a brilliant sun in a speckled sky. On the left, the Mediterranean, a slatey grey just now but with here and there a fugitive gleam of the later universal blue. On our right, olive groves and vineyards in russet soil, and beyond them the snow-covered teeth of the coast sierras.

Below Barcelona the olive gives way to mile after mile of orange groves. To our unaccustomed eyes there was something fantastic about the sight of snow on the slopes of the mountains and oranges on the foot-hills below. But the soil here is the richest in Europe. We were told that it often yields three crops of different kinds in the same year.

SEE FOR OURSELVES

Nevertheless, pleasant as these things are to dwell upon, they are what every tourist sees and it was not as tourists we went to Spain.

We went at the invitation of the Spanish Government to see for ourselves what was being accomplished in Republican Spain and to try to get some idea of the prospects of the Government in the fight against the Fascists. We hoped also to learn in what way we could best assist the Government so that we might give intelligent direction to our own efforts.

In what I shall say I am speaking for myself alone and without consultation with the rest of the Members of Parliament who went with me; but I have no reason to suppose that I shall say anything with which they will disagree.

DAILY BOMBING

The whole coast from the French frontier right down to Almeria is under daily bombing from the air, invariably by planes from the Balearic Isles. We were told that they were Italian planes manned by Italian airmen.

The Government is helpless to defend itself against these raids. The planes come up over the sea at a great height and before they can be seen they swoop down over the defenceless cities of Barcelona, Valencia, and other smaller towns along the coast, drop their loads of death and are gone before there is time for the chase planes to take off and engage them.

In any case such fighter planes as the Government possesses are almost all at the front where they are needed to defend the Government troops from machine-gunning from the air.

We had several experiences of these visits of the 'Black Planes,' as the Spaniards call them, giving us some idea of what it must be like to the civilian population. Tom Williams and I had arrived back in Barcelona at 2:30 a.m. after an adventurous motor journey from Valencia which included an air raid just outside Valencia, a burst tyre and a skid into a ditch.

We were just getting into bed dog tired and thankful to have escaped so far when the siren sounded the alarm, all the lights of the city went out, and the traffic outside stopped dead. There being nothing we could do, we finished our undressing and got into bed.

In the darkness and hush which followed the siren, we waited for the coming of the bombs. The night before one hundred and fifty had been killed and wounded in an air raid on that city and we had no reason to suppose that there was any special providence watching over Labour Members of Parliament. All over that city hundreds and thousands of men, women and children were in our position.

The worst part of the experience is the feeling of helplessness. It is one thing to fight and struggle against danger; it is another to await the coming of danger knowing that one can do nothing to avert it.

For us this was a passing experience and on the morrow we were setting out on our journey homewards to safety and comfort. But to the populations of these cities that we were leaving behind this was a daily and nightly terror.

NO PANIC

For their conduct in these circumstances we can have nothing but unbounded admiration. There was no sign of panic or any loss of self-control. Immediately the sirens sounded the 'All Clear' the lights went on and the traffic started once more.

One young officer of the Republican army to whom we spoke said rather wistfully, 'It would be so nice to see a city with all the lights on once more.'

One aspect of these air raids impressed all the members of the party. During our stay in Valencia we examined the reinforced concrete shelters which the Government have made for the protection of the population. They were commodious, strong and even elegant. More than half the population of the city of Valencia can find refuge in them and others are being constructed.

It is a significant side light on the efficiency and drive of the Government that even in the midst of waging a civil war involving an immense strain on their resources they can carry out works of this kind.

The high spot of our visit and the one which gave us more insight into the fortunes of the Government than any other was the visit that Tom Williams and I made to Teruel.

Teruel lies upwards of a hundred miles inland from the coast, and the road we took is the only good approach to Teruel that lies in Government territory. For the most part it winds its way among the foot-hills of the mountains until it reaches a height of more than three thousand feet. At this altitude it continues with slight undulations to Teruel itself.

CONCRETE EVIDENCE

The temperature was several degrees below zero and a heavy fall of snow had frozen hard on the road.

It was here that we had first hand evidence of the wonderfully efficient organisation of the Government. Early in the morning though it was, thousands of troops and field workers were at work clearing the snow and cutting the ice from the surface of the road. The men were working cheerfully and swiftly, obviously fully conscious of the need to get the road clear for traffic.

This was the main artery for the Government forces and carried two endless streams of lorries. The drivers of these lorries performed feats of daring driving. Whether they were going to or coming from Teruel they refused to give way to anyone except staff officers.

Lorry loads of prisoners now met us as we drew near to Teruel, concrete evidence of the Government victory. From the demeanour of the prisoners we gathered that they were by no means sorry to be away from Franco.

About ten miles from the front we stopped at the headquarters of the General Staff, and there we met General Rojo, the Chief of the Government forces. As we entered the room, the position of which for obvious reasons we cannot disclose, we heard the field telephone announce that another two thousand prisoners had been captured and we heard the orders being transmitted to the front ordering that all lives must be spared.

We then went on to the front, but that is part of a story that I have not the space to tell.

On our return to Valencia we had an opportunity to test the reliability of the Government wireless news, with what we knew had actually occurred at the front. In all respects the broadcast was a sober statement of the truth.

On all sides we naturally heard rejoicing at the victory of Teruel, but nowhere did we find credulous optimism. Everyone appeared certain of ultimate victory, though all were conscious that they still had a long road to travel to attain it.

The bearing of the people is confident and there is immense pride in the new Republican Army. The fact that Prieto, the Minister of War, had remained in the front line trenches during the battle was commented on frequently.

The offensive has definitely passed to the Government and the opinion was universally expressed that Teruel marks the turning point in the war.

We must redouble our efforts to see that the Republican Government is provided with arms, and to prevent any more assistance going to Franco from Italy and Germany.

I returned home with pride in the working class of Spain and a feeling of shame that the British working class has given them so little assistance in their heroic struggle.

The blackest page in Britain's history – 3 March 1939

On Sunday the Labour Party held a vast demonstration in Trafalgar Square to protest against the Government's intention to recognise General Franco. On Monday the Government announced their decision to accord recognition. On Tuesday the Parliamentary Labour Party moved a Vote of Censure on the Government. It was, of course, heavily defeated in the division lobbies.

In 1920 a far smaller Parliamentary Opposition, acting in co-operation with the Trade Unions, did succeed in preventing the British Government from destroying the Russian Revolution.

These facts have a sombre significance for all of us. It is better that we face them and extract from them the last bitter drop of revelation.

In particular, let those who still believe that Labour can win the next election unaided, consider one further fact. The National Government is in its fourth year. The General Election is almost certain to take place some time this year. Despite this, the Government feels strong enough, and confident enough, of the results of the Election, to offend the deep feelings which have been aroused in the country in support of the Spanish Republican Government.

It is able to disregard the wishes of the Opposition because it does not fear the Opposition at the polls.

***

This was the silent argument which dominated the Debate on the Vote of Censure on Tuesday. It explained the jauntiness of Chamberlain and the high spirits of the Tories. Clem Attlee used bitter language in his opening speech, and I for one, was glad of it. But, as I listened to him, I thought how much more effective it would have sounded if it had come from strength and not from weakness.

A united Opposition would have worried the Government supporters and given point to the many excellent speeches which were made from our side of the House. It is little comfort to win the argument and lose the victory.

As I listened to the Debate and thought of the hundreds of thousands of brave men and women in Spain who have fought so nobly and for so long against such terrible odds, my heart grew heavy within me. The exultant faces of the Tories opposite showed the glee with which the supporters of the Government welcomed the defeat of freedom and the triumph of their champion Franco.

I knew then more completely than I have ever known before that one argument, and one argument only, would impress them – power.

I KNEW THEN THAT OUR TASK LIES IN THE COUNTRY, AND IN PARLIAMENT ONLY TO THE EXTENT THAT PARLIAMENT CAN INFLUENCE WHAT THE COUNTRY WILL DO.

***

In a short and splendid speech Seymour Cocks expressed my feelings. He began by quoting A. E. Housman: –

'Be still, be still, my soul, it is but for a season.
'Let us abide a-while and see injustice done.'

After narrating the story of the pressure brought upon the French by the British Government to close the French frontiers to Spain, he went on:

'I do not know whether the members of the House of Commons believe that this world is ruled by some Divine agency and that there is some pattern to which nations and individuals must conform. I do not know whether they believe that national crimes and national apostasy are followed in the long run by national retribution. There is much in history to support that view. The most celebrated example is the case of Melos. The Athenian people, at the height of their power, forsook their principles and destroyed the inhabitants of that island. There followed the expedition to Syracuse and the destruction of the Athenian Empire.

'Britain and France today are surrounded by enormous dangers, and we shall survive them only if our people are animated by high and noble causes. As both the British and French Governments have sacrificed the high traditions of their countries, in Abyssinia, in Czechoslovakia and in Spain, our peoples, if war should come, would go into battle inspired by no noble ideal of liberty and democracy, but fighting only in the spirit of self-defence, which even the lowest animal will show when it is attacked. In the day of stress and danger we shall be haunted by the spectres of the nations we have betrayed, and the gods of freedom, liberty and democracy will not be there to steel our soldiers' hearts.

'It may be that as a result of this moral surrender, we shall be defeated and that we shall lie at the foot of a foreign conqueror as we have never yet done. If that be the decree of Providence, I can only trust that in the struggle that will follow to liberate ourselves from foreign domination, the British people will regain that spirit of freedom and liberty which our ancestors possessed, but which their degenerate successors in the Cabinet have forgotten.

'Today I feel that this house should be closed, and that our churches should be thronged by multitudes praying for the restoration of that national honour which the Prime Minister has betrayed.'

***

I make no apology for that long quotation, nor do I accept the implication that the history of this country is by any means free from crimes against the liberty of other peoples. But there are two parallel histories of Britain, one of oppression and one of continuous struggle against it, at home and abroad.

It is this second history that Cocks invoked. It is to this more splendid tradition that we must appeal in this dark hour.

In their obscene haste to accord recognition to General Franco, the Government have made no great effort to obtain an amnesty for the brave workers who have fought so heroically against him. Indeed, the Prime Minister went so far as to justify Franco's desire for revenge; only he drew a distinction between political and other crimes – a distinction which we know is blurred in the minds of Franco and his followers.

This surely must be the blackest page in the history of Great Britain. It is certainly not the brightest in the history of the British working-class movement. We have seen the ideals of our movement, and the gallant workers who have fought for them, harried and slaughtered all over Europe, and we have not helped them to victory or succoured them in their defeat. We may indeed pray that when our time comes we shall not be similarly requitted.

Are you a traitor? – answer now – 24 May 1940

There are but two tiny sections of the people who now doubt what is their duty. All others have nothing in their hearts but a determination to aid in every way the young men of Britain and France who are the sole barrier against the Nazi conquest of the world.

Those two tiny sections are what are conventionally called the Extreme Left and the Extreme Right – though they are extreme in nothing but ignorance, impudence and folly. On the one side we have the group that still calls itself Communist, which has not had the guts to stand up to a real war, though it talked bigger than anyone else. These people relied on Stalin to do their thinking for them: now he has travelled his own road they can do nothing but snarl and whine. No honest, anti-Fascist worker cares for them at all. They shame their own dead in Spain.

FOOLS ON THE RIGHT

And the Extreme Right? They do not read the *Tribune* and our words will not reach them. But those who still think that they can conserve their investments if Hitler is victorious are dwindling day by day. The rich are stupid, politically, but they are not so stupid as to fail to see that the Nazis will rob them to the last penny when they can. Gangsters kill off first the best and most courageous members of society. True, but the fat people are the ones they feed on.

Even *The Times* and the *Daily Express* nowadays print leaders, warning us about the dangers of Quislings and the circles in which they are really to be found, which a month or two ago only Socialist papers would have published.

But as the last of the stragglers fall in, as the most stupid and greedy slowly realise the truth, it is for us as Socialists to proclaim again that we more than any others must be – have the honour to be – the vanguard and the shock troops in this struggle. It is the very choice of the enemy himself which declares this.

WHOM DO THEY HATE?

On what countries has the savagery of the Nazis fallen most fiercely and earliest? Upon the countries where the workers had advanced furthest – whose trade unions and whose Press were freest – where social reform, under the pressure of the Socialist workers, had been most successful.

Read the list of their victims: Czechoslovakia, Denmark, Norway, Holland, Belgium; it might be a roll of honour of the countries where the organised workers, thrusting towards the light, had made life most civilised and tolerable for all.

Fascism is something from the blackness of the past. It is the power of darkness fighting against the light which was slowly illumining the cottage as well as the castle wall. How significant it is that the first blows fell upon just those countries where the light was brightest!

Hitler and his hordes hate one thing above all else. That thing is the whole way of life made possible by the institutions and organisations of the working class painfully constructed in this century and the last. These institutions – trade unions, parties, local councils, co-ops and all the complex of social services and parliamentary freedom – arouse in the Nazis a special ferocity. For they are the living answer to their creed which proclaims that ordinary folk are innately stupid and born to be slaves. In the countries conquered by the Nazis as well as in Germany herself all trade unions, co-operative societies, independent political parties and allied activities are immediately suppressed. Freedom of speech and writing becomes treason punishable by death.

All this we know. But let me add to it this. As it is the institutions and status of the workers which are first attacked by Hitler, so it is the workers who must give him his answer. The Nazis make war first against the people, and only secondarily against the capitalist interests of France and Britain. One of the main reasons why the mighty economic and military strength of France and Britain have not been effectively mobilised as yet is because they were so long partly paralysed by the secret sympathy which the governing classes of both countries felt for the anti-working-class activities of Hitler. He sapped their virility by sharing their hates. They have learned the truth very late and their imbecility has had the effect of obscuring in many workers' minds the real nature of the war which is now raging. It has made many workers see it as another example of capitalist rivalries and consequently as none of their business. Even yet many do not fully realise that the workers are the main enemy against which the Nazis are launching their hosts.

LITTLE TIME IS LEFT

There is only one force which can retrieve the fortunes of war, and that is an awakened working class. There is very little time left us. We must be prepared to set aside every consideration except the paramount one of exerting ourselves to the utmost first to hold the Nazis and then hurl them back in defeat. If we all have to work harder and longer for a short time what of it? If the Nazis win we shall work harder and longer not for a short time but for ever. Any holding back now is more than treachery to the State.

It is unforgivable and direct treason against the workers and against our fathers who sacrificed so much for the democratic institutions which are now in danger. Are you or are you not a traitor? That question has to be answered by every worker this day, this very hour.

LET US ANSWER NOW

It is suggested by some that if the workers surrender any of their cherished rights during war-time they will never get them back again. There are two answers to this. First, it is unreal. Nothing can stop the workers getting back all they want after the war except themselves. No fear that the workers will emerge from the war weaker in organisation than they are now – if we win! If this war is won by us it will be won because the workers will have become strong enough to dominate the war effort. Their organisation (as in 1919) will be stronger, and they will know better how to use it. They certainly will be able to enforce the full restoration of their rights. The second answer is conclusive. *If the Nazis win the workers will have no rights*. Don't forget Italy and Germany where for long years not a spark of effective working-class resistance has shown itself.

THIS IS OUR DUTY

It is the duty of us all in these days to make the workers aware of the issues which are at stake. Once the workers see their way clearly they will produce an invincible determination. From the factories, workshops and mines of

Britain will flow a ceaseless stream of arms and munitions to support our soldiers, sailors and airmen who for the first time in British history are really and incontrovertibly fighting for the welfare of the common people against the most deadly enemy of civilisation since the Vandals swept across Europe.

The way to win through – 31 May 1940

We are passing through days of great tribulation. Each day, almost each hour, deals a fresh blow against us and against our cause. Before these words appear new calamities may have befallen us. To many of us these will bring personal loss and an abiding sorrow. To many more these are days of agonising uncertainty. Hope and fear strive for mastery in our hearts as we weigh the import of what we hear in its bearing on the fate of those we love. Grief and pain immeasurable breaks like a tidal wave upon Europe engulfing alike the busy city and the quiet village. No island of peace and serenity survives its dark and swirling waters. The hideous doctrine of Total War respects no sanctuary and venerates no abode of ancient peace.

There is no halting place, no accommodation, no compromise possible. The issue is stark. It is either total victory or total defeat. The goal the Nazis have set themselves is not the redress of grievances, nor the expansion of national opportunities, nor even revenge for real or imagined wrongs. The prize they march to win is world conquest; the subjugation, first of Europe, and then of the rest of the world.

THE NEW VANDALS

To meet this challenge of the new Vandals the pulse of civilisation is at last quickening. At first that pulse was sluggish. It is difficult for the civilised mind to conceive an issue in simple terms of black and white. It knows that the truth is never all one side, and that to distrust the universal application of any generalisation is the beginning of wisdom.

Consequently, it is not easy for the civilised intelligence to achieve the complete dedication to a single-minded purpose that the waging of total war demands. We are always inclined to keep something back, to reserve a little, if it is only a part of our mind, rather than allow ourselves to be wholly absorbed and spent in the purpose of the moment. It is this qualifying habit of mind that the Nazis call the decadence of the democracies, and on which they ultimately rely for their hopes of victory. Of course it is not decadence, but the by-product of an established way of life, in which the essentials of existence were so secure that we felt free to indulge the luxury of scepticism.

We are no longer free to do so, for the very foundations of our lives are assailed by the onrush of the Nazi hordes. We have already dallied too long and it will require every effort of which we are capable if we are to hurl to defeat this new threat to civilisation. The first step in this direction was taken a few weeks ago when the Chamberlain Administration was thrown down and the Labour and Liberal Parties joined the Government of Mr. Churchill. Had it not been for the invigorating effect of this change it may well have happened that the disasters of the past fortnight would have produced a despondency too deep for recovery. Fortunately we acted in time and under a new leadership new hope rises in the hearts of the people.

The Government gave immediate evidence of its recognition of the gravity of the crisis. Unprecedented powers were asked from Parliament and were given with a whole-hearted promptitude which showed that the House of Commons was also awake to the urgency of the times. By these powers all persons and property are placed at the disposal of the Government. We are assured that no private interest shall be allowed to stand in the way of the public need. At last the total resources of the nation are available for the waging of total war.

The workers' organisations have agreed to waive many of their most cherished protections, under a solemn undertaking that no attempt will be made to resist their restoration when the need is passed. We expect the undertaking to be honoured when the time comes, but our surest guarantee will lie in the strength of the workers themselves. We do not fear for the status of the workers when victory is won, for the victory of our cause and the dominance of Labour will occur together.

It is in the use of the powers in the mobilising of property that I feel misgivings. It must not be forgotten that vested interests are entrenched in the vast Conservative majority in the House of Commons and it will be used to fight a rear-guard action in defence of property against every invasion of the new Government. In what way does the Government intend to apply its power? Already the suggestion is being made that, with some exceptions, the right to take over property will be kept in the background, to be used as a threat against any who show reluctance to fall into line with the Government's plans. I hear from many quarters that the Government expects the persuasive effect of the powers to be sufficient for most of their needs and an elaborate system of State control is being used to marshal industry in accordance with the needs of the war effort. If this be so I can see trouble ahead. Two considerations should be kept in mind. One, the utmost use and exertion of the nation's resources to win the war. Two, the necessity to prepare for the economic dislocations arising from the crossover from a war to a peace footing when the war is over. To those who say the second consideration is academic, I reply that the same methods which will serve best for winning the war will apply equally well for the change-over. They are not opposed but rather complementary.

Experience has taught us that control is not enough when applied to the basic industries. Full State control was achieved over the coal industry in the last war. It did not get the best results from the coal mines during the war and it proved calamitous when the war ended.

State control without State ownership makes the worst of both worlds. And this for reasons which must be obvious to anyone who thinks for a moment. Under State control the whole personnel of an industry comes under the direction of the Government, but it remains in the employment of the same employers, and, what is even more to the point, the staff knows that when the war is over their continued employment will depend upon the good-will of the owner. In these circumstances to whom will the staff give first allegiance? The State or the employer? Obviously the employer will always come first, and where the interests of the two conflict the State will take second place. In any case, the State is far away and the employer or his manager is on the spot. It is difficult to conceive conditions more conducive to unconscious sabotage. Divided loyalties are never good. They may be disastrous in times like these.

COAL AND THE NATION

If we consider the case from the standpoint of the employer the position is even worse. He looks forward to his industry being restored to him after the war and this becomes his main concern. The classic case again is coal mining. In the last war certain coal owners practised direct sabotage. They deliberately allowed the most productive seams to remain undeveloped and concentrated on more expensive and less productive ones. Some even went so far as to open up good seams and then left them idle, so as to exploit them immediately control ended. It is no use complaining about their lack of patriotism. A state of affairs ought not to be allowed in which private acquisitiveness is set in opposition to the national interest.

If David Grenfell wants, as I am sure he does, the last ounce out of the coal industry, he should insist upon the Government taking over the coal mines and discuss the terms of compensation when the war is won. Until it is done much of the drive he strives to impart to coal production will be intercepted and cushioned by the coal owners.

What is true of coal production holds with equal force for coal distribution. Coal, priced at 80/- a ton, sold in bags in our great cities, is a monstrous outrage and generates a most dangerous and unfair friction between those workers who pay it and the coal miners, for the latter are unjustly blamed for prices which go to swell middle men's profits and are never reflected in miners' wages.

What of the railways? Is it not intended to unify them at once under national ownership? Are the accounts of the railway companies being kept separate so that they can revert to the same old silly system after the war?

An even more urgent case is the distribution of electricity. For many years the chaos and corruption there has been a scandal. If air raids on a great scale occur, as they are certain to, the central ownership and direction of our electrical supply will become a matter of vital national importance. Here is a first-class opportunity to cut through a whole jungle of vested interests, which would have a wholesome influence on industry and politics and at the same time put in the hands of the Governments the instruments of effective economic organisation. The problems of rural housing, food production, and evacuation to the remote countryside, are all bound up with the scientific organisation of electrical supply at uniform tariffs.

Now is the accepted time to do it. I know that Herbert Morrison has for years yearned for the chance to put the electricity industry right. I do most earnestly hope that he, and his Labour colleagues in the Government, will not lack the courage to apply the remedy boldly.

What is needed now is to nationalise enough basic industries so as to provide the State with a sort of publicly owned economic backbone. This will immensely add to the efficiency of the war effort now and provide an invaluable instrument with which to guide the economic life of the nation after the war. It would build up under war pressure a *vested interest in public ownership* which would resist all attempts to get back to economic anarchy after the war. Unless the wide powers given to the Government are going to be used in this way they are nothing but a masquerade. Their effects would differ in no way from what happened in the last war. And they would lead to no better result in the war's aftermath.

RECIPE FOR VICTORY

The leaders of the nation need to learn at once that what we did in the last war is no model for this one. It is because they had to have this lesson burned into them that the Nazis have succeeded so far.

We are hearing too much of how we have in the past surmounted disasters and won through to victory. Victory comes not through disasters but in spite of them. Disaster is no recipe for victory. Only by bold and sweeping measures, improvisations and daring experiments can the Nazi flood be made to recoil upon itself. The nation has willingly armed the Government with final powers. It must use them for total victory.

We and the Germans – 25 June 1943

Europe is seething. The first effects of the sustained bombing of German centres, of the Allied victories in North Africa, leading to the growing threat to Italy, all reinforced by the delayed-action shock of the failures on the Russian front have broken down the German people's confidence in the Military sagacity of their Nazi rulers. From many parts of Europe, for some months past, evidence has come showing that the people of the occupied countries have regained their self-confidence and are beginning to hit back. The most significant admission of the new mood, however, comes from Germany itself. On June 13th the *Voelkischer Beobachter*, the official Nazi newspaper, carried a leading article in which appeared this statement: –

> 'We in particular must acknowledge our close links with the Party, even though this may require a good deal of "Civic courage." It is easy and it may appear advantageous to profess membership of the Party on festive occasions; to appear and act as a *Parteigenosse* (Party Comrade) in everyday life and at all times is incomparably harder and by no means always pleasant.'

Here we have an admission that it is now unpopular to belong to the Nazi Party, and that if one does belong, an excuse is the best way to justify it. This, then, is the moment when the political arm can so powerfully supercharge the effectiveness of the military arm as to bring the war to an earlier end and save countless thousands of lives, both here and on the Continent. To talk, at this moment, of the general guilt of the German people, as a whole, for the behaviour of the Nazis is both unwise and inexpedient. Nor is it a decent spectacle to see certain people indulge their blood pressure at the expense of young men who have to do their will in the plane, the battleship and on the battlefield. Let us do what we must. But no more, lest every excess be paid for in the suffering and bloodshed of the innocent.

HITLER – THE BEST WITNESS

If we are to take advantage of these fissiparous tendencies within Germany it is first necessary to clear our own minds of certain misconceptions about the general responsibility of the German people for the events of the past ten years. For our conclusions will guide our conduct – and our ultimate fate. Nor is it necessary to dip deep into history in order to find guidance. Each generation is inclined to rewrite history to suit its own purposes, and it would, indeed, be sad if we had to ask historians, who disagree so much with each other, to agree on the advice they should give to us. A little applied intelligence to the known facts is sufficient for our purpose.

The best witness of the guilt of the masses of the German people for the war and for the bestiality with which the Nazis have conducted it is Hitler himself. He is an admitted authority on the psychology of the German people. This being the case, a question arises. If he was convinced that the generality of Germans could be relied upon to co-operate enthusiastically in preparing and making war on the world, why did he consider that his first task was to gag, bully and intimidate the German people? Surely if they are what the hate merchants make them out to be, the Brown House, the concentration camp, the suppression of all free institutions in Germany, the burning of books, the punishment for listening to the foreign radio and the manipulation the Press – all these were utterly unnecessary. The fact is Hitler could not trust the German people to follow him in his maniac intentions if he left them to the free exercise of their informed judgment. The fact is – and it is the basic fact from which our reasoning must proceed – the ordinary German was the first victim of Nazi aggression, and when he lost his freedom ours was immediately threatened. It would have been as immediately threatened by the Italian people's loss of liberty if Mussolini had the material strength at his disposal that Hitler has at his. Mussolini had to content himself with the comparatively weak Abyssinia because he dared not loose his hate on bigger prey. If he been able to do so we should have seen every pimp with a classical education serving up the inequities of the Italian people through Machiavelli, the Borgias, to the time-serving eloquence of Cicero, and missing Garibaldi and Mazzini on the way.

A HUMAN PROBLEM

It is essential to grasp firmly on to the principle that men and women are more the creatures of their social institutions and the political machinery than they are of their blood stream and of their remote history.

Nor must we forget that there are powerful people amongst us who have a real vested interest in this attempt to prove that social and political behaviour have their roots in immutable racial or individual qualities. They are the same ones who seek to prove that labour troubles are caused by the evil dispositions of agitators and not by the wrongs done to the workers. They are the ones who argue that if you put slum dwellers into good houses they would put coal into the baths. It is necessary for them to seek to prove that poverty and social evils are caused by the shape of our heads, our ancestral inheritance, the colour of our skins – anything but the maldistribution of wealth or the defects of our economic, political and social institutions. For these last are within our power to change, and they dread the changes lest they be dispossessed of their power and privileges.

Therefore our attitude towards the future of the German people is at bottom the same as the question of our attitude to our own future, and to the kind of society we want to emerge from the anguish now searing the whole world. They are not two different issues. Either we are all free and safe, or none of us can be. Nor is it wise to allow those good people who talk of the need to re-educate Germany after the war to indulge their false paternalism. Who is to do the re-educating? Britain? Have we made such a good job of educating the 350 million Indians that we can take on 80 million Germans? It seems that a little introspective humility is called for from us at this moment. The only people who can be safely entrusted to make over the bad Germans are the good Germans. If they cannot do it no one can, for no nation will accept its cultural education compulsorily at the hands of another.

It all, therefore, comes down to this: there is no German problem nor an Italian problem. There is a human problem of how the peoples of the world are going to live in peace, freedom and prosperity, and inside that general problem there is the problem of how we in Europe are going to settle our affairs. As I have already said, it is urgent that we make up our minds about this now for the moment of decision is upon us.

TORY POWER OF BLACKMAIL

We already have an example of how not to do it. The protracted and acrimonious negotiations between de Gaulle and Giraud in Algiers reveal the evil of taking short views on such a vital matter. We elevated to power in

North Africa all the anti-democratic and neo-Fascist elements to be found there, and then thrust upon the Free French the task of coming to terms with them. We put our friends at a great disadvantage, and because they find the situation intolerable we shrug our shoulders and talk of these 'impossible French.'

There is one unpleasant fact we must face, and for that we in this country are responsible. The Tories are in power here, and therefore when our Armies land on the European mainland their Tory leaders will seek to come to terms with their opposite numbers in the countries we occupy. In short, the Tories here will try to put back into power the reactionary elements there. It is natural that they should do so. If we Socialists were in power in this country we should promote the ascendancy of Socialists in Europe. When the guilt comes to be apportioned we shall bear a heavy share for our failure to defeat reaction in this country.

It follows from this that the more the Tories assist with the reshaping of European Governments the more those Governments will tend to take on a reactionary character under the guidance and pressure of London and Washington. The efforts of progressives here must consequently be directed to reducing Tory interference to a minimum. We must have confidence in the belief that the European masses will move in a revolutionary direction as soon as the military weight of Germany is removed. In short, we must have confidence in the political aspirations of the ordinary people in all the countries of Europe immediately their opportunity comes to them.

The Tory powers of blackmail and coercion will be enormous, for in addition to the presence of our Armies, the victors will be the bearers of food in large quantities for the relief of the half-starved multitudes.

If a revolutionary movement seizes power Wall Street and the City will be tempted either to starve it into submission or suppress it by force of arms under the pretext of preserving order and civil conditions. What starts as a campaign of liberation will tend to develop into a counter-revolutionary occupying force. Nor are we entitled to be surprised if and when this happens. If the people of Europe declare the railways, the land, the banks, the mines and the factories public property the owners of similar properties here and in America will take alarm and will try to suppress a revolution which might have unpleasant repercussions for them.

Then will come for us a time for the utmost vigilance and political activity, for our own hopes for the future are bound up in the success of the revolutionary movements on the Continent. We have shown our own incapacity to achieve victory for the progressive forces in this country, and the most we can do now is to neutralise the influence of our own reactionaries when we come to land on the Continent.

It should now begin to be clear why certain interests in this country seek to inflame our passions against the whole German people and prepare for a prolonged occupation under the guise of re-education. They are taking steps to keep the ordinary people of Europe under control, for they are grimly aware that if German tanks stopped short at the English Channel revolutionary ideas would not.

The last war gave us the Russian Revolution, although the prolonged opposition of the capitalist nations deprived the Russians and us of some of the finest fruits of it. This war can give us the European Revolution if the arm that strikes down the Nazis is not allowed to crush the insurgent spirit of Europe.

GUARDIANS OF THE REVOLUTION

Unfortunately, we labour under disadvantages which were not present at the end of the last war. There was a strong, militant, and independent Labour Party in this country in 1920, and through its exertions Mr. Churchill and his friends were prevented from doing the infant Russian Revolution to death. The Soldiers' and Sailors' Councils, which sprang up almost overnight, kept guard over the fate of their Russian comrades who were striving to establish their revolution in the midst of interventionist civil war and the hostility of all the governments of the world. Where are the guardians of the coming European Revolution? The Labour Party is enmeshed in the Coalition and has never shown less evidence of revolutionary ardour. A generation of Labour leadership has grown up with its feet deeply rooted in the maintenance of the existing social order. The rest of the Left forces are divided, whereas at the end of the last war they were united within the Labour Party and the trade unions. Is there not here a task on which all the Left can unite? At home our domestic rivalries seem to divide us hopelessly at the moment. Where in Britain are those to whom the workers of Europe can look for help when their hour strikes?

The City will look after its own. Cannot we look after ours?

What Eden cannot do – 14 April 1944

'Realistic' discussions about the future of international relations assure four Great Powers, after the defeat of Germany and Japan. They are America, Russia, the British Empire and China. We can take it for granted that China is included as a courtesy, for it will take more than a generation before her huge material and man-power resources can be organised for their deployment on a world stage. She is a world power in potential only, and much will happen before that potential is enabled to mature into the actual. That leaves three, America, Russia and ourselves.

What about the British Empire? Remember we are talking with the 'realists' in terms of the new power politics. Can we truthfully say in those terms that we measure up to Russia and America? For the purpose of these comparisons we must leave out the coloured populations of the British Empire, for the war has shown that, both in disposition and distribution, they cannot be relied upon as fighting assets. Why they are not, and whether they should, lies outside our present discussion. That leaves us with a white population of something like 70 millions.

TWO GREAT POWERS ONLY

But even that figure is too optimistic in terms of world strategy of tomorrow, for New Zealand, Australia, and Canada could co-operate effectively with the Mother Country in the event of war only with the permission of the United States. That leaves us with a population, massed around its own base, of about 50 millions in these islands. This compares with populations of 170 millions in Russia and 130 millions in the United States. No doubt this is subject to a hundred-and-one modifications in detail, but it is nevertheless the overall picture, and from it no objective mind could insist that Great Britain is a great power in any sense which includes Russia and the U.S.A.

So those who demand we consider the future in terms of 'realism' and power are speaking of the two great powers of America and Russia, with all other nations grouped around them in obedience of the centripetal or centrifugal influence of the dominant two. These are the material facts which underlie the paralysis of British foreign policy, and to which I referred here last week.

The position of Great Britain in all this is unique, for she has interests and possessions in all parts of the world. That is probably what Mr. Ernest Bevin meant when he said the other day that Britain is the bridge between Russia and America. The choice of metaphor here is important, for in certain circumstances the bridge could become a football, a decoy, a makeweight, or even a rich prey to be hunted down and shared out. In any event the conception that the future of international relations is merely to be a continuation of the past, with other nations playing the dominant roles, is not one to excite enthusiasm in any of us.

Nor can we fall back on the peaceful if humble role of small spectator of the power game of the great ones. The development of the present war has shown that the occupants of the grandstand seats are eventually tumbled into the arena. Neutrality has become a historical reminiscence, and its defence only a little less burdensome than war. Then again, in a world bent on power politics, even small nations like to take a hand in the game, for there is always the chance of pickings in the company of the bigger beasts of prey, and the mammoths are often ready to throw a few prizes to the little ones who hunt by their side. So, whether we are great nations or small, preparing for war and fighting it when it comes will be the lot of all of us if the hard-headed 'realists' of power have their way.

There is another consideration to which I should like to call the attention of Labour people here and our friends in America. To what extent will it prove possible to preserve civil liberties and democratic institutions in such a world? The mental readiness of a population to engage in war is at least as militarily important as its material preparation. Hitler proved that. Modern war is total war. It involves the mobilisation of all the resources of the nation into a single striking force. Not only does the bomber bring the civil population to the fighting front, but the modern fighting machine recruits general industry into its service. These are commonplaces, but their significance for peace-time conditions have not yet been realised.

INDIVISIBLE FREEDOM

Waging total war means total preparation for it. And that means mental as well as physical preparation. Hitler did not talk idly when he declared the internationalist at home to be as much an enemy of Germany as the opponent in the field. His logic was ruthless, but it was well founded.

In terms of modern power politics the international propagandist who tries to disarm your people mentally is a real danger to your power unless your possible enemy also allows him similar freedom in his country. Freedom is nowhere safe unless it is everywhere enjoyed. This was partially true in the past. It is wholly true now if only because the technique of modern war demands it.

Before the twentieth century wars could, and indeed were, carried on, and still left a considerable proportion of the population comparatively unaffected. If power politics are to rule the world war will therefore be an ever-present reality, pervading the whole population and creating a permanent psychosis. This condition of affairs will be so shocking a violation of the manifest oneness of the world in culture and economics that only political repression of the worst sort will prevent ordinary people from resenting so monstrous a contradiction. *Suppression of civil liberty is consequently an inevitable accompaniment of the 20th century power politics.*

Those who talk glibly of looking for our security to the size and efficiency of our war machine have not taken the trouble to examine what it will mean as a social burden. A modern navy, army and air force involve a colossal drain on economic and manpower resources. Nor will it prove possible for power politics to limit their size by agreement. That method was tried and failed. The French thesis that security must precede disarmament was wholly sound. Men must first feel safe before they will throw away their arms, and it is just this feeling of safety that power politics inhibits. America will not feel safe in the size of the Russian war machine, and Russia will look askance at every increase in America's. And the rest of the world will follow suit.

A further irony will be added to the situation by the fact that the more successful and civilised a nation becomes in the ordering of its domestic affairs the less safe it will feel. If we are to achieve full employment in the arts of peace, any of our resources we set aside for war preparation will be resented and consequently resisted. This was so in the Liberal era. An expanding economy resents war preparation. A contracting economy welcomes it. Prolonged unemployment in Britain favoured war preparation in 1937–8–9. In Germany the Nazis made it into their principal economic programme. Power politics will make the Nazi principle universal. This then is the outlook before us if the 'realists' have their way, and at the moment no authoritative voice is raised against them.

WEIGHT OF MASS OPINION

But is it quite certain the 'realists' will have their way? The professors of 'real politik' have been wrong before, both on the Right and the Left. Many of these believed it was inevitable that Russia would have to meet the attack of the Fascist powers alone, instead of which she is in alliance with the two great capitalist powers of Britain and America. At the last moment the opinion of the masses made itself felt, unexpectedly, and the victim turned out to be not Russia as was confidently anticipated, but Nazi Germany and Fascist Italy.

This factor of mass opinion is of importance just to the extent that the whole population of a nation is now involved in modern war. There is therefore this negative restraint on the freedom of action of the power politicians – they must carry the people with them. In extreme cases like Germany it is done by the complete suppression of all opinion not 100 per cent 'official.' In its way it is a tribute to ordinary people that they have to be systematically deceived before they can be persuaded to co-operate in stupid policies.

But an ill-informed, and undirected public opinion is not sufficient in itself to check the drift to universal anarchy. Leadership and the sustained presentation of an alternative approach is now more needed than ever. From where is it to come? And what is it?

The nation best situated to provide it is Great Britain. First, because it has more to give as a contribution to world organisation in imperial spirit, and therefore more to lose by world anarchy; and second, because the mood of her people incline them to a more enlightened approach to social problems than at any time in her history.

By Great Britain I do not mean the existing Government. Nothing can be expected from them but a repetition of past ruling class policies in more and more debilitated terms. Fortunately it is now fairly clear that their period of political power is going to suffer an eclipse, of long or short duration depending upon how we use our opportunities. In these circumstances the British Labour Party will come to power at a time when the whole world will be looking for a lead. That is to say, it will have a world audience listening to its guidance. It is therefore of the utmost importance that it should not be committed now on the lines of its future policy.

It should take the earliest opportunity of stating in general terms its attitude to the central problems of world reconstruction. It has already gone too far in maintaining silence on a number of questions of first importance. It allowed itself to be compromised by agreeing to the appointment of Darlan, and it looks like committing itself to further folly by agreeing to allow General Eisenhower the right to nominate the French authorities with whom he will co-operate when we land in France. Labour people here are also uneasy about what Lord Beaverbrook is cooking in the matter of the future of civil aviation. His Lordship's past reassures no one concerned about world peace.

Its authority as the practically certain Party to form the next Government of Great Britain therefore gives the Labour Party a unique position at this moment. It can talk over the heads of existing governments to the people of the world, and by so doing it can put a healthy check on many of the schemes now being hatched.

INTERNATIONAL CO-OPERATION

In writing this I am bound to confess to some doubts as to whether the existing leadership of the Labour Party will seize its chance. Nevertheless that does not absolve us from the obligation to say what we think it should do, for by it we perform our task of education and so raise the level of political consciousness. Also there is another reflection which comes to console me; the next General Election should see an influx of fresh minds and more vigorous and adventurous men and women to the ranks of the Parliamentary Labour Party. Still another reflection occurs to me and it should also occur to those responsible for the shaping of Labour policy. It is this:

The British people will be in no mood to accept any more fighting in the pursuit of illusory power adventures. They went into this war cold, they are fighting it cold, and they will emerge from it determined to pursue another course. It is the universal experience of those who move about the country that flag-wagging and its associated appeals rouse no enthusiasm among the masses. Their devotees exist in newspaper offices and nowhere else. In the absence of an enlightened appeal to their idealism the people will relapse into a condition of cynical apathy, unhealthy for any form of social action.

But this is no reason why we should despair of the prospects before us. All over the world there are millions of men and women eagerly awaiting the lead we can give. The remarkable and growing support American Vice-President Henry Wallace is getting among his countrymen is evidence that millions of Americans are not prepared to support the prophets of the American Century. The supporters of world co-operation outnumber overwhelmingly the army behind the power politicians.

Part of our task now is to re-establish contact with them wherever they can be found, and in every way open to us. As soon as circumstances permit the broken strands of international working-class organisation must be reknit, so that people of like mind can take counsel together and decide common action to meet what lies before us. For a long time to come we must expect that governments will try to prevent this, because they fear the spread of enlightened ideas among the peoples of the world. Already the British trade unions are reaching out to meet and assist in rebuilding the trade unions of the Continent. We shall get from them at least as much as they will get from us, for our defect of insularity has been dangerously reinforced by the ruptures of war.

So, whilst there is no doubting the difficulties ahead let us at the same time not forget to add up our advantages. And if that does not prove sufficient let us consider the black outlook for mankind if the troglodytes once more get their way. The world is weary of war and the ways of the war-makers. It is time the architects of peace took charge of the site.

We asked for it – 18 September 1953

World politics present a depressing spectacle of leaderlessness. The two most powerful Western leaders, Churchill and Eisenhower, seem overwhelmed by events; Churchill because of age and Eisenhower because he just does not know the reckoning.

Last May, Churchill, in calling for a meeting at the highest level with the Soviet Union, grasped the initiative. He probably would have followed it up, despite the opposition of many of the most powerful of his colleagues, if he had not been suddenly taken ill.

Since then the only indication of an independent British line was the support given to India for membership of the Korean Conference.

Eden is still too ill to take full charge of foreign affairs. This has left Butler in effective control, and the result is that Britain has relapsed into docile acceptance of American leadership.

Even the friendliness of the Tory press for the British Government has not been able completely to conceal the significance of all this from the British people. Apart from resentment against rising food prices, the issue on which the ordinary men and women of Britain are most sensitive is the prospect of peace or war.

The longing for secure peace is profound, and no statesman who fails to take it into account can hope to have influence. This has not resulted in 'neutralism,' as so many foolishly believe. Rather it expresses itself in a demand that British policy should align itself with all those forces in the world that make for a peaceful solution of problems.

The failure of the British Government to follow up the lead given by Churchill has resulted in a fall in their political stock. Nor is it possible to see how the Government can recover favour. They have no Bills before Parliament that can do any other than add to their embarrassment.

If the coming Labour Conference is able to hammer out a programme which unites the Labour movement, then Labour faces a winter session which will see an accession to its strength.

Recent events in Germany are not likely to reduce the headaches of statesmen dealing with international affairs. The decisive victory of Dr. Adenauer was hailed here with an astonishing inability to see its inner significance.

Adenauer was supported and financed by the same big industrial interests which had been responsible for Hitler's climb to power. His success is applauded in Britain by the same elements that saw in German fascism only an answer to the threat of Communism.

The chickens will now come home to roost with a vengeance. We have asked for it and we are going to get it.

At the end of the war the British Labour Government wanted the Ruhr industries to be given over into public ownership. America under General Marshall refused to agree. Once more the British allowed themselves to be bullied. The price now falls to be paid.

Some have seen in Dr. Adenauer's victory new hopes of European integration after the fashion of American ideals, along with twelve German divisions for the European Defence Community (E.D.C.).

Adenauer does not quite see it that way. Already he begins to manoeuvre Germany into a position where she is courted by both East and West. This is exactly what some of us prophesied.

Adenauer has already used ominous language. He speaks now not of German unity but of the 'liberation of the Eastern provinces.' He tells his Western backers that European unity means for Germany unity of all Germany.

If, he hints, the Western Powers cannot get this for him, then he may fall back upon direct negotiations with Russia with the same end in view and, in exchange, give Russia guarantees in Europe. Adenauer is therefore sitting pretty.

The U.S.A. thought his victory would mean the integration of Western Germany in the E.D.C. with the hope that a powerful defence force would be built up against the Soviet Union. But Adenauer will not accept absorption in the West at the cost of permanent German division. Germany is quite unable to reconcile herself to the prospect of indefinite mutilation.

This is what Adenauer is now saying. In effect he declares, 'Get it for me by force or I will buy it.' If he buys it at any price acceptable to Russia, then the U.S.A. will have lost what she so badly wanted, a German army in Europe poised against the Soviet bloc.

Nor has the Soviet Union any cause to congratulate itself on the result. By making himself the champion of German unity at all cost, Adenauer rallied to him a majority of the German voters, including many who already romanticise the memory of Hitler.

By comparison with this red-blooded programme, the Social Democrats seemed feeble and uninspiring. Soviet behaviour accomplished the defeat of the Social Democrats, and so insured the triumph of those Germans who are both capitalist and chauvinist. All the Social Democrats hoped to achieve was sufficient votes to force Adenauer to include them in his Government and thus assist in modifying extreme nationalist elements. By maintaining a divided Germany the Soviet Union guaranteed Adenauer's electoral success, because most potential Socialist votes are in Eastern Germany.

Since the end of the war Western diplomacy has struggled to re-establish in Europe the same social pattern that preceded the triumph of the Nazis. How can it expect that the same result will not follow?

By insisting on the dismemberment of Germany the Soviet leaders worked to the same end. A united Germany would have resulted in the success of a moderate type of Socialism after the fashion of British Labour. But this does not suit the Soviet leaders any more than it suits the United States.

By destroying civilised alternatives these two misleaders of mankind have recreated just those conditions that led to the second world war. It makes no difference that the personalities in the drama have different names. The play is the same, and if we do not take care it will have the same dreadful last act.

Of course, we are told Adenauer has no such intentions. That is of little or no importance. He has let loose the same forces that carried Hitler irresistibly to power.

The energies of the German people will be diverted from the peaceful transformation of their society by the struggle for inclusion of Eastern Germany in a Fourth Reich. Soon we shall see marching and countermarching.

Nor will the appetite of German chauvinism be satisfied with the mere inclusion of Eastern Germany. There are the lost provinces to be considered. Here the Soviet Union will be caught in a painful dilemma, for German claims could only be satisfied at the expense of Poland. This would cost the Soviet Union a fatal loss of face.

Such a cynical sacrifice of a satellite might lead to the disintegration of the Soviet bloc and the decline of Soviet power.

OUR BEST HOPE

The conclusion of all this is clear. If social changes are frustrated, a resurgent nationalism takes its place.

Another illustration of this is to be seen in Italy. Finding himself faced with a precarious parliamentary majority dedicated to the maintenance of the economic status quo, Signor Pella, the Italian Prime Minister, discovers 'a Yugoslav plot' to incorporate Trieste in Yugoslavia by force of arms.

So he makes bellicose speeches, moves armies and warships, and demands a conference on terms that he knows the Yugoslavs will not agree to.

Does he want a solution of the Trieste problem? It may be. But there is a shrewd suspicion that he wants, even more, a political diversion from the paucity of his own social and economic policies.

It certainly is desirable that the Trieste problem should be considered and a solution found. But if the main cause of the trouble is in the refusal of Italian ruling circles to face the problems arising from the poverty of the Italian people, a solution of Trieste would be followed by another claim somewhere else.

A morbid national psychology is not to be cured by a series of concessions at the expense of other nations.

These are some, but only some, of the problems that loom large on the international scene as we approach the closing months of 1953. The picture begins to look ominously like the middle thirties, when statesmanship proved bankrupt and policies drifted until we were all caught in the tragic currents that moved remorselessly to the second world war.

That we are aware of them and can see them in such a historical perspective is perhaps our best hope that the same terrible conclusion may not once more be reached.

Aneurin Bevan attacks radioactive nonsense – 15 July 1955

[...]

The leading articles in the *Manchester Guardian* and the *Daily Telegraph*, dealing with the statement of the scientists, make painful reading. They might have been written by Foster Dulles.

The *Guardian* writes, 'The existence of Western bombs has contributed to making the Russian Government more cautious and conciliatory.' Perhaps so. But is the Russian possession of bombs making the Western Powers more cautious and conciliatory?

We have had the bombs for some time, the Russians have only just come into possession of them. As the U.S.S.R. begins to match us in capacity for mutual destruction she grows more conciliatory. Might it not be that she, for her part, now recognises that the role of force in international affairs is receding?

Would it not be better to proceed to reason from that basis rather than to conclude in the old-fashioned and now outmoded way that Russia is ready to negotiate only because she is conscious of relative inferiority?

The Western Powers used to argue that it was not safe nor prudent to negotiate with Russia until they could 'talk out of strength.' But they apply the opposite reasoning to Russia. She, apparently, is ready to talk out of weakness.

Would it not be better to start with the assumption that both sides are now evenly matched, in the sense that both are now capable of reducing the world to radioactive rubble? And that consequently, in the language of the Appeal, we must 'use peaceful means for the settlement of all matters of dispute between nations.'

The *Daily Telegraph* outbids the *Manchester Guardian* in demonology. Its leader states, 'The whole problem arises from the determination of free peoples that life on this earth would not be worth living under Communist domination, and from the Communist conviction that life will be worth living only when Communism is universal.' In that one sentence the possibilities of peaceful co-existence are ruled out.

The 'free peoples' apparently include Spain, Portugal, Guatemala, and our colonial possessions such as Kenya and British Guiana, not to mention the coloured people of the Union of South Africa and Algeria.

The colonial people are unable to bring us to the conference table, not because we have rejected the role of force in human affairs but simply and solely because they cannot threaten us with hydrogen bombs. The same can be said about the Russian satellites, but this is just a matter of the pot calling the kettle black and not a question of dividing the world into God and Devil nations.

The inhabitants of Cyprus, for instance, have just brought us to a round table conference, not because we recognised the justice of their cause from the outset, but because they have made us dangerously uncomfortable there. Is that proof of the 'new thinking' the scientists are asking of us?

It would be better for the *Daily Telegraph* to drop its unctuous humbug and recognise that the nuclear age has caught all of us unprepared, both morally and politically.

In their effort to state the issue before us in the least contentious terms the scientists avoided classifying us in political categories and suggested that what is now in issue is the survival of mankind as a 'biological species.' One would have thought that here at least is common ground for all of us, including the Communist part of the world.

But the *Daily Telegraph* will have none of it. It complains that they – the scientists – 'assume continuation of the human species as the crucial consideration.' Well, is it not?

It is precisely because war would lead to the extinction of the 'human species' that there is every hope that war as an 'instrument of revolution' is in process of being discarded by Communists. This, we are led to understand, is the 'revolution' now taking place in Communist theoretical thinking. No theory of human society can be rationally pursued to the point where it would result in the destruction of the human race.

Instead of appreciating that in this thought we have reached a stage where all mankind has a common interest which could result in common action the *Telegraph* resorts to a frenzied intolerance that his Holiness the Pope has himself warned us against. The *Telegraph says*, 'But we do not and should not, regard ourselves simply as members of a species and nothing more.'

But that is precisely as we should regard ourselves when faced with the possibility of universal destruction. We have yet to learn of a Communist or capitalist thought without a head to hold it in.

'Ah,' but we are told, 'this exposes the West to the possibilities of endless blackmail by the Communist nations, for the latter will threaten the human race with extinction unless it embraces Communism.' Where is the evidence for that?

It is possible to build up such a case on certain interpretations of Russian behaviour since the end of the war. It is also possible to see the opposite in certain demands now canvassed that Russia should surrender all influence over her satellites and in the persistent refusal to bring Peking China into the United Nations.

The argument of the scientists is that there is nothing the nations have at issue with each other that transcends the duty of preserving mankind as a 'biological species.' Therefore, because war is now clearly seen to be a 'universal enemy' it should now be universally outlawed.

It is as much a cause for hope, as it is for fear, that a common morality has now become a common interest.

The disarmament breakdown – 11 May 1956

The breakdown of the disarmament talks is an unqualified disaster. Both sides are once more engaged in the old game of putting the blame on the other.

Both sides have shifted their ground so frequently that public opinion has given up the task of keeping pace in despair. Nevertheless, it would be fatal to surrender to such a mood.

Efforts to reach agreement must go on, if not in this way then in that, if not by means of formal conference then by searching out each other's position in ways familiar to the arts of diplomacy.

At all costs it must not be assumed that the London Conference registered a final failure to reach agreement.

But if future discussions are to prove more fruitful, there must be a clear conception of what it is the great powers are to attempt. At first sight this may sound curious; for surely everyone is now agreed on the objectives, even though they might still be far apart on the means and methods employed.

Ordinary men and women have assumed that the main purpose of the London Conference was to agree on the level of arms and then to proceed to their orderly reduction by stages. It was further assumed that measures of inspection and control were indispensable to the creation of an atmosphere of confidence and trust.

Heaven knows these are difficult enough of achievement, as we have been made to realise all too frequently. But they are sufficiently precise to be capable of practical examination.

Actual figures about the size of armies have been mentioned, if not agreed, and points of control and even limited areas of inspection were brought up in the discussion. All this offered the hope that at last a start was possible. Why was it not made?

Has the leading American delegate to the Conference, Mr. Harold Stassen, given us the real answer? In a statement made in London, before the Conference reported failure, he said that there were two major differences between Russia and the Western powers.

These were the extent and nature of the inspection system and *the necessity for political settlements before a low level of armaments can be contemplated.*

Mr. Stassen mentioned four outstanding political differences, as requiring settlement, before there could be full-scale disarmament – *the reunification of Germany in freedom and peace, the reunification of Korea on the same terms and agreements on the Far East and the Middle East.*

AN UGLY SOUND

At the conclusion of the Conference he stated: 'I think the question of political settlement has been brought more into focus in these talks.' There we have it, and it has an ugly sound.

We had all understood that there was one principle which is basic in these discussions on disarmament. The point has been reached in the development of modern weapons of war, we thought, when their employment for the settlement of political differences could not be contemplated; that in consequence they have become a nonsensical and intolerable burden; therefore, what is now required is an agreed way of dismantling the war machine.

Without this overriding and governing principle being accepted throughout the discussions even partial disarmament would merely amount to the abolition of outmoded weapons, with the more formidable ones kept in the background as a possible means of eventual coercion.

If Mr. Stassen's words do not mean that then they mean nothing. They imply clearly that even if the London Conference achieved complete agreement on everything connected with a general plan for disarmament, the United States would still have held out for a political settlement on its own terms as a prior condition.

In short, political surrender by Russia is regarded by the United States as a pre-condition for general disarmament. Apparently Mr. Stassen is delighted that the disarmament talks have succeeded in bringing this 'into focus.'

Is this also the British, Canadian and French view? That is certainly the impression given by the answer on the same subject which Mr. Anthony Nutting has given in the House of Commons this week.

When the United Nations referred the question of disarmament to its sub-committee did it contemplate that issues of such high political moment should be included on the agenda or that they would be permitted to be raised?

Is it conceivable that a sub-committee of comparatively low status could have the right, or the obligation, to discuss, much less negotiate, questions that can only usefully be discussed by heads of state? If this is not the case what on earth does Mr. Stassen mean?

JUST TALKING

Or does he mean that he made it clear that whatever progress might be made at the London Conference, he felt obliged to lay it down, on behalf of his Government, that everything must be considered in the context of a political settlement which involved the abandonment by Russia of all her major political positions?

Or was Mr. Stassen just talking for the benefit of the American press – and, of course, through it to the various American 'lobbies,' all now in a ferment of activity during a Presidential election year?

Was it this he meant when he said: 'I continue to believe that the remaining gap will be closed. I do not think anyone today can describe the precise manner, but I think *the next year holds the best prospect of closing it.*'

In the meantime the British position grows desperate. It is common knowledge that British opinion is hardening in the direction of limiting expenditure on outmoded weapons and concentrating her waning financial resources on nuclear weapons and thermonuclear research.

The British Chancellor of the Exchequer has pledged himself to a reduction of the order of one hundred million pounds in the projected expenditure for the forthcoming year. It is assumed that most of this will be found from the Service Estimates.

BREAK LOOSE

Soviet Russia is likely to take the same line. Consequently what could have come from an international agreement will now flow from other considerations.

Because of her immense material resources America is not compelled by the same urgency. She can afford to take her time and she is indifferent to the more straitened circumstances of her Allies.

At some time or other Britain and France will have to break loose from the clamp in which they are held to the United States. Their position is becoming more and more humiliating.

Unless they take the initiative soon the opportunity will pass. Soviet Russia is prepared at any rate to do a deal with the United States. When the Presidential election is over America will be ready to play with Russia. There are distinct signs already that she is moving in that direction.

Marshal Bulganin and Mr. Khrushchev made it clear during their London visit that they looked upon it mainly as a bridge on which to cross to the United States.

When that happens neither Britain nor France may be in the company. They may find that they will not even be paid the reward of prolonged servility.

Destroy the bombs before they destroy us! – 24 May 1957

So Britain has now got her own H-bomb. Thus, as some newspapers have said, she once more takes her place 'among the great nations'. The argument that Britain must herself possess the Great Deterrent has won.

Apparently, however, it will be some years before she will have the bombs in sufficient quantities along with the essential modern apparatus to deliver them on to target. In the meantime – or so it seems – America deters Russia, and Russia deters America, while we propose to hurry up so that we can form one of the deterred three.

During this period, unless some agreement can be reached either on the abolition of the bomb or on general disarmament, other nations will almost certainly wish to qualify for membership of the H-bomb Club. For the argument that Britain applies to herself is one of universal application.

The spectacle of one nation after another insisting upon having its own H-bomb tests is a fearful one to contemplate. Some scientists, like Lord Cherwell, have been attempting to assuage our fears by claiming that our tests contribute only a small and comparatively innocuous fraction to the levels of radio-activity.

He admits that there might be a few more cases of bone cancer caused by our own experiments. At this point, however, he dispenses with his role of scientist and assumes that of the moralist, and tells us that this would be a small price to pay for the British possession of the bomb.

I am not competent to pass judgment on Lord Cherwell as a scientist. But we are all of us equally equipped to comment on his moralisings.

Lord Cherwell's reasoning, and those who think as he does, might be described as the morality of numbers. Some innocent people must be condemned to a horrible disease and to death in order that a large number of unknown people might live. It would follow from this that Lord Cherwell becomes guilty of immorality only at the point where his conduct would condemn more people to death than would be saved.

If this is not the case, what proportion of innocent people should be condemned to die in this way before it would constitute an offence under the moral code? Lord Cherwell doesn't tell us. Nevertheless, it is a question that he should be asked to face.

It is a good principle that you should judge your own conduct by the consequences that would follow if others did the same. If it be a fact also that what we have already done will condemn some innocent people to pain and death, if also by the same reasoning other nations are entitled to make their macabre contribution to the total, will Lord Cherwell and his accomplices tell us what the roll of murder must be before their consciences are pricked into action?

It must be borne in mind that the apologia of this group of scientists is put forward on behalf of the nations who claim to be dedicated to the sanctity of individual life. But it seems the anonymity of the condemned absolves us from guilt.

If we could display the victims of our behaviour before, say, a television screen so that they could be identified and their sufferings made manifest, would that make any difference to the nature of our deeds? Of course not. It would merely serve to quicken our imagination so as to bring home to us the enormity of our conduct.

Now that the scientists have had their say and the moralists have been worsted, the soldiers come forward to play their part. They are beginning to address their minds to the strategic consequences of the British possession of the bomb. Lt. General Sir Frederick Morgan attempted to face the problem in an article written in the *Daily Mail* on May 17.

The conclusion he reached was not very original. It had been reached in the House of Commons some years ago, but then, of course, it was more or less an abstract question. Now it is becoming a concrete reality.

As Sir Frederick puts it: 'One man, if the worst comes to the worst, is going to have to say "Shoot". That terrible decision has now become a real-life problem.'

Then, as though to make sure that the silenced moralists are kept silent, Sir Frederick goes on to comment: 'We are going to come up against all those nice-minded people who will say we must not be the first to use the bomb in the event of war.'

'In the event of war' is a question-begging phrase. For Sir Frederick himself insists that there would be no period of time during which the hydrogen powers can make up their minds whether or not to use the bomb. As Sir Frederick writes: 'If we are not the first to use it, we shall never use it at all.'

The same logic, of course, applies to the other hydrogen bomb nations. According to Sir Frederick, half a dozen hydrogen bombs would be sufficient to wipe out Britain. Twenty or thirty would be required to do the same for the Soviet Union.

Consider, therefore, the picture which is conjured up for us. The first purpose of arms is to win a war if you have to wage one. The second is to deter an attack. The third is to influence diplomatic relations.

The first can now be ruled out. Despite what Sir Frederick says, it is inconceivable that any great nation will be so completely destroyed in one attack as to be unable to deliver a counter-blow from some base or another not immediately affected by the first onslaught. The country most immediately exposed to such a possibility is, of course, Great Britain.

In these circumstances we are, therefore, confronted with the situation described by Lord Attlee some years ago as the danger of impossibility of anticipation. That is to say, some nation will take Sir Frederick Morgan's advice and get in with the bomb before the others. The logic that he applies to us, applies, of course, equally to others, although it is a curious fact that this never appears to have weight with people like Sir Frederick.

Bearing in mind all these facts, the only conclusion that a calm appraisal justifies is that the existence of nuclear weapons can no longer be regarded as a deterrent to war, but as making war a certainty.

In any major crisis between the great powers the mounting tension will tend to become unbearable. Frayed nerves will be screaming for action, and statesmen will get into the same state of mind that we saw in Britain last November.

It is in these conditions that the fear of anticipation will be at its height. In the very nature of things, public discussion about what to do will be ruled out. For this would destroy surprise.

As Sir Frederick Morgan rightly points out, someone would have to make the decision. This is to say, decisions about life or death, about the future of the human race, have passed out of the control of civil political institutions so long as weapons of this character are in the possession of governments.

The conclusion is inescapable. If the peoples are to recover control over those issues that are central, not only to the future of civilisation, but to its proper functioning, then we must apply our minds to the destruction of nuclear weapons before they have the chance to destroy us.

The clash of the giants –
23 August 1957

The cauldron of the Middle East continues to boil and bubble. Egypt, the Yemen, Jordan, Oman, and now Syria. These names flicker across the world, each carrying its own message of warning and foreboding.

There never was a time in all history when the statesmen of the world were more clearly presented with premonitions of disaster unless they took action in time.

No reason exists for the hope that, if left to themselves, the affairs of the Middle East will develop into a condition of peaceful stability, for of course, they are not, and cannot be, left to themselves. It is not an area that can be ringed off or walled in so that its embers are not allowed to ignite inflammable material elsewhere.

Unfortunately, both by a legacy from history and by economic necessities, the rest of the world, and in particular Western Europe – including Britain – are dependent upon the Middle East for oil.

PRIVATE GREED

If this dependence upon oil was an affair only of governments it would be sufficiently difficult to handle. But, of course, private oil interests, especially those of the United States and of European countries, are in competition with one another for the oil that they know exists and especially for the oil that they hope to find.

Thus, private greed and ambition exacerbate a situation already dangerously complicated.

When to these ingredients you add ostentatious opulence, cheek by jowl with appalling poverty and ignorance, gimcrack political constitutions, religious bigotry and flaming nationalism, it is scarcely conceivable that the whole area will not blow itself up.

In these circumstances you would think that the statesmen of the world, anxious as they continually declare themselves to be to preserve the peace and settle their differences amicably, would be in almost constant conclave, seeking to mute the succession of incidents and work out a long-term policy of settlement.

The very opposite is the case. This area, so full of menace for the peace of the world, is continually being goaded into aggressive action by this or that power in pursuit of its own ambitions.

Where international co-operation is manifestly a paramount necessity, we have instead intense rivalry and, most insane of all, competition in the supply of arms to nations that do not murder themselves and others only because so far they have lacked the means to do so.

At the time of writing, the newspaper headline is Syria. It may be that before these words appear in print, Syria will have definitely passed within the Russian orbit.

As *The Times* mordantly observes, if this happens, it will be the first time that Russia will have leap-frogged across other countries and established her paramountcy within the territorial area of her diplomatic enemies.

The Times adds, with refreshing candour, that this was prevented in British Guiana and Guatemala.

The main reason for the intractability of this problem is because the statesmen, especially of the Western nations, do not possess the courage of simplicity – that quality which is always to be found in greatness.

If we stand back for a moment from the immediate scene, and ask ourselves what is the one common concern of mankind, surely the answer will be found in seven words. At all costs, the avoidance of war.

I repeat, *at all costs*, because it is now universally acknowledged that war is the final catastrophe. This conclusion embraces the Communist nations, as well as every other.

It follows from this that the great powers ought not to push their claims and intensify their rivalries anywhere to such an extent as may imperil peace. Yet that is precisely what they are doing at this very moment in the Middle East.

The main burden of guilt rests upon the Western Powers. They have persistently based their policy on the assumption that Russia and Russian interests can be ignored in this area.

In the years immediately following the conclusion of the war, it was understood that Britain would look after the Middle East, whilst the United States devoted its attention to the Pacific.

It was an old-fashioned conception which took no account of the new distribution of world forces that war and revolution had produced.

NEW JOCKEY

It soon became clear that Britain could not fill the role. Elements in the United States came to the conclusion that this was because Britain was a decaying world power, that the imperial reins were slipping from her hands, and that therefore the time had come for Uncle Sam to occupy the driver's seat.

In short, the roles in the play were to remain the same, but the casting was to be different. This development naturally offended imperialistically-minded Britons. At the same time, it delighted their American counterparts.

The Eisenhower doctrine was the result.

Whatever may have been its short term effects in the case of Jordan, its long term consequences are likely to prove disastrous. All it really does is to bring the two great powers, Russia and the United States, into daily collision in the most sensitive area in the world.

At the same time, Britain continues to try to salvage what she has left of her historical legacy from being trampled under by the feet of the two manoeuvring giants.

The architects of the Charter of the United Nations recognised one over-riding principle which, although vexatious in many of its results, holds as true today as when it was first formulated.

This principle is that what the great powers cannot agree to do, cannot be done. Among those great powers, of course, are the United States and the Soviet Union.

CLEAR VISION

When, therefore, the United States refuses to recognise the possibility of reaching agreement with the Soviet Union in the Middle East, she is in effect saying that here, in the most dangerous part of the world, the advantages of the Charter must be withheld. The logic of this is that peace is not a paramount concern where Middle Eastern questions are involved.

It is just at this point that we are denied the courage of simplicity.

If we kept our vision clear and our purpose constant in the conviction that nothing at all matters so much as the preservation of peace, then we should bring the Soviet Union to the conference table with all the other powers concerned, in an effort to unwind the tangle of the Middle East before we all become hopelessly ensnared.

It is not necessary – nor indeed is it wise at this stage – to set out the particulars for a Middle East settlement. It is, however, a prerequisite to any settlement that the Soviet Union should be one of its main pillars.

TALK TO RUSSIA

The Soviet leaders are well aware that the U.S.S.R. can also burn her fingers at this particular fire. Russia knows that she may go in to such an extent that she may not be able to draw back without what she may consider to be a fatal loss of face. The same is true of the rest. It is here the danger arises.

These incidents flickering up, now here, now there, cannot always be relied upon to die down.

Unless they are brought under effective control, it is quite certain that some day one of them will set the world alight.

Platitudes won't save mankind – 13 December 1957

Very soon the N.A.T.O. powers will be meeting in what has been described as their most critical conference for many years. Nevertheless, few informed people expect anything very definite to be decided during its deliberations.

The American delegation will, after all, now be led by President Eisenhower; but, as distinct from the situation which existed only a few short weeks ago, the presence of the President is a matter of little importance.

Naturally we are glad that his health will allow him to attend, but it is not the personality of the President which is now undergoing critical examination; it is the posture and the politics of the United States itself.

POWER BLOCS

The Russian possession of the continental ballistic missile may not have profoundly affected the balance of military forces between the two great power blocs. But this, accompanied by the spectacular success of the Soviet Union in launching their satellite, has made the United States – in the language of George Orwell – more equal among equals.

Ever since 1950 the principal theme in the West has been the necessity to foster American intervention in European affairs as the best, indeed the only guarantee against the Russian conquest of Europe, including the United Kingdom.

This was a proposition to which I never subscribed, although I also did not see why there should be any objection to the Western nations concerting among themselves for their mutual defence.

REAL CHANGE

The situation has now changed. The United States needs European co-operation for her own defence.

Until she develops the equivalent of the Russian ballistic missile she will continue to need bases in Europe, especially in Britain, for her own shorter range rockets and presumably, for a time, for heavy bombers.

There has, therefore, taken place within the Western Alliance, a certain shift of authority. There is no longer complete ascendancy by one power over all the others. As a consequence, they are all the more inter-dependent.

The term that has come to express this new set of circumstances is integration. In practice, this means that the integrated nations will lose at least part of their authority over the use of their own armed forces.

FORCE

The employment of physical force by a nation against others, and the use of the powers of coercion by a nation over its own citizens are, between them, the final symbols and expressions of full sovereignty. When a nation has reached that position, it has achieved full nation-hood.

The seriousness of the argument which has now started among the Western powers, is therefore obvious. It is true that when nations enter into treaties with one another, they invariably accept some limitation of sovereignty according to the terms of the treaty. But there is no comparison between this and what is now being contemplated.

ALLIANCES

Traditional alliances did not undermine absolute authority of the armed forces of a nation. Treaties could be annulled, modified or allowed to pass into desuetude.

The frontiers of sovereignty were not blurred. They remained clearly defined.

Integration means something quite different. The deployment of such armed forces as are integrated is possible only by the consent of all the integrated powers.

INTEGRATION

It is true that the powers of coercion within the States, the police or the judiciary, for example, remain intact. But even here, sovereign rights might be threatened if domestic conditions look like impairing the objects of integration.

Many people will not look upon these developments as in any way alarming. They argue, and with considerable justification, that in a world which is growing so perceptibly smaller, the perpetuation of the nation state is becoming more and more anomalous.

Here there is a danger of the issues becoming confused. Complete control over its own physical powers is the last phase in the development of a nation, not the first. The proposals put forward for integration within N.A.T.O. reverse the natural order of growth.

Somebody, not yet defined, is presumably to have the disposal of the integrated forces, while all the other trappings of sovereignty remain intact.

This is really the nub of the question. In the context of the present world situation, we are here discussing nothing less than the survival of mankind. If, therefore, sovereign powers are to take flight from the parliaments of the Western world, where is it proposed that they should alight?

The situation is already sufficiently obscure to cause general alarm. It is by no means clear who is exercising control over the bombing planes loaded with hydrogen bombs that patrol the skies incessantly throughout the twenty-four hours.

JOINT CONTROL

These bombers take off from British bases and are presumed to be under the joint control of the United States and British Governments, but if they take off from Spanish bases or from American bases, who exercises authority over them? And if any of them are used for destructive purposes, will not the bases in Britain become immediately involved?

These are all questions that need to be answered now, before integration becomes the accepted thesis.

It is essential that we should be clear about where we want to arrive before we travel any further along this road. But a question of even greater importance has to be answered.

SELF-DEFENCE?

In the service of what policies are these military preparations being made?

It might be replied: 'Self-defence and nothing more.' NA.T.O., we might be told, is nothing more than a defensive military alliance, and its authority is confined to discussing only those political questions which fall within the military field.

But this merely sets the limitations of N.A.T.O., not the limitations of the question. We must be told what steps are contemplated to seek a lessening of the tensions which have led to the creation of this unprecedented military apparatus.

The question should be put and should be answered *now* before we part with any power whose loss may make it impossible for us ever to put the question again.

NO SURRENDER

We should refuse to surrender the ability to act independently, except in a cause which promises wider and more beneficial consequences than are likely to be obtained by adherence to our traditional powers.

It is not that we should seek to act alone, for that is neither permissible nor practicable in the world as it is today.

But if we are asked to merge our sovereign rights with those of other nations, we should be clear, not only about the conditions on which it is done, but on the objectives at which we are aiming.

It is because there appears neither the disposition nor the capacity to consider contemporary issues in this wider framework, that the N.A.T.O. conference is scarcely likely to produce anything other than a series of idle platitudes.

Arms and the slump – 31 January 1958

Once more the economists are gazing into their crystals. For surely what they describe as an analysis of the economic and financial situation deserves no more respectful description.

Perhaps it is unfair to blame them too much. The world of reality bears little relationship to what they were taught in their textbooks.

The automatism of market forces working through the laws of supply and demand, although always a fiction, nevertheless formed a useful working hypothesis so long as it was regarded as no more than that.

It can no longer be accorded even that status. The impact of political decisions upon economic decisions is such that economic prediction is at the same time political prophecy.

ANYBODY CAN MAKE A GUESS

This state of affairs is shown most clearly in the United States. Certain facts are known, but what significance to attach to them is anybody's guess. Ignorant laymen can make the guesses as well as statistical economists.

Unemployment in the States has reached a post-war record of about four millions. Industrial production has fallen about six per cent. since August.

Personal incomes have declined in the region of about one per cent. Not much you may say. But the economy of the United States is geared to a high, indeed it might be said, to an hysterical rate of personal spending.

Coupled with a fall in industrial investment, the decline in personal spending can be expected to continue. Where the bottom will be, no one knows. When I was visiting the United States at the beginning of November last, all these facts had not fully revealed themselves. But already the outlook was gloomy and the soothsayers pessimistic.

There was also a feeling of defeatism in the air. The Western Way of Life did not look so successful and attractive as it once did. The appearance of the Russian sputniks dealt a sharp shock to the ingrained complacency of the majority of Americans.

ANOTHER RECESSION COMING?

If on the top of the evidence of Russian technical advance, the Western world plunged into yet another disastrous economic recession, then the claims of Communism would take on a different complexion.

The comparison would appear to be between economic stability and progress accompanied by spectacular scientific achievement in the Communist world and economic chaos shadowed by technical failure in the Capitalist world.

That is an over-statement of the position. Nevertheless I found many in Washington who were worried by these considerations. They were asking themselves what answer could the West make to a situation so obviously favouring the Soviet challenge.

RESTORING THE BALANCE

In the meantime the accomplishment of the British Harwell team of scientists has gone some way to restoring the balance, even if it does not completely re-establish the self-confidence of American public opinion.

All other considerations apart, having regard to the necessity of making some reply to Soviet ascendancy, it is astonishing that American influence prevented the Harwell discoveries from being made public much earlier.

Curiously enough it is interesting to note that it was Mr. Khrushchev himself who put a check on Soviet exuberance. He repeated in public what he had already told my wife and myself when we saw him at Yalta in September.

TO EVERYONE'S ADVANTAGE

He pointed out that in the sphere of science now one, now another, of the advanced industrial nations would get ahead. It was 'all very healthy,' he said, 'and to everybody's advantage.'

This was, of course, before the Harwell achievement. The wisdom of Khrushchev's restraint is therefore underlined.

The most depressing feature of the American scene is the extent to which all the prophets are accepting an increase in American defence expenditure as the most hopeful way out of the growing depression.

The expenditure is expected to amount to 23 billion dollars for 1958 as compared with 17 billion dollars for the whole of 1957. These are colossal figures.

The pundits are divided in their estimates of how soon the projected new spending will begin to affect the industrial decline.

Some argue that the mere decision to embark on such an increase will of itself produce a more optimistic tone and encourage investment in anticipation of rising demand.

Others take the view that work must actually begin on defence contracts before any great response can be expected.

SOME TRUTH IN BOTH VIEWS

There is probably some truth in both views with the greater emphasis on the argument that contracts will have to be in hand before fresh investment risks are taken. Everyone, however, seems to be agreed that the recession will show no improvement until the last third of 1958.

If this proves to be the case – and it is the more hopeful view – it is highly improbable that the rest of what is called the free world will begin to benefit from the American recovery until well into 1959.

The time lag could scarcely be less than that. In the meantime Britain has already begun to suffer from a recession not directly connected with events in the United States, but arising largely from frantic attempts on the part of the Government to fight inflation by a general restriction of credit.

These British policies and the effects of the American trade situation are likely to join together towards the middle of this year.

A YEAR OF BITTERNESS

What the total effect will be it is impossible to estimate. It is, however, certain to be a year of economic frustration, political bitterness, accompanied by a percentage of unemployment of an order no one has ventured to assess.

No small part of the trouble arises from the fact that Britain has a Government which demonstrably does not enjoy the support of the majority of the people. At the same time it is committed to policies involving attacks on the social services which are bound to offend public opinion even more.

For me, the most deeply depressing aspect of all this lies in the fact that the United States is set on an enlarged arms expenditure.

DO THEY FEAR DISARMAMENT?

This is seen not only in terms of defence, but as a way of rescuing the economy from what otherwise might become a crisis as bad as that of the thirties.

In these circumstances it is fair to ask what plans the American administration has in hand in the event of an agreement on disarmament.

Or is everything based on the assumption that no agreement of any substance is expected?

Expected or feared? It is not possible to resist the thought that there are obvious resistances of all kinds to disarmament in a society where increased expenditure on arms gives rise, not, as it should, to deep foreboding, but to feelings of relief.

Obsessed by the immediate fear of trade recession and unemployment, the larger danger – that an intensification of the arms race might lead to the destruction of our whole world – appears to be a mere background consideration.

5
INTERNATIONAL RELATIONS
*Stop that nonsense now! –
20 December 1940*

The great debate has begun. It has been going on in a fashion since the war started, but now it is in full voice. What is it about? It is about our attitude towards our enemies and towards the populations under their control. But more particularly about our attitude towards our enemies, because if we can get that right the rest follows naturally.

The debate can be said to centre around one issue: are we fighting the German people or the Nazis? Or to put it another way, have these calamities been brought upon Europe by something which is intrinsic in the nature of the German people, or is it the product of German political institutions and of the German Nazi Party?

Some people find it very easy to make generalisations about peoples and about nations. These generalisations form the common stock of a great deal of political discussion. These people reduce the world to the size of a pill and then swallow it with great éclat, looking around for the admiration of their observers. I have heard them during my political life dismiss this and that nation with a sweeping statement, and although very shortly events falsify them, it does not discourage them from repeating the same mistake.

THEY LEARN NOTHING

They used to tell us that we could not expect anything from the Russian revolution, because the Russians were dreamers and poets, or *kulaks* and *moujiks*, and could not possibly understand modern machinery. When in the course of years the Russians did produce a great mechanised army and an air-fleet they said this was because the Russians were robots.

They made sneering references to the Portuguese for their lack of valour, forgetting that the Portuguese have a most magnificent history of maritime adventure and intrepidity.

It was not so long ago that Dean Inge, writing in the *Evening Standard*, told us that we could not expect much from the modern Greeks, because, after all, what had they in common with their reputed ancestors, who made the glory of Athens and Sparta? These same Greeks are now amazing the world in the Albanian mountains.

Now these cretins, again forgetting, or perhaps never having learned any of these lessons, are making sneering remarks about the cowardice of the Italians, as though Garibaldi and Mazzini had never existed.

How wickedly absurd it is to sneer at the Italian soldiers, sailors and airmen! It is not only that these sneers are a slur on the courage of our own men. It is that instead of sneering we should rejoice. Rejoice, not because the Italians are cowards, for this they are not. Rejoice, because the Italian workers and peasants and lower middle class, do not find it in their hearts to sacrifice their lives and their homes for the things for which Mussolini stands. It is not that they lack courage, it is that he, and what he stands for, cannot inspire it.

All through the years since 1922, when Mussolini took advantage of the hesitancy of the Italian Socialists and Liberals, seized power in Italy, and shut out the Italian people from control of their own country's policy, we have said that the Fascist State did not have its roots in the affections of the people and that when it was put to the test it would fail.

All that has happened is that we have been proved right. Why should we now neglect to harvest the fruits of our prophesy? Why should we not speak to the Italian people and applaud them for their refusal to be made the instruments of Mussolini's mad schemes? Why do we not try to unite them with us, making them our friends in a common fight against the things we hate?

I was very much encouraged the other day to hear Mr. Attlee say, presumably on behalf of the Government, that this was a war of ideas. If that be so, then our allies are wherever men believe in those ideas. And we know that men share them in Italy, in France, in Holland, in Belgium, in Austria, in Czecho-Slovakia, in Poland, in Denmark and Norway, aye and in Germany itself. It is therefore the most powerful weapon in the arsenal of the democracies so to behave, so to speak, so to conduct ourselves that we inspire our friends, wherever these are to be found, to hope for our victory and when opportunity offers to work for it.

That is why I regard Sir Robert Vansittart's broadcast to America as profoundly mistaken, and as doing a great disservice to the Allied cause. We must base our whole policy on the assumption, justified by all history remote and recent, that there are millions in Germany who hate Hitler and all his works as much as we do. We must also not forget that the peril to Britain began only when these millions of Germans lost the right to be consulted. War started to threaten Europe when freedom died in Germany. When the German people lost their right to be consulted in the shaping of German state policy, it was then that the threat of war raised its head in Europe.

WHAT WE SHOULD SAY

It is probably true, and it will be one of our most delicate post-war problems, that since Hitler's rise to power he has used that power to poison the German youth. I admit it will take some time for knowledge of other values to penetrate to the darkened minds of these victims of Hitler's mania.

But that means we must tell the German people now by every means at our disposal that we mourn with them that they and we are the common victims of a loathsome tyranny, and that it is one of our war aims to destroy that tyranny, and to restore to the German people the widest exercise of political liberty.

The last war was fought mainly for the right of national 'self-determination.' Or in plainer words, national freedom. We now see how wrong that aim was. This war should be fought for the right of individual self-determination, of individual freedom. The nations of the world are so closely interwoven that the welfare of one is determined by the behaviour of another. There cannot be any absolute national freedom.

If we are right, and we insist we are, that ordinary folk left to themselves do not want to make war upon their neighbours, then it is the first principle of modern civilised society that the people should never be deprived of that right.

No nation should have the right to take individual freedom away from its citizens, and the citizens of no nation have the right to give their freedom away, for as we have seen, when they do so, tyrants arise and by the abuse of their power bring war upon the world.

From this point of view it will be seen that our real danger arose, not when Hitler militarised the Rhineland, nor when he invaded Austria, nor when he invaded Prague, but long before. It arose when Hitler became Chancellor, for when he came to power he silenced our friends in Germany. He deprived us of our natural allies among the common German people.

WHO ARE OUR ENEMIES?

It is the institution of tyranny that is our enemy and not the people who permit it or suffer under it.

Thus I hope the great debate to which so many able and enlightened minds, as well as others not so able and not so enlightened, are now contributing, will end in the decision that our only enemies are Hitler and Mussolini, the Fascist and Nazi Parties, the institutions by which they live, the ideas by which they seduce men's minds, and the machinery by which they perpetuate their rule. That we shall exorcise all this from the soul of Europe. That we shall turn our backs upon the arid conception of national self-determination, and insist that there is one right that all men shall share in common, and shall be interwoven into their institutions: that individual men and women shall have accorded to them, and reserved to them, the unchangeable right of directing policies of those who govern them.

Why is Duff Cooper so bad? – 4 April 1941

Last week the *Tribune* rejoiced in a victory over the reactionary elements in the B.B.C. But do not let us blame the B.B.C. for what they did for they were not wholly responsible. The responsible party was the Minister of Information. It is true that the B.B.C. is technically supposed to be a self-governing body, but that, of course, in war time, is a fiction. The real boss is Mr. Duff Cooper.

Now it is not good enough merely to prevent the B.B.C. from making a fool of itself from time to time, for whenever it does so it creates bad feeling in the country. People say: 'there you are, that's the sort of rulers we have got. If they are not watched like a cat watching a mouse, they behave like Nazis.' It is no virtue in the B.B.C. or in our present system of propaganda, that we can, by repeated exertions, prevent them from doing harm to our cause. We would much prefer to praise them for a positive contribution.

Now do not entirely blame the Minister of Information, because he is only one Minister among many. The ultimate responsibility lies with the War Cabinet, for it is this body that lays down the high policy of the Allies. All the Minister of Information can do is to tell to the world the story they give him to tell. If it is a poor story, he still has to say it; although I am bound to add that even a poor story can be well told, and in many respects the Ministry of Information fails to do even that.

Nevertheless, it is time we faced the fact that the propaganda of the British Government is poor stuff, precisely because the War Cabinet baulks at the responsibility for setting out the main aims which are animating the Allies in this war. These aims, if they were stated, would be the guiding principles for the Minister of Propaganda, for the B.B.C., for the newspapers, and for every good friend the Allies have throughout the world.

Towards the end of last year I had hopes that the War Cabinet were about to face up to the task. The Lord Privy Seal threw out several hints that he and his colleagues were labouring at it, and that a pronouncement could be expected quite soon.

To our intense disappointment not only have we not had a declaration of enlightened war aims, but the Prime Minister has, on more than one occasion, gone out of his way to rebuke those who ask for them. Our war aim, he says, is to win the war.

***

Now I don't doubt that millions of people find this answer perfectly satisfactory. On the other hand there are many millions who are deeply disturbed by it.

Most of those who have spoken about the necessity for declaring our war aims have based their case mainly on the ground that it is necessary to do so in order to win to our side the millions of people who are now subject to Nazi rule in Europe. Certainly I do not underestimate the importance of doing that. But there is a great wisdom in the old saying that 'The eyes of the fool are upon the ends of earth.' I believe in keeping mine fixed a little nearer home. My association with the industrial population of Great Britain teaches me that a declaration of War Aims, of an enlightened and progressive nature, is at least as much needed to fortify the spirit of our own people, as to rally the peoples of other lands.

It is true that the last week has brought us news which has lifted up our hearts. The remorseless destruction of Italy's African empire; the resurgence of Yugoslavia; the quickening mastication of Italy's Mediterranean fleet by the British Navy; the increased warmth of Soviet Russia towards the Allied cause in the Balkans; all these have lifted a dull weight from our spirits, which were naturally depressed by the appalling winter.

But it must not be forgotten that the ordinary men and women of Great Britain are about to undergo great trials and perils. In many of our great industrial cities a shortage of food is causing much hardship and anxiety. The compulsions of labour that Mr. Ernest Bevin is finding it necessary to introduce, will be accepted by the workers, but with great misgivings. The thought of another winter throws a shadow over even the dawning spring.

It must be remembered too, that the generation which is fighting this war is of a different stuff from any other. It is old enough to remember the last war, and the tragic disappointment of the hopes that were then raised. It is a literate, and, to an extent that many people underestimate, an informed generation. For the first time in history it forms an active audience of the things which its rulers are doing in its name.

The question is everywhere on men's lips: 'What is the kind of world that we want to make, if and when victory is ours? And why is it that its outlines are not stated to us by our national spokesmen?'

I will tell them some of the reasons.

***

If we are to have a Europe organised for peace, what must be its foundations? National sovereignties must be limited, and part of their powers vested in an over-riding international authority. The implications of this frighten the Tory mind, for they threaten the rights of private exploitation in the British Colonial Empire. It is inconsistent to deny full sovereignty to the peoples of Europe, and claim it in respect of Great Britain's Empire.

International means of communication, such as the great Continental railroad systems, must clearly be owned and directed by a public international authority. Ominous words for the transport bosses of the British railways.

Raw materials are unequally distributed over the land masses of the world, and the fight for them has been behind the evil diplomacy of war makers. Their internationalisation and equitable distribution is an essential condition for a world at peace. Look through the directories of the businesses of the City of London and see how many vested interests will be upset by this principle.

A world mercantile marine, publicly directed by an international corporation, is an essential instrument for the scientific distribution of commerce across the waterways of the world. The shareholders of the British mercantile lines will look with no enthusiasm on such a scheme.

Modern war needs steel more than anything else, but iron ore is not to be found everywhere. And as nations go to war for steel, the public international ownership of steel is inseparable from a peace structure.

Steel is no use without coal, and coal also is unequally distributed throughout the world. Consequently, if the struggle for this essential raw material is not to be a cause of international enmity, coal too must be publicly owned on international lines. How can we possibly argue this, in face of the opposition of the coal masters of Great Britain, even to the nationalisation of the coal industry of this country?

Then again the student of modern diplomacy knows full well how the ownership of oil has been behind a series of sinister conspiracies in the Embassies of the great world powers. The big oil companies of Great Britain and of Holland will bitterly oppose any proposal to take this highly profitable industry out of their hands.

***

Does the reader begin to see why the Tory mind which dominates the War Cabinet is inhibited from any statement of war aims which would satisfy the people of Britain? We cannot think of war aims in the 1914 or 1918 sense of the term. Everything we say about what is needed in the rest of the world for peace, reflects upon and condemns the economic practice of Great Britain.

That is why the Prime Minister, the leader of the Tory Party, says that to win the war is enough, for to say more than that frightens all the vested interests and century-old privileges of private propertied interest in Great Britain.

Students of politics have been asking in the last few months: 'Upon what is the opposition to the existing Government going to arise?' I say it is here on this issue. For this question embraces every other upon which men are beginning to doubt the direction in which our Government is going.

Complacency will not win the war – 5 September 1941

Public opinion in Britain is passing through an interesting and dangerous phase. Interesting because so many and diverse elements drift disconnectedly through it, and dangerous because it might congeal into a shape fatal for the conduct of the war and the moulding of peace. Some of the elements bear a close resemblance to the first period of the war, now classified for all time as the Sitzkrieg, or the Phoney War.

Many people are beginning to feel that the Government is as much out of touch with the real feeling in the country as was the Administration of Mr. Chamberlain. There is the same suspicion that the Government is drifting before events, and is substituting brave speeches for a cold will and imaginative action.

The Prime Minister is still undoubtedly very popular, but his defenders fall back increasingly on the risky argument that there is no obvious person to take his place. Among the people there is a strange mixture of lassitude and irritation. The one feeds on the other. The lassitude arises from the absence of any large scale enterprise which enlists the energies and devotion of the people, and irritation against the privations, inconveniences and disturbances inseparable from war. It is not easy for jaded spirits to bear the petty prickings of sordid circumstance.

There was one advantage which was present in the early part of the war which is absent now – there is no great political party waiting in the wings ready to take the stage and carry on the drama with new vision and fresh energy.

National unity, so essential to sustain the nation in perilous emergency, has the disadvantage that it removes the alternative leadership whose provision is not the least of democracies' contributions to good government. Let us hope that in the months immediately ahead the House of Commons will reveal an independence and austerity from which a new leadership may be expected when the time for a change comes upon us.

***

There are a number of definite reasons for the listless spirit now existing. The Government appears to be trying to nerve the people by a story in which they no longer believe. Indeed, they suspect that the Government itself does not believe it. We have been told to make every preparation for an invasion that may occur at any time. In this way the Government is attempting to re-create the mood of last summer and autumn. At the same time that these warnings and fearsome prophecy come from Whitehall, the people read in the newspapers that President Roosevelt has expressed the opinion that the attack on the Soviet Union makes it highly improbable that Britain will be invaded this year.

Mr. Menzies, in Australia, spoke in much the same strain. What are the people to make of it? These two statesmen know the facts just as well as our own Ministers, and it seems to most of us that the opinion of the President and Mr. Menzies is more closely in accord with reasonable expectations than the somewhat worn-out alarmism of our own discredited Brass Hats. What is the use of trying to galvanise the people by a story which is endorsed neither by our spirit nor by the known facts? The Government cry 'Wolf, Wolf,' at the very moment when the people can see the wolf engaged in a life and death struggle with a bear at the other end of the field. The general view is that the best way to deal with the danger from the wolf is to give the bear a hand.

It is just here that there is another explanation for the widening gulf between the Government and public opinion. The attack on the Soviet Union has given us a totally unexpected opportunity to give a death blow to the Nazis and the Government seems terribly slow to take advantage of it. A common front and means of supply with the Soviet Union was an immediate necessity and the obvious way was through Iran.

Why were we so slow in acting? Mr. Eden says we acted with exemplary patience. Why were we patient? No one really believes in the possibility of sovereign independent states after the war. Why then should we be so tender with them during the war? Especially in a case where the whole issue of the war is desperately involved. It would be silly to fail to appreciate the formidable difficulties that face us in making use of the Iran route to send supplies to the Soviet Union. But the British people expect those difficulties to be tackled with supreme urgency and vigour. They are deeply moved and inspired by the sacrifice and courage of the men and women of the Soviet Union. They will exact a terrible revenge if it should be proved that anything is allowed to stand in the way of giving all we can to mitigate those sacrifices and sustain that courage.

***

In addition to the limits that geography imposes on our joining forces with Russia there is our continuing lack of war materials. Ministers persist in telling sunshine stories about the output of our war factories. So far from brightening my life they fill me with gloom.

What on earth is meant by saying we are breaking records? All that means is that we are producing more than we were. But did anyone think we might be producing less? You expect our war production to increase in war time. What matters is the *rate of increase* and the *absolute mass* of war materials. Everyone who is entitled to speak on the subject agrees that performance is lagging behind possibilities, and there is profound dissatisfaction and disquiet throughout the country. One of these days that disquiet will burst under the Government and blow it apart. Mr. Eden did no good to himself or to the country when he said the other day that we did not send an armoured division to France before Dunkirk. The answer to him is that he was a member of the Government responsible, and if he says the cause lay with the previous Government, the further answer is that many of the guilty ministers were retained by Mr. Churchill and are still enjoying office. Another purge is long overdue if we are to shorten the war and lessen its horrors.

***

Another and important cause for the popular unrest is the feeling that the Soviet Union is not being taken into full consultation and co-operation. The people of Britain noted that the Soviet Union was not a party to the conferences which led to the Atlantic Declaration. There is a growing suspicion that influential persons are engaged in a conspiracy to form an Anglo-Saxon bloc to rule the world after the war. That way lies world tragedy of unimaginable dimensions. We are not fighting this war in order to substitute a stupid Anglo-Saxon myth for the barbaric cult of the *Herrenvolk*.

There has always been a lot of nonsense talked in America about the domination of Anglo-Saxon blood. Even Jack London was tainted by it, and there are lots of social illiterates in this country who take pride in the shape of their skulls. Civilized minds all over the world are looking to the new alignment with the Soviet Union as a means not only of defeating the modern Vandals led by Hitler, but of making a peace which will embody the best contributions of the most diverse cultures. We will not surrender this hope for an adolescent myth which has no roots in anything but the intellectual and moral bankruptcy of the old capitalistic world.

In political affairs people are moved either by fear or by hope. For the moment the fine resistance of the Soviet Union has lifted the fear from our hearts. If our people are listless it is because they hardly yet dare to hope. If the Government can place before the people a conception of the future which will take into its sweep the infinite possibilities now opened up to us then hope will come and from it the dynamics of victory.

Here is a real plan to put the war machine in reverse – 7 August 1953

For some time past two main themes have dominated discussions about international affairs. These are rearmament and World Mutual Aid. The one is the enemy of the other. The burden of arms production has kept aid to underdeveloped countries down to a microscopic percentage of what is required.

It would be unjust and certainly unwise to write down what has been done. In the Colombo Plan, by Marshall Aid, and immediately after the war, by UNRRA, vital assistance has been provided both to the nations impoverished by the war and to others not yet furnished with the products of technical science. Without this help the condition of hundreds of millions would be much worse than it is.

Unfortunately the outbreak of hostilities in Korea led to a sharp rise in expenditure on arms, and in consequence World Mutual Aid took a bad second place.

WITH STRINGS

Another consequence was almost as bad. Assistance from the United States was increasingly conceived as a weapon in the fight to contain world Communism, and so a conception which began in a spirit of idealism became tainted and diverted from its original purpose.

To the extent that the United States attached strings to its gifts, to that extent the gifts themselves were resented, and where still accepted, the atmosphere became poisoned by a sullen sense of dependence on the one side and of patronage on the other.

Burma, though weak, ailing and desperately poor, refused any further American help.

In Italy the Communist vote increased, stimulated by American reproaches of ingratitude accompanied by threats that further aid might be cut off.

In America the Pentagon, with the usual blindness of soldiers faced with the mysteries of civil psychology, despaired of France and started to woo Western Germany with an ardour undiminished by the experience of repulses elsewhere.

WAR WEAPON

Military assistance to Chiang Kai-shek exceeded the amount set aside for civil aid in the Far East.

In short the grand conception of a World Plan for poor nations degenerated into merely another weapon in the cold war.

There is real tragedy in this not only for backward nations but for the whole world, because the conception of World Mutual Aid is the one hope of peace and of civilised progress.

There is no real prospect that the undeveloped parts of the world will be able to attract private capital on a scale sufficient either for their own needs or to take off the surpluses of countries like the United States and Canada, not to speak of Britain and other contributors. Only inter-governmental action on an unprecedented scale will suffice.

Nations weighed down by insupportable military budgets have neither the mood nor the means to take part in a scheme of economic development in other countries. At the same time, as we saw last week, they do not see how they can cut their arms programmes without finding an outlet in world trade for the resources thus set free.

The solution is clear. A period of years should be agreed by the nations concerned, including of course Russia, during which annual contributions to a world pool should be made. These agreed contributions should be on such a scale that no nation could afford to make them and still maintain its existing expenditure on arms.

A POOL PLAN

The ideal arrangement would be for the pool to receive the percentage by which the participating nations agreed to reduce their military budgets. But this would not be absolutely essential if the contribution was fixed high enough. The world Pool of Mutual Aid would become the enemy of the arms expenditure instead of the reverse, as is now the case.

This in its turn would go some way to meeting the case for mutual inspection of the arms production of the nations taking part, for the good and simple reason that payment into the Pool would be itself a reasonable guarantee that no secret increase in arms production was taking place.

Naturally, there is no absolute guarantee here, but if we are looking for absolute assurances we are not likely to get them.

The word 'payment' here is a kind of shorthand, for the actual contributions would have to be assessed in physical terms, such as so much corn, wheat, tractors.

Nations would be expected to give the sort of things that could be reasonably asked of them, having regard to the character of their economy. In the same way the recipient nations would take from the Pool what they are most short of.

There is no insuperable difficulty in this. We have already had some experience, though on a more limited scale than I am proposing.

Russian participation in such a scheme might be objected to on the ground that the standard of living of her people is still much lower than that of many Western nations. This objection cannot be sustained, because Russia maintains a vast military establishment and the whole idea is to get this reduced at the same time as others reduce theirs and this by a method that creates confidence all round.

But Germany has no military establishment to dismantle. What about her?

The answer is that Germany should be required to make a contribution to the Pool equal to a percentage of what her military expenditure would have been if she had been allowed to re-arm. Her contribution would start as soon as she had been united under free elections.

It is generally accepted that some armed forces should be permitted her at once. If the whole conception is carried out, then by the expiry of an agreed number of years the other nations would have disarmed to her level and she would be enjoying the same degree of national sovereignty as all the other nations.

NO GUARANTEE

In the meantime, and long before the period set for the carrying out of this operation, Russian and Allied occupying forces in Germany should be withdrawn to zones to be agreed.

The further apart, the better. The nearer they are to each other, the more the number of points of friction and the greater the danger of 'incidents.'

There, briefly, is the proposal. It meets all nine conditions which, last week, I stated had to be satisfied if the problem of the future of Germany is to be solved in a way that does not endanger peace.

It means that the German question is only a facet of the world problem and cannot be settled by itself. It is useless to suggest, as Mr. Churchill hinted, that Russia should agree to Germany re-arming and rest content with a kind of Locarno guarantee against aggression from the West. Russia is too realist to give arms and take paper in exchange.

The world has got itself snarled up in what appears to be an insoluble enigma. It is an epic problem which can only be resolved by a design which matches up to its own scale.

What of the objections to the proposals? It may be said that the people will not obtain any relief for themselves if all that happens is to make them substitute a contribution to a Pool for world development for what they are now paying for arms.

That is true, but the one promises peace, the other is certain war, with the end of civilisation as the probable result.

Also, I am convinced that if the statesmen of the world could bring themselves to adopt such a scheme there would follow a great release of productive energy everywhere from which we would all benefit.

The war machine not only saps our material resources, it crushes our spirit, shadows our lives and fills the future with dread.

'Ah, but,' I shall be told, 'America would never agree, so it's a non-starter.' Are we quite so sure?

THEIR VISION

Senators Flanders and Sparkman and thirty-two other Senators recently introduced a resolution into the American Senate which expresses the American desire for peace and disarmament and reaffirms the nation's objective of obtaining universal agreement for enforceable disarmament.

It proposed that the President should develop a plan in accordance with his pledge of April 16th for the transfer of resources and manpower now used for arms for constructive ends at home and abroad.

The Americans have shown more than once a capacity for spacious vision and a quality of idealism which is the other and more agreeable side of a nation that too often appears to be wholly engrossed in material success.

It is folly to forget that America like Britain is made up of many diverse elements. The worst are not bound always to win.

Another and perhaps more dangerous line of attack is that the proposal is too neat, too obviously tailored to all the requirements of the various problems set out, and therefore too artificial in its conception.

The answer is that we are dealing with a problem which is itself highly artificial in character, and that some master design is called for to make all the pieces fit into their proper places if men and women all over the world are to realise the self-confidence needed to fulfil the task.

There is nothing more defeating to the human spirit than the niggling, fiddling and altogether inadequate approach we are witnessing at the present time.

Another aspect of the proposal worth special attention is this. If by negotiations between the Great Powers we could decide upon a definite period of years when the plan would start, and proceed through all the orderly phases of its development, an entirely new climate of opinion would be created throughout the world.

Constructive tasks induce an optimistic and buoyant mood. As we have already witnessed in India and Pakistan, and as we shall eventually see in Malaya, the fixing of definite dates in place of vague generalities has the effect of concentrating the energies of those involved, energies otherwise dissipated in mutual recriminations and endless speculation.

Nor should we underestimate the urgency and gravity of the threat to the whole of mankind arising from the growing population of the world and the relatively declining supplies of food. I invite the reader to get hold of a book by Harold Wilson, just published by Gollancz, *The War on World Poverty*, if he wishes to read a detailed analysis of the question.

There is no need for us to approach these issues in a mood of despair. They are not insoluble. A resolute attack on world poverty along the lines I have indicated would at the same time be a recipe for world peace.

Empire and the Tories – 18 December 1953

Sir Winston Churchill once remarked that he had not been appointed Her Majesty's First Minister in order to preside over the liquidation of the British Empire. This characteristic piece of romantic bombast is now beginning to haunt its author.

As the negotiations in Egypt draw towards their close, many Tories are reminding the British Prime Minister of his words. They regard the withdrawal of the British forces from the Canal Zone as yet another and important step in the 'liquidation of the British Empire.'

It is nothing to them that Egypt was never in the Empire and that we are there by treaty only. All they can see is the spectacle of a great empire in decline, with whole chunks of territory being torn from the tortured body, as it writhes and twists in the agony of decay.

IMPERIAL OBSESSION

The Tory mind is obsessed by the imperial tradition. A world without the British Empire is not one they care to face.

People nurtured in classical history and minds stored with the legends of old and dead empires are conditioned to the thought of decay, even as they bitterly resent it when it occurs. The rise and fall of empires, that is how they see the pageant of history.

For these, the form of history is also its content. They do not see the continuity of the life of ordinary men and women, for they have never been concerned with these. Those ordinary men and women are mere phantom, shadowy figures moving in the background as the imperial procession moved onwards – Egypt, Carthage, Rome, Ottoman, France, Spain, Britain.

And now what? Does Britain become a memory like the others? Will new powers take her place, wield the sceptre she held so firmly for so long? In the Tory heart there is nothing but nostalgia for the mighty past and a determination to postpone the inevitable future as long as possible.

This classical preoccupation with the history of the rise and fall of empires helps to conceal the real nature of what is taking place today. We are not witnessing the substitution of one imperial power for another. What is happening in the modern world is the death of the idea of empire.

It is true the United States emerged from the last war as one of the two leading nations, with Britain falling behind. But that does not mean that what Britain relinquishes America takes.

The conception of nationalism is now in conflict with that of imperialism and the latter is losing the struggle. The imperial legacy now falls to be inherited, not by a conqueror successor, but by the nationalities of the constituent parts.

America did not take over India – it was India. Who wields the sceptre once held by Britain on the Gold Coast? The inhabitants. When the British walk out of Egypt, the Egyptians, and only the Egyptians, will walk in.

It is true that the Soviet Union, in defiance of the trend of history, and in violation of its stated creed, did reach out and clutch to her many of the small nations on her borders. But they move restlessly in the hug of the bear and nothing is more certain than that they will never be reconciled to their oppressor.

The classical scholars are wrong when they insist that when one empire falls its place is necessarily taken by another. They try to explain what is happening by reference to historical parallels. What they fail to see is that there are precipitates in the present world situation which have no parallels in past history.

It is true that some nations will have more influence and authority than others and that this will be so because of possession of greater material power. But the exercise of this superiority will not, in the future, take the traditional form of physical occupation and domination. Pride in nationhood is too strong to permit it.

The presence of the troops of another's nation on one's own national soil is a circumstance to be borne only when it is voluntarily conceded. Even then, it has definite disadvantages. The presence of American airmen is tolerated in Britain but not accepted. If their presence comes to be actively resented, then they will have to withdraw; and, for much the same reason as we shall have to withdraw from Egypt, because a military base is useless if it is surrounded by a hostile population.

CO-OPERATION

Of course, the conflict between imperialism and nationalism is an old one. But there is this difference – the co-operation of the local population is more necessary to good government than ever before.

In our more complicated societies of today, with their greater degree of literacy, wider diffusion of culture, and the use of novel industrial techniques, non-co-operation by the inhabitants of the occupied country can bring political administration to a standstill.

When such a situation is reached, the position of the imperial power becomes impossible. It is only a matter of time before it is bound to recognise the facts and withdraw. It is always better to do this as a recognition of the justice of the claim to nationhood, rather than to have to go eventually, simply because to stay any longer is made untenable.

In the past, the imperial master wanted only obedience from the defeated in the performance of simple physical tasks, and this he could command. Today, in the context of a modern community, he requires the willing co-operation of the mind as well.

If this is not accorded him voluntarily, he has no way of getting it. By the use of fear you can get more work out of your victim, but, for the more recondite processes of the mind, fear is an inhibiting condition. And it is in these processes that the modern community most differs from those of the past.

Because of these reasons, there is little or no disposition for a new imperial power to take the place of the old one when the latter is compelled to relax on account of successful rebellion against it. The same reasons would make the successor power incapable of effective rule.

Thus, Britain surrenders – reluctantly it is true – but still surrenders, not to the sword of a new world conqueror, but to the persuasive influences of a mounting nationalism, which in its very nature, renders imperialism old-fashioned and worthless. That she does this so reluctantly, is due as much to outmoded conceptions of government as to a desire to hold on to inherited possessions.

It is difficult for the Tory to believe that principles of government which have dominated men for so many centuries are now irrelevant. It is easier for him to accept that, perhaps, Britain is now too weak to hold what his ancestors won for him, than it is to adjust his whole philosophy to a new situation.

The first calls only for resignation; the second requires the rejection of all he has ever stood for. And if he was capable of this – then, of course, he would not be a Tory.

America must be told: 'you go it alone' – 16 April 1954

Ever since the war, British diplomacy has been influenced by one dominant consideration – fear of American isolationism.

Ernest Bevin believed it was his main task to prevent America from withdrawing into its traditional aloofness. This was the mainspring of his diplomatic strategy, the source of its strengths and of its weaknesses.

In those days there was a lot to be said on both sides. But about one aspect of it there is no question. It lays us open to indefinite blackmail.

If the United States is led to believe that, in the last resort, we shall always bow to her wishes, then from the outset we exert no leverage on her policy.

In Washington they have become quite cynical about it. 'They'll tag along in the end,' they say.

We have paid a heavy price for this nightmare fear of American isolation.

We succumbed to pressure from the United States and allowed the Ruhr industries to be restored to their former owners. We did this against the facts of history and in spite of our instinctive distrust of the consequences.

NOW WE PAY THE PRICE

The fruit of this folly is now apparent. A reactionary government has been financed into existence in Western Germany, and all the evidence available points to a revival of Nazism.

Schumacher, the leader of the German Socialists, reproached us – the British Socialists – for this policy, and the reproach was justified.

So dominant was our fear that America would once more desert us that we preferred to offend our Socialist comrades rather than risk the anger of the ruling circles in the U.S.A. It is a sad story and bitterly shall we repent it.

Again, we permitted ourselves to be rushed into the acceptance of an inflated arms programme which was beyond our means. To this we sacrificed a part of our cherished social services, faced rising prices, and in the end it proved impossible to carry out. But it weakened the Labour movement in Britain by creating dissensions among its members.

The same panic caused the U.S.A. to believe that a German army was essential to the defence of Europe. To that we have sacrificed whatever prospects there were of working-class unity in France, and we are in danger of seeing the same lamentable result in Britain.

We were led to stigmatise Revolutionary China as an 'aggressor' in Korea, and this is now held to stand in the way of her formal recognition.

I am not here attempting a description of American foreign policy since the war. I confine myself only to a few of the positions we were led to adopt because we were reluctant to carry our opposition to American pressure to the point of possible rupture.

Nor do I withhold tribute to the assistance given under Marshall Aid. Unfortunately that imaginative and generous enterprise has now degenerated into a programme of military assistance only.

The threat now comes from Washington that the paymaster will stop payment unless we dance to tunes approved by him.

And now the squalid and pitiful story is working up to its climax. We are to be invited to scupper the Geneva Conference before it assembles.

This Conference was the only hopeful thing that emerged from the Berlin Conference. But this was scarcely ended before the United States made it clear that in no circumstances would recognition for Revolutionary China be traded for peace in Indo-China.

WE WANT TO KNOW

Why then is China invited to Geneva? Is it only to give her a venue for surrender?

Are we to have negotiation or bullying? Peace-making or war-making? The hand of friendship or the threat of the H-bomb?

We want to know. And we want to know now before the Conference starts.

In the meantime Mr. Foster Dulles visits Europe, ostensibly to seek agreement with Britain and France concerning the policy to be adopted at Geneva. Or is it submission he is after? Because, unless it is submission, he must retreat from the position he has taken up.

The only card we can play at Geneva is recognition of China, in return for peace in Indo-China. And that means peace on the basis of national independence for the Indo-Chinese.

They must be independent of everybody, France as well as China, and that goes for the United States as well. The independence of Indo-China cannot be traded away.

Peace cannot be based permanently on colonial exploitation. Peace is not to be founded on the assumption that the status of the colonial peoples can be frozen where it is now.

The rule of collective peace in the world must provide for social progress and for the attainment of self-government by subject peoples. Otherwise their legitimate struggles for nationhood will endanger peace. Peace and injustice can never live long together.

THE RIGHT TO BE COMMUNIST

There are no qualifications to this. If the Indo-Chinese elect to go Communist, they should be allowed to do so.

It is here that the collision with American policy occurs. She regards every extension of Communism as an accession of strength to the Soviet Union. And so it well may be, if the treatment accorded to China is the pattern to be followed.

British thinking has never followed this line. When the Revolution occurred in China, we took the view that it was a matter for the Chinese.

It was possible to conceive circumstances where the presence of Revolutionary China on the Security Council of the United Nations might modify the attitude of the Soviet Union. It would end her complete dominance of the Communist world and compel her to adjust her conduct to conform with the needs of other nations.

The United States refused to accept this view, and we are now paying part of the price for her stubbornness and blindness.

We must now refuse to pay the rest of the price. The demand that we should join an alliance for the containment of Communism in South East Asia is not sought as an instrument for the prevention of war, but rather as an extension, into the international field, of the defence of American social, political and economic values.

The military threat is a cover for counter-revolutionary measures. We are being asked to join, not an alliance for the preservation of peace, but a bulwark against political and social progress.

Where that progress is arrested by colonial powers or by black reaction the struggle takes on a more and more revolutionary colour. We are then asked to oppose it in the shape of resistance to Communist aggression.

It is an old story and by now we should be familiar with it.

This new move by the United States, therefore, brings us up against the old dilemma. Should we agree in the end, or should we carry our opposition to the point where it might mean a break?

The answer is quite simply that we shall never be able to make America understand our attitude and adjust herself to it until we are prepared to break with her unless she does.

The Alliance with America was forged in the hope of preventing war. It was not intended as opposition to Communism as such. If America wishes this, then the Alliance is distorted beyond its original purpose.

We should tell America so in the plainest possible terms. If after that she persists, then she must do so alone.

The second Cold War – 23 December 1955

The war of bluster and threat, of charge and counter-charge, has broken out again in full spate.

Mr. Khrushchev's denunciation of the imperialist nations has been seized on eagerly by the spokesmen of the Western powers. It was too tempting a chance for there to be any hope of them ignoring it, for it provided a means of diverting attention from the poverty of their own policies. Mr. Khrushchev also appeared to feel the need for diversionary exercises.

The 'Geneva spirit' did not provide either side with a congenial climate, so at the first opportunity both have reverted to their wonted bellicosity. It must therefore, I am afraid, be assumed that the cold war is on again.

*

Responsibility for this situation must be fixed before we can hope to see any way out of it. First we must try to comprehend the general character of the problem, and it can be stated quite simply.

The Western powers must reconcile themselves to the fact that the framework of the past has been irretrievably broken, and the second half of the 20th century will see the building of the outlines of the future pattern of society.

This is a hard decision for them to make since the West is composed of vast congeries of vested interests, the fortunes of private individuals being involved as well as the fate of principalities.

Nevertheless the Western powers must realise that the forces of change now at work in the world are too compulsive to be held in check. The task of statesmanship is to guide those forces to their natural destination without courting disaster on the way.

The case of the Communist nations is different. They form part of the yeast of change and so see their role as the prodders of progress everywhere. Consequently wherever a people is moving restlessly against the weight of tradition and the injustice of exploitation, the Soviet Union and its associates see in such a situation their natural, and, as they would put it, their historical opportunity.

But the Communist bloc will make a fatal blunder if it allows itself to be guided too much by historical parallels. Social revolution may now be consummated in circumstances of complete and utter tragedy.

We are not today in the presence of the comparatively simple social organisms which existed when the classic principles of Communism were formulated. The world today is not only infinitely more complicated and inter-related than it was in the 19th century, but also the simple arms that were then relied on have now been replaced by nuclear weapons of appalling destructiveness.

No one should understand better than Communists that this technical change has altered the whole character of social revolution and that it is madness to refuse to take account of it.

The dynamics of social change are, therefore, entirely different from what they were, and the tactics of previous revolutions offer no real guide.

The leaders of the Soviet Union do not appear to have appreciated the significance of this development, and so they stoke up the embers of social revolt with a recklessness which alarms even those who might otherwise be sympathetic with their main aspirations. To press the pace of social change to the point of general conflagration would be fatal to Communism as well as to every other social creed.

Before the new outburst of recrimination, it seemed as though the Communists had come to appreciate the truth of this, but, as with the Western powers, 19th century habits of thought appear to have reasserted themselves.

The general conclusion we are compelled to draw from these considerations is clear. Whereas the Western powers must accept the fact of social change, the Communist powers must seek to accommodate it to peaceful purposes.

If the first see only a threat to their privileges, and the second only a means to the expansion of their authority, then the world is doomed. The situation is a challenge to the imaginative statesmanship of both, for both are involved in the outcome.

If this general conclusion is accepted, then the area where co-operation could be most fruitful is where the dangers are greatest – the Middle

East. It is here where the interests of East and West clash most sensitively, and it is here also where social changes are being made with the greatest rapidity and where the social and political structure is straining and cracking.

It is here where the present is breaking with the past, under the pressure of poverty contrasted with flaunting opulence. It is here, consequently, where the prodding of Communism and the resistance to it can blow up the whole world.

This situation has come at a time when Russia feels able to offer economic help and technical aid. If these are proffered only in competition with the Western powers, then it is merely just another aspect of the cold war and carries us no further on the road to peace.

If, on the other hand, both sides could be brought to pool the assistance they are ready to give in great schemes of economic reconstruction, especially of irrigation accompanied by electrical generation, then the whole Middle East could be transformed in a decade or so.

The land space is there, the people are there; all that is required are the economic resources and the willingness to apply them.

Instead of proceeding on these lines, the Western powers have embraced Iraq and Iran in the Northern tier; that is, in an outpost of their defence system. The Russians have responded in like manner, and dangle their offers of help before the eyes of the starving masses. What could be the most imaginative example of international co-operation the world has yet seen, is becoming a frontier of mounting friction.

This is an appalling illustration of the dangers I have stressed in this article. Here we see the exploitation of social revolution for the aggrandisement of power. Here is the manipulation of people to serve ends beyond themselves – as though there can be any desirable end in which individual people are not the ultimate wards of statesmanship.

The spokesmen of the West claim that Russia would not respond to an offer of mutual co-operation in the Middle East. But has the offer been made?

Until it has, the guilt lies with the West; for it is the West which is in effective occupation of the area.

It must be world control for all the commercial waterways – 3 August 1956

For the moment President Nasser is riding high. He is the hero of the Egyptian masses and of most of the Arab world. It is a heady position. It is, however, apt to be temporary.

Unless a political revolt seizes upon social positions of vital importance for its future when it is at the height of its power, its days are numbered.

If a social movement elects to take the path of revolution, it must pursue it to the end, and the end is a complete transformation of society, accompanied by a transference of power from the old to the new social forces.

Judged by this criterion, the movement first led by General Neguib and then by Nasser has not as yet added up to a social revolution, or anything like it.

It has been marked by a series of palace revolutions, first against King Farouk, then within the National Movement itself, when Neguib was deposed from the leadership; and now its energies are directed against the West by the seizure of the Suez Canal.

There has been no radical transformation of Egyptian society. Some land has been redistributed with doubtful economic benefits to the Egyptian economy and opposition parties have been suppressed. In the main, the structure of Egyptian society has remained what it was before all these dramatic events took place.

No doubt a great deal of corruption has been rooted out from the public administration, and a start made in the development of industry.

But from the beginning, the Movement was strongly nationalistic, with social and economic objectives playing a secondary role. It derived its driving power from resentment against Western imperialism, and as this attitude was shared with the Arab oil states, Egypt became the champion of the Arab world against the Western Powers.

President Nasser and the army officers around him were and are idealists who resented the presence of British troops on Egyptian soil and were outraged by the extravagance and decadence of King Farouk and his entourage.

True, they also resented the extremes of wealth and poverty around them, but – and here is the nub of the question – they saw the solution not as beginning with a root and branch redistribution of property, but as depending on the building up of a modern state, to a large extent with outside aid.

Thus from the outset the National Movement has been torn between two extreme passions, realism and evangelism.

In the hands of more experienced social engineers these need not have been uncomplimentary. Nationalist resurgence could have been canalised for economic purposes. Its energies might have sustained Egypt through the years of inevitable sacrifice as industries were built by which to raise living standards.

But this would have involved patience, restraint, long term planning, and above all, an avoidance of dramatic postures and political upheavals.

Long term investment requires above all things, a degree of political tranquillity, especially when a great deal of it must come from outside, and much of it in the form of grants or long term loans.

The Aswan Dam is a classic example of this sort of investment. Nasser made it a symbol of his success.

When I met him a few years ago in Cairo he could speak of little else, apart from getting the British out of the Canal Zone.

The astonishing thing is that he has not appeared to realise that it was obligatory upon him to assemble the internal political conditions necessary to bring the Dam to fruition.

He has not realised that to keep on stirring the pot of nationalist passions is not conducive to the creation of conditions favourable to long term economic projects.

It was hoped, at one time, that getting the British out of the Canal Zone would have sufficiently sated national pride, and that Egypt would then settle down to a period of economic construction. But having tasted the heady wine of nationalist success, Nasser wanted more and more draughts of the same stimulant.

He desired to see himself at the head of the Arab states and in particular to champion them against Israel. He permitted, and certainly connived at, the most virulent anti-Western propaganda from Cairo. He devoted a considerable amount of Egyptian revenues to building up his armed forces although millions of his people live in the direst poverty.

When he could not get what he wanted from the West, he got it from Russia, thus permitting himself to be exposed to the charge of the most dangerous form of international blackmail.

In short, he has sought to subordinate prosaic economic facts to the seductive attractions of the nationalist sword. And now, to cap it all, he has stated in the most categorical language, that the Suez Canal, being on Egyptian Soil, is therefore Egyptian property.

Of course he is right in a narrow and perhaps legalistic sense of the term, providing that one accepts the right of sovereign states to repudiate international contracts.

Pravda has hastened to claim that there is no essential difference between the action of Nasser in nationalising the Suez Canal with compensation and that of the British Labour Government in nationalising iron and steel and coal with compensation.

This is the first time that a 'Marxist' has been heard to place juridical forms before economic necessities. But when from Communist China we are told that the Egyptian action is a contribution to world peace, we have left the world of realities for Wonderland.

It is also difficult to see how Egypt can claim that she needs the revenues for economic construction and, at the same time, that she intends to pay compensation, unless she has it in mind to extract higher dues from ships passing through the Canal. In short, that she intends treating the Canal like a medieval caravan route, and levying toll for right of way.

The Socialist reply to all this is clear. It is to internationalise all these water ways through which the commerce of the world is articulated. And this goes for those in British possession as well as those in the control and possession of other countries.

If Nasser's action has brought this on to the world agenda, it is all to the good. It means that all these means of access on which the world depends for its trade and commerce transcend the claims of national sovereignties, and have reached the stage when they should be entrusted to a world authority to be policed and administered by that authority.

On that basis we should have an answer to Egypt on which we could stand. When the British Prime Minister asserts that no one nation should be able to hold up the commerce of the world, he is on good ground.

But the logic falls short of what is required unless he goes on to the position that what is vital for the world, the world should claim for itself.

In the meantime, Nasser and all Egypt should realise that they have done great damage to the cause of aid to under-developed countries, including their own.

Nations should be set free so that they may freely come together. National independence is the basis for international co-operation, not for the indulgence of rabid nationalist excesses.

Egypt has the right to come into her own, but not into someone else's. As for Nasser, he is acclaimed in Egypt as the champion of his country. It is a proud title. But a prouder one is to be his country's saviour.

That title he has yet to earn.

Give the United Nations a real job to do – 5 October 1956

When the immediate issue of the future of the Suez Canal is settled it will be found that the controversy has opened up considerations of far greater import than the Canal itself.

The most important of these is the character and volume of international investment, especially investment in economically backward nations.

The questions involved are complex and delicate, for they concern not only problems of finance but feelings of national pride and independence.

It is natural that when colonial peoples free themselves from imperial oppression they object to putting themselves in financial bondage, often to the same imperial power. If loans or grants are made to them for the development of their resources, it is essential they should be free of political strings which would limit or condition their newly won national independence.

This is obviously so when the arrangements are between government and government, but scarcely less important when the investment in the new nation is through private sources.

Private capital will flow only to areas where there is security against political disturbances, immunity from expropriation, and an expectation of high profits. But the new nations cannot guarantee such immunity, for it carries the assumption that foreign capital is exempt from its own domestic legislation.

This is the issue raised by the action of Egypt in nationalising the Suez Canal Company. Nasser takes his stand on Egypt's national right to take over any property on its soil, foreign-owned or otherwise.

In this he is supported by all Asian countries and, needless to say, by Socialists everywhere. It is an essential condition for the political development of liberated countries that they should be entirely free to do what they like with what lies within their own borders, whether placed there from an outside source or built by their own efforts.

It is by appearing to contest this principle that France, Britain, and the United States have offended the emergent nations.

Foreign capital is often suspect, just because it is foreign, especially if it arrives in a country with only a colonial status. It becomes intolerably offensive to the local population if it claims special exemptions.

So much is clear or at least should be to anyone looking at the problem with unprejudiced eyes. But there are further difficulties.

It almost invariably happens that the new nations are backward economically and therefore lack the means for their own development. Their peoples are too poor to provide surpluses for investment in the advanced techniques of a modern industrialised society.

GUARANTEES?

There is here a dilemma of the first magnitude. It cannot be resolved by reliance on conventional methods. Private capital will not flow in sufficient volume to backward countries without guarantees against revolutionary action, and these cannot be provided without, at the very least, appearing to infringe the newly won sovereign rights.

If the government of the receiving nation does give the guarantees, it exposes itself to attack from its own freshly released revolutionary forces.

It is the common pattern in such circumstances for political independence to be followed by economic action.

If this action takes the form of expropriation either with or without compensation, it dries up the flow of foreign capital. Nevertheless, it often happens that only by such expropriation can the government seize on the means necessary for its plans of industrial expansion.

There is another aspect of the problem in which the Western nations are particularly concerned. It is hoped that the emancipated nations will put their faith in the institutions of political democracy after the fashion of the West.

But these depend on popular support, and this will not be forthcoming to a government which appears unable to provide for an improvement in the material conditions of its people.

CRUEL TEST

This is frequently impracticable if the production of goods of personal consumption is held down in the interests of ambitious plans of fixed capital investment. Nevertheless, it is upon just this investment that the government must rely if it plans for the permanent betterment of the condition of the nation.

These circumstances expose the institutions of political democracy to a cruel test. Sometimes they fail to survive it, as in the case of Egypt.

The institutions of democracy are rooted in economic surplus, and the sooner liberal thinking accepts the conclusion and acts upon it, the nearer we shall be to a solution of many of the difficulties facing us.

It is no use preaching the virtues of democracy to people living near subsistence levels and expect them at the same time to set aside surpluses for economic expansion. It is equally useless to ask them to exchange their national independence for economic aid.

The first is impracticable, and the second is immoral. Nor should the situation be seen as just another aspect of the cold war with economic aid as an auxiliary weapon.

LAGGING BEHIND

Once more the case of Egypt has shown how foolish that is, and it is none the less foolish because Nasser tried to play the game that way.

The problem should be seen in its proper historical setting. It arises from the fact that one part of the world – the greater part of it – has lagged behind the other in the application of the industrial sciences.

The psychology of the situation is made worse by the fact that the part which has lagged behind was for centuries the prey of the nations which have advanced. The solution is obvious and has long been recognised, but it has been applied piecemeal and often used to serve national ambitions.

The surpluses of the advanced nations should be made available to those which are backward, but it should be done in a way that avoids any taint of national subordination on the one hand or 'big nation' condescension on the other.

The best way would be to canalise the surpluses through the medium of an agency of the United Nations. The contribution of any one nation would therefore be merged in the whole, and no one's pride would be hurt.

DOUBLE PURPOSE

This method would serve a double purpose. It would help to shore up democratic processes in the receiving countries, and it would give the United Nations organisation an authority and substantiality it sorely needs.

What is the good of continually complaining that the United Nations lacks authority to impose its will on recalcitrant nations if it is always by-passed and deprived of the activities for which it is best fitted?

It is no use only praying for peace. The institutions of peace must be strengthened and clothed with power and dignity, so that all men can see in them both the source of their material well-being and the hope of its continuance.

If the provision of financial assistance to Egypt had been the concern of the United Nations and not a bequest of the United States, the whole miserable squabble over the Suez Canal would probably never have arisen.

It is time we learned this lesson and applied it to the many similar problems that are bound to arise.

Crisis time for United Nations – 1 February 1957

'We must uphold the rule of law in the world ...'

'Collective security is the sheet anchor of peace and we must stand by the decisions of the United Nations as expressions of this principle.'

These affirmations, which appear to be unexceptionable, have become so much a part of progressive thinking about international affairs that we are in danger of mistaking the form for the reality.

It is a mistake, frequently committed, to confound an aspiration with a principle.

Because we aspire to see the rule of law established in the world, we jump to the assumption that it has been reached through the agency of the United Nations.

It follows from this that obedience to the decisions of the United Nations is the hallmark of the good world citizen.

How simple international affairs would be if they were really like that. All that would be left for us to do would be to employ the most persuasive of lawyers to plead our case before the world courts – as we do in the national courts – and accept the verdict; with pleasure if it were in our favour, but with obedience, however glum, if it went against us.

Unfortunately, these are not the facts and it does no good to the cause of peace and to the eventual establishment of the rule of law to assume otherwise.

The United Nations is not a law court issuing dispassionate decisions. It is an arena of contending nations where the more civilised statesmen are attempting to build up a code of international conduct which, we must all hope, will eventually win universal approval and acceptance.

Its actions must therefore be judged by its success in establishing just that state of things.

When the British Labour Party opposed the action of the Tory Government in the case of Egypt, it was not because the rule of international law was violated.

TOWARDS ANARCHY

It was because, among other things, the invasion of Egypt weakened the authority of the United Nations, and so retarded the eventual establishment of the rule of law. We were taking a step back towards the old anarchy and not forward to a new world of peace backed by the institutions of international law.

It was not because, we said, the law is there – we must obey it. It was because what the Tories tried to do would prevent it from ever being established.

It follows from this that the conduct of the United Nations must itself be judged by the extent to which its actions have the result in winning respect for its decisions and in promoting peace with justice.

In the present stage of its existence, it is therefore not enough that the United Nations has reached a decision. The decision itself must be subjected to a prior test, which is, will it promote peace and limit the anarchical claims of national sovereignties?

The United Nations is an institution in process of becoming what it not yet is, an international court universally revered.

This is vividly illustrated in the case of Israel.

When the United Nations called upon Israel to go back behind the armistice lines, it asserted the unquestionable principle that no nation should benefit by an act of aggression.

But if it stops at that, it will be merely an act of arid, judicial primness. It will leave untouched and, therefore, unremedied, the conditions that led to an outbreak of violence.

It will assert the claims of Egyptian national sovereignty over and above the creation of conditions making for peace.

It will be a form of law without its essential content, for law is not to be judged by itself alone, but by its success in fostering the conditions that have led men to support its exercise.

It is here where the Afro-Asian bloc in the United Nations is taking the wrong attitude.

The causes why this is so are obvious.

Most of the countries included in it won their nationhood in struggles against imperialism. They are, therefore, inclined to insist upon their national rights, even where these conflict with the conditions making for peace.

They are jealous of rights so recently acquired, and they appear to be ready to cling to these, even where they violate the principles essential to their own preservation.

They make claims on Israel. What do they demand from Egypt?

Do they agree with Egypt when she says that a state of war exists with Israel, has existed, and will continue to exist after Israel withdraws behind the armistice lines?

PRO-EGYPTIAN?

Do they support Egypt's blockade of the Gulf of Aqaba against Israeli shipping, and her persistent refusal to allow Israeli ships to use the Suez Canal?

Do they, in short, support war by Egypt on Israel, and at the same time express horror and condemnation if Israel takes Egypt at her word?

Is this the rule of law, or the exploitation of the United Nations for reasons which invalidate its very existence?

When the Afro-Asian nations contend that Egypt is within her national rights in allowing, or refusing to allow, shipping to pass through the Suez Canal, they are asserting the sanctity, not of law, but of the anarchy of nationalisms intent on building walls around themselves in violation of the manifest inter-dependence of all nations.

For make no mistake about it; implicit in the principle of complete self-determination is the claim of a nation to make war on any other, if it believes its very existence to be in danger.

Mankind has never believed that respect for a principle, enshrined in the most sanctified law, should be carried to the point of personal or national extinction.

Ask that question of any man starving to death in front of a shop window full of food. Respect for the policeman is apt to diminish in such a situation.

Keeping all this in mind, I am convinced that the opinion of most people is behind the spokesmen of Israel when they demand that the United Nations has the obligation to see that the condition of affairs which existed before the invasion should not be revived.

GUARANTEES

Egyptian belligerent rights over the Gulf of Aqaba should be denied her. The Gaza Strip should be administered by the United Nations. The passage of Israeli ships through the Suez Canal – and of all other shipping – should be guaranteed.

It may not be necessary that these should be accorded Israel before she withdraws her troops. But it is essential that both operations should proceed simultaneously.

Private assurances by Egypt are not sufficient. They are not binding, for they are not recorded and can be easily repudiated or not admitted.

Nothing less than this can win respect for the United Nations and convince public opinion that the purpose of law, as well as its forms, are to be implemented.

The task of the United Nations is not to freeze the relations of nations where they are, but to change and mould them in a way in which force, or the threat of force, becomes progressively infrequent.

Warning to the wreckers – 28 June 1957

The present Commonwealth Conference is probably the most important of its kind ever held. I say that for three reasons.

First, this conference will inevitably be a post-mortem on the British Government's Suez policy. Second, it is the first at which an African independent state will be numbered among the members – a harbinger of more to follow shortly. And third, it occurs at time when demands upon sterling balances will compel a re-examination of British financial policy. This involves our financial relations with the other members of the Commonwealth.

The first matter is scarcely likely to occupy the Conference for long. The British Government has no case on Suez which will stand examination; the sooner it recognises this fact and hopes that bygones will be bygones, the better the chance for the success of the Conference.

It is with the second and the third matters, the reasons for the uniqueness of the Conference, that we should mainly concern ourselves.

The promotion of Ghana to full independence and her willingness to accept membership of the Commonwealth mean more than just another additional member. The nature of the Commonwealth is undergoing a profound change. This will test both its flexibility and its strength.

In particular, the older and 'white' members will need to show an imaginative awareness of what is taking place. Nothing in their own experience is available to guide them.

DIFFERENCE

Canada, New Zealand, South Africa and Australia have histories with many common features, and they share few, if any, of these with India, Ceylon, Ghana, and soon Nigeria, the Malay States and the Caribbean Federation. The difference is not one of colour, nor indeed of race, for these are superficial, and most civilised people have now come to recognise the fundamental equality of all races.

But the difference in historical origins is important, if only because independence is being realised by the new Dominions in quite a different social context to that of their fellow members. This different context is bound to influence the course of development of the new Dominions, and, therefore, to distinguish them sharply from the others.

The two main differences are the existence of Communism in Russia and in China and the fact that the new Dominions are passing through, or have still to undergo, their own industrial revolutions.

BACKWARDNESS

In the case of India, there is another difference of equally great importance, due to the pressure of her huge population combined with their economic backwardness.

Compare this feature of the situation with what happened in the older Dominions. They were, in many respects, the by-products of the industrial revolution in Britain at various stages of its growth. The people who populated the 'white' Dominions were usually literate, often men of education, artisans, and already acquainted with the technical equipment of a modern state.

EMIGRATION

Their migration from the mother country in wave after wave eased the tensions caused by the dislocations of the industrial revolution in Britain. It is probably true to say that, were it not for emigration, the industrial revolution in Britain and in the rest of Europe would have been marked, not only by the minor rebellions which did occur, but by wholesale revolution.

There was another difference of equal, if not greater, importance. The older Dominions were empty countries. The indigenous population was small and unable to offer any effective resistance to the immigrants from Europe.

This comparative emptiness did for them what they had done for the industrial revolution in Europe. It offered endless opportunities of escape when the social tensions of their own society became unendurable.

DISCONTENTED

All these facts are, of course, well known. But it is wise to recall them when we are facing the task of framing Commonwealth policy for nations with a totally different experience and, therefore, with entirely different problems.

If the industrial revolution is injected into the Indian society in the same fashion as it was into European society, where could the discontented masses emigrate? What cushion, what shock-absorber, is available to India?

KEEP TRADITIONS

An industrial and technical revolution carried out by private enterprise, as happened in Britain, would produce a host of quite insoluble problems. Indian village life would be destroyed. The displaced peasants would throng the Indian cities in scores of millions without prospect of employment, and would live in indescribable misery and filth.

The problem facing India is, therefore, how to avail herself of modern industrial techniques, while at the same time preserving the stability and much of the traditional texture of Indian Society.

India suffers from another disability, and this she shares with most of her new fellow members of the Commonwealth.

Not only does she lack a technically trained population, but she is also without the financial surpluses which were accumulated by Britain over centuries, and which, when the time came, were available to finance the industrial revolution. (It should also be noted that much of this surplus was provided by the rape of India.)

CONSENT NEEDED

Yet another fact must be mentioned to show how different are the histories of the young as compared with the older Dominions. They have adopted the full range of democratic institutions at the outset of their careers as independent nations.

They have, therefore, to accomplish the accumulation of great industries in all the circumstances I have described, not only with the willing consent, but necessarily with the active co-operation of their peoples. They have to do this against the background of the industrial revolution carried out in Russia and in China under quite different political institutions.

ONLY CHOICE

It should be obvious to anyone not blinded by political prejudice that the young Dominions are irresistibly compelled to plan the transformation of their societies under some form of state direction and control. Even if they wished it, the road of traditional capitalism is not open to them. *They have* to choose either democratic Socialism or Communism.

Certain British critics of Mr. Nehru should learn to understand this. If they do not, and if their criticism is allowed to affect Commonwealth financial policy, the Commonwealth will disintegrate.

IGNORANCE

India is being criticised for her share in running down sterling balances. Even journals like *The Economist* write of India having had 'a spending spree.' Such language shows a lamentable ignorance, not so much of the financial facts of the situation, for these *The Economist* knows well enough, but of the deeper inwardness of the Indian social and political situation.

If the financing of the industrial revolution imposes too great a strain upon the populations of the younger Dominions, it must be realised in London and New York that they will go Communist.

THEY FOLLOW

They will follow, not the example of Europe and North America, but of Russia and of China, particularly China.

One conclusion flows inevitably from what I have written. If by 'our way of life' we mean the urbanities, the tolerance, and the free institutions to which we are accustomed, then it can be defended not by massed armies nor by Hydrogen Bombs, but by economic policies which assist the peoples of the young Dominions to win their way to better material conditions without suffering intolerable privations.

Back to free markets – and the jungle – 30 August 1957

In European political circles the argument about the Common Market is hotting up. If Conservatives get their way we shall soon be talking about nothing else.

On the European continent it has been a major political preoccupation for some years now, but so far the British have been inclined to discuss it in the minor key.

As the term implies, the common market conception is nothing more or less than free trade among those European nations that choose to take part in it.

This is expected to be brought about gradually over twelve to fifteen years, that being the period in which industry and commerce are expected to adjust themselves to the emerging pattern of competition.

In contrast with the Continent, opinion in Britain has welcomed the idea with marked caution.

Not even Conservatives are wholly enthusiastic about it although they are edging their way to its acceptance like a timid bather testing the temperature of the water with a tentative toe.

SHY OFF

There are a number of reasons for this caution. One of them and by no means the least influential is the traditional British dislike for propositions put forward on abstract grounds.

The Continental exponents of the Common Market have claimed so much for it that the British, who are empiricists by history, and now by disposition, are inclined to shy off.

Any idea about such prosaic matters as trade and commerce, when decked out with a mystical nimbus, is looked at askance by the typical conventional business man in striped trousers and rolled-up umbrella.

He is exhorted to be a 'good European' when all he wants is to be financially successful. Where the success is found is a matter of indifference to him.

Nor is this attitude surprising in a business world that for several centuries has been as cosmopolitan as the British. There is a natural reluctance to be too deeply committed to any particular area.

This reluctance is increased when Continental supporters attach to the common market concept arguments about the need to diminish the authority of the various sovereignties of Europe and merge them in a wider 'Europe over All.'

There is in fact no Europe in that sense to which the abrogated sovereign rights could be entrusted.

There can be no doubt that tariffs, proscriptions on trade and restrictions of various kinds imposed by a congeries of sovereign Parliaments are vexatious and may constrict productive forces.

SUSPICIOUS

But, in the absence of a wider sovereignty, all the conception of a common market does is to elevate the market place to the status now enjoyed by the various European Parliaments.

It is at this point that Socialists become suspicious of what is intended.

Is it the disenfranchisement of the people and the enfranchisement of market forces?

Are we now expected to go back almost a century, reject Socialism and clasp free trade to our bosom as though it were the one solution of our social evils?

Does it not happen to be the fact that most of the social conditions against which Socialists have fought and in which Socialism was conceived, arose in countries which practised free trade as well as trade restrictions?

The 'Europeans' point to the United States as an example of what a 'Continental market' can accomplish in the way of releasing productive forces.

The parallel is false. The creation of the United States was unique and its subsequent history entirely different from that of any other country with perhaps the exceptions of Canada, Australia and New Zealand.

These countries were the recipients and the beneficiaries of a series of migrations from Europe consisting often of skilled workers.

Also, they were, in the main, empty countries where there was consequently no churning up and destruction of old patterns of living such as Europe experienced during the Industrial Revolution.

In addition they escaped the physical impact of two World Wars. Indeed, they benefitted by them, because their productive forces were immensely stimulated by the role they played in those wars.

It should also be remembered that the 'Continentalism' of industry and commerce in the United States was consistent for more than a century with conditions of appalling poverty in the South.

If I am told that these very wars originated in Europe and might have been prevented if the 'European' idea had been adopted earlier, I reply that free trade nations have been neither less nor more belligerent than restrictive ones.

COST OF WARS

Both have made wars and the idea that an interwoven pattern of trade makes wars less likely unfortunately is not borne out by history as Sir Norman Angell discovered after he had written his *Great Illusion*.

To be just to him his contention was that the cost in terms of the destruction of trade made wars in the modern world not worth the candle.

But candles are not what war is about: at least not in the minds of those who fight them.

There is an argument for negotiated reduction of trade restrictions where restrictions can be shown to be mutually disadvantageous.

But the conception of a Common Market for Europe is not a blue print for European prosperity and stability. It is the result of a political malaise following upon the failure of Socialists to use the sovereign power of their Parliaments to plan their economic life.

It is an escapist conception in which the play of market forces will take the place of political responsibility.

SUPPLY AND DEMAND

If times are prosperous the Parliaments will be inactive for there will be no call for them to act. If times are bad economic forces will be blamed.

Parliaments will remain inert, for if they attempt to exert themselves it will be an offence against the authority of the market which by then will have been endowed with the sacrosanctity of a totem.

Our old friend the law of supply and demand will be back with all its old authority.

Socialists cannot at one and the same time call for economic planning and accept the verdict of free competition, no matter how extensive the area it covers.

The jungle is not made more acceptable just because it is almost limitless.

It is also necessary to point out that competition between goods results in competition between standards of living unless these are supported and sustained by *powerful and uniform social services*. The latter flow from the use of political power exerted by pressure on political institutions.

This is anathema to all conceptions of universal competition.

We must save India – or lose democracy's hope – 5 September 1958

In Britain economists are reconciled to the view that there will be rising unemployment this autumn and winter and a consequent fall in production.

Some measures are being taken to lessen the decline as much as is thought possible, such as the recent reductions in the bank rate and easier money for hire purchase. But no responsible authority believes these will prove sufficient to do more than cushion the depression.

WHAT LEVEL?

Nor is there any inclination in Government circles to do much more. They have made their choice. They believe there are two courses open to them: inflation or a permanent percentage of unemployment. They have chosen the latter.

What the percentage should be is undecided. Indeed it is not easy to come to a decision on such a question. And this for the good and simple reason that there are no really effective means available in capitalist economy to control the level of unemployment except within very wide limits.

Financial restrictions and expansion operate slowly, clumsily and with uneven effects, depending on whether industries are in a position to finance themselves or have to resort to banks or to the open market.

EXPORTS FALLING

Right wing politicians will blame the recession on the delayed results of the industrial depression in the United States. For some time the United Kingdom benefited by the American setback. The cost of primary and raw materials fell and so the cost of imports to Britain was reduced.

But now the usual consequences of such a situation are being met in a fall in exports because exporters of primary materials are compelled to reduce their purchases from abroad.

For almost the first time since the end of the war British industrialists are faced with thin order books, workers are either working a shorter week, being laid off, or dismissed.

In a few areas the degree of unemployment has already reached serious proportions.

Nevertheless, it is a significant fact that prices to the ultimate consumer have not so far shown any inclination to respond to the decline in production. In particular, they have failed to reflect the reduction in import prices. Nor does it seem to be expected that they will do so to the full extent.

In my opinion, this demonstrates the existence of a permanent crisis in Western economy. When expansion does take place it begins at a higher price level than the previous one so that each fresh expansion is accompanied by immediate inflation.

This situation is brought about by the fact that final consumer prices are able to offer greater resistance to a fall in costs than the rest of the economy.

This is due to changes in the structure of the distributive processes and to the spread of the practice of 'administrative prices.'

Individual competition becomes rarer and rarer as firms defend their margins of profit by trying to make the same profit on smaller turnovers.

This is, of course, poison to the capitalist system for not only does it limit the creation of mass demand but it maintains in production firms that should, by the old laws of capitalist economy, have gone bankrupt.

WORSE TO COME

If the situation worsens these trends will no doubt be upset and wholesale bankruptcies follow. But for the present the rigidities in the capitalist system are considerable. They constitute a major defect and operate to deprive the whole economy of effective self-correcting mechanisms.

The new banking policy of making credit easier to obtain does not undermine the argument. Indeed, this development reinforces my point.

INDIA'S PROBLEMS

Facilities for easier credit will stimulate demand from a small section of the population. In doing so, it will help to restrain competition and to keep up prices.

It is against this background that the foreign exchange crisis of India must be seen. On the one hand the economy of the West possesses unused industrial resources, while on the other, India is compelled to cut back her development plans because of [a] shortage of foreign exchange.

This is a contrast that cannot continue without the gravest consequences for the democratic world. It must also be borne in mind that this state of affairs exists side by side with continued expansion of the industrial capacities of the Sino-Soviet Bloc. The political and psychological consequences are obvious.

HELP NEEDED

It is a challenge of such magnitude that the Western nations dare not let it go by default without admitting defeat. In the West the defeat would be demoralising; in the East it would be decisive.

There are signs that the significance of all this is at last being appreciated. The question is whether the appreciation is quick enough, massive enough or sufficiently influential.

The major challenge is, of course, to the United States. But the European countries, including Great Britain, are equally involved even though their resources are not on the same scale as those of the United States.

WAVERING ANSWER

Apart from the material issues raised, a philosophical question of the utmost importance is brought to the front. Put shortly, it is whether an economically backward nation can build up its capital equipment and technical resources and at the same time enjoy democratic institutions.

The Communists' answer is no. The democratic nations have not yet replied; at least the reply has been wavering, inadequate, and so far, less than effective. India, under the leadership of Nehru, replied, yes.

But he was never under any delusion about the nature or magnitude of the task facing his people. He was also aware that India could not by herself, out of her own resources, fully meet the challenge.

Nor could she be expected to do so. No other nation has done it. Certainly not Great Britain or the United States. They achieved their industrial expansion in a different century, under totally different conditions.

NEHRU'S REQUEST

The British effort was spread over centuries and the United States benefited by migrations of skilled workers from Europe accompanied, at the same time, by investments from Europe in the most advanced industrial techniques developed there. It should not be forgotten that the workers of Europe did not enjoy the full range of political liberty possessed today by the people of India.

The building of the capital equipment of Europe was largely an involuntary act by the workers of Europe. Nehru is asking the people of India to do it voluntarily. He asks them freely to forego immediate advantages for more distant gains when the plans have matured.

OUR RESPONSIBILITY

If assistance to India from the Western democracies was based only on grounds of political expediency, mixed as we hope with some altruism, it would be enough. But there are obvious material advantages also to be gained by the West through coming to the help of India in her present difficulties. It would give a much needed fillip to its languishing industries.

If the internal rigidities I have described above inhibit the economy of the West from self-created expansion, an injection of demand from outside might start it off again.

The sceptic may say 'A fool's eyes are always on the ends of the earth.' But only fools nowadays refuse to see that the ends of the earth are on our own door step.

Independence – then hard work: how to maintain the frontiers of liberty – 21 November 1958

Milovan Djilas, himself a Montenegrin, once told me a story illustrating the general distaste for hard work among his fellow countrymen.

Marshal Tito was addressing a large gathering in Montenegro. In the course of his address, he shared their rejoicing over achieving national independence and then went on to warn them that the time had come to consolidate their liberty by hard work.

When the Marshal sat down, a tall Montenegrin got up from the back of the audience and said: 'When Marshal Tito talked about our national independence, he stole the words from my heart. But what is all this talk about work?'

I am reminded of the story by the news that yet another country, recently emancipated from colonial rule, has succumbed to a military coup. The list is now long. Syria, Iraq, Pakistan, Egypt, now the Sudan.

LONG LIST

Even in Ceylon the elected government found it necessary, or thought it was necessary, to employ unusual powers for a long period. Happily, at least as seen from this distance, public affairs there have settled once more into a democratic mode.

Each one of this list of nations has its own separate history and its own local reasons for failing to enable democratic institutions to take sufficiently deep root.

But the list is too long, and the emerging pattern too uniform for there to be no underlying common factor.

One feature, of course, they have in common. They are all Muslims. But that can hardly be the explanation.

Islam is one of the most democratic religions in the world. No priest interposes himself between Muslim and Allah. The communication is simple and direct. There is no closely knit hierarchy, conspiring to share or command governmental authority.

STATE OF MIND

The Mullahs have, from time to time, as in the process of constitution-making in Pakistan, attempted to impose their stamp on the nature of proposed legislation, but it did not go far, for the needs of a modern state cannot be bound in the clamp of Islamic law, particularly as there are a number of different interpretations of it.

Part of the explanation is to be found in the state of mind that is created in the course of the struggle against the occupying colonial power.

A curious kind of double mentality is created. If things go wrong the colonial power is not only blamed for it, but is also expected to put it right. It comes to be regarded as both God and the devil at one and the same time.

Privations, vicissitudes, hardship and poverty, all of which could fairly be said to be caused wholly or in part by natural and historical causes, are the mind of a subject population attributed to the hated foreign rule.

This is not to say that there was not and is not economic exploitation by colonial powers. There was and there still is. But it seldom amounted to the magnitude ascribed to it.

I refer now to comparatively recent colonial rule and not to the period of mercantilism when plain loot was the main purpose of the conquering power, for example, in the early Spanish conquests and in the earlier phases of the British occupation of India.

The charge against the colonial powers during the late 19th, and the first part of this century, is not primarily one of economic exploitation, but of neglect – failure to educate, and on the basis of that failure, an inability to identify sufficient numbers of the indigenous inhabitants with the machinery of administration. And, in particular, neglect to develop natural resources.

The physical preserve of the alien power is reflected in the psychology of the subject people to an extent even more obtrusive than the facts themselves would seem to justify.

When the colonial power is withdrawn by agreement, as in the case of India, Pakistan, Ceylon, Burma, and Ghana, or driven out by successful revolt, the change is profound – so profound as to constitute for a while almost a trauma.

The sudden onrush of responsibility, although accompanied by the delirious delight of liberty, finds many of the emancipated people unprepared. It had seemed to them, in the years of struggle, that when the hated power left, their lot would be suddenly and dramatically improved. It is then they discover, like the Montenegrin, that national liberty implies work and self-reliance.

TASKS AHEAD

In the circumstances of the modern world, it involves still more. It might even mean a lower immediate standard of living in order to mobilise the nation's resources in the building of the industrial establishments characteristic of a modern advanced community.

After the first rejoicings over independence comes a sober realisation of the tasks ahead. Unlike India which has enjoyed two enormous advantages – the spiritual thrust of Gandhi and the genius of Nehru – many of the leaders who led the struggle for independence are ill-equipped for the tasks of national construction. In place of the departed rulers, they soon find themselves the whipping boys of disillusionment.

The political parties, newly created and shallow rooted, find themselves faced with tasks for which they did not have adequate preparation. The sudden accession of their leaders to power and greater material well-being, leaves a gap between them and their former associates in the earlier days of heroic struggle.

Charges of corruption find easy credence against such a background. Corruption there probably is, but not on the scale usually described.

Parliamentary democracies do not decline and fall because of corruption alone. If they did, the British parliamentary system would never have survived the days of the House of Hanover.

No. The plain fact is that recently emancipated colonial peoples can rarely hope to continue to enjoy personal liberty as well as national independence unless some aid from outside is available.

This modern phenomenon of emancipated colonial peoples succumbing to Military dictatorships must be explained not by the classical answers, but by more mundane causes.

Political liberty, as distinct from national independence, is rooted in economic surplus. The flower of liberty does not flourish on barren soil.

HELP NEEDED

It is no accident that modern democracies occurred among nations of advancing material prosperity. Political liberty commended itself to the people of these countries because it coexisted with improved welfare.

The lesson of all this is clear. If the Western democracies are not prepared to see the frontiers of liberty continually contracting, they must do more than merely withdraw from the countries they once dominated.

They must be prepared to compensate for the years of neglect, and to underpin the political institutions of the new nations with part of their own wealth.

Bibliography

BBC, *Bevan is ultimate Welsh hero* (2004), http://news.bbc.co.uk/1/hi/wales/3523363.stm (accessed 20 December 2021).

Beckett, Clare and Beckett, Francis, *Bevan* (London: Haus Publishing, 2004).

Belam, M., 'Jeremy Corbyn's Nye Bevan quote is pure fiction', *The Guardian* (2017), https://www.theguardian.com/politics/2017/may/17/jeremy-corbyn-tweets-fake-nye-bevan-quote-on-fighting-for-the-nhs (accessed 20 December 2021).

Bevan, A., 'Socialist Classics: The Communist Manifesto', *The Plebs*, 13/1 (1921), 19–21.

Bevan, Aneurin, *Why Not Trust the Tories?* (London: Victor Gollancz, 1944).

Bevan, A., 'Ten years – Tribune, 1937–1947', *Tribune* (31 January 1947), p. 7.

Bevan, A., 'July 5th and the Socialist Advance', *Tribune* (2 July 1948), p. 7.

Bevan, Aneurin, *In Place of Fear* (London: William Heinemann, 1952).

Bevan, A., 'Rationed – or "free"?', *Tribune* (29 October 1954), pp. 1–2.

Blair, T., 'Foreword', in G. Goodman (ed.), *The State of the Nation: The Political Legacy of Aneurin Bevan* (London: Victor Gollancz, 1997), pp. 11–13.

Brome, Vincent, *Aneurin Bevan: A Biography* (London: Longmans, Green and Co., 1953).

Campbell, John, *Nye Bevan and the Mirage of British Socialism* (London: Weidenfeld and Nicolson, 1987).

Corbyn, J., *We must include everybody and exclude nobody. They were Nye Bevan's values, they are Labour's values. #NHS70* (Twitter, 2018), https://twitter.com/jeremycorbyn/status/1014026451299942406 (accessed 20 December 2021).

Craik, W. W., *The Central Labour College: A chapter in the history of adult working-class education 1909–29* (London: Lawrence and Wishart, 1964).

Crines, A. S. and Laybourn, K., 'The oratory of Aneurin Bevan', in A. S. Crines and R. Hayton (eds), *Labour orators from Bevan to Miliband* (Manchester: Manchester University Press, 2015), pp. 14–30.

Davies, N., 'Why does Jeremy Hunt keep comparing himself to Aneurin Bevan?', *Left Foot Forward* (2016), https://leftfootforward.org/2016/07/why-does-jeremy-hunt-keep-comparing-himself-to-aneurin-bevan/ (accessed 20 December 2021).

Davies, N., 'Liberty, Bevan and Welsh Labour', *Thinking Wales* (2017), https://blogs.cardiff.ac.uk/thinking-wales/liberty-bevan-and-welsh-labour/ (accessed 20 December 2021).

Davies, N., 'Top Marx: Bevan and the importance of Karl', *Thinking Wales* (2017), https://blogs.cardiff.ac.uk/thinking-wales/top-marx-bevan-and-the-importance-of-karl/ (accessed 20 December 2021).

Demont, S. E., 'Tredegar and Aneurin Bevan: A Society and its Political Articulation 1890 – 1929' (unpublished PhD thesis, University of Wales, 1990).

Foot, Michael, *Aneurin Bevan: 1897–1945* (London: Granada Publishing, 1975).

Foot, Michael, *Aneurin Bevan: 1945–1960* (London: Granada Publishing, 1975).

Foote, Geoffrey, *The Labour Party's Political Thought* (London: Croom Helm, 1986).

Griffiths, Robert, *S. O. Davies: A Socialist Faith* (Llandysul, Dyfed: Gomer Press, 1983), p. 51.

HC Deb., 16 July 1929, vol. 230, col. 339.

HC Deb., 27 February 1930, vol. 235, col. 2468.

Krug, Mark M., *Aneurin Bevan: Cautious Rebel* (New York: Thomas Yoseloff, 1961).

Lee, Jennie, *My Life with Nye* (Middlesex: Penguin, 1981).

Morgan, K. O., 'Nye Bevan', in R. L. Louis (ed.), *Resurgent Adventures with Britannia: Personalities, Politics and Culture in Britain* (London: I. B. Tauris, 2011), pp. 181–95.
Nairn, T., 'The nature of the Labour Party – 2', *New Left Review*, 1/28 (1964), 33–62.
Smith, Dai, *Aneurin Bevan and the World of South Wales* (Cardiff: University of Wales Press, 1993).
Sparrow, A., 'Who is Labour's greatest hero?', *The Guardian* (2008), *https://www.theguardian.com/politics/blog/2008/sep/22/labour.labourconference1* (accessed 20 December 2021).
Strachey, John, *The Coming Struggle for Power* (London: Victor Gollancz, 1932).
Thomas, Elizabeth (ed.), *Tribune 21* (London: MacGibbon and Kee, 1958).
Thomas-Symonds, Nicklaus, *Nye: The Political Life of Aneurin Bevan* (London: I. B. Tauris, 2015).
Wilson, Harold, *Memoirs: The Making of a Prime Minister 1916–64* (London: Weidenfeld and Nicolson, 1986).

INDEX

A
Ablett, Noah 3, 4
Abyssinia 207, 219
Adenauer, Konrad 171, 229–31
Africa 88, 218, 221, 260, 291–2, 294
Algeria 181, 233
Anderson, Evelyn 7
Anglo-Soviet Alliance 141–4
Arms 9, 11, 13, 14, 69, 76, 141–2,
    165, 175, 188, 193–4, 205, 212,
    225, 236, 242, 244, 247, 251–4,
    267–71, 275, 280
    and capitalism 251–4
    bombs 194, 233–4, 240–2, 249,
        276, 297
    disarmament 9, 175, 181, 188,
        225, 236–9, 240, 254, 270
Asia 115, 163–4, 277, 286, 291–2
Assheton, Ralph 148, 150
Astor, David 125
Astor, Nancy 132
Attlee, Clement 6, 8, 75, 138, 140,
    163, 206, 242, 256
Australia 48, 223, 264, 294, 299
Austria 171, 257-258
Authoritarianism *see* Totalitarianism
Automation 62–7

B
Baldwin, Stanley 1, 20, 131
Bank of England 186
Beaverbrook, Lord 149, 227
Belgium 138, 210, 257
Beria, Lavrentiy 173
Bevan, Aneurin
    Bevanites 9, 12
    Deputy Leader of the Labour
        Party 9
    early life 3–5
    editor of 'Tribune' 7–8
    election as MP 5–6
    'In Place of Fear' (1952) 2, 9, 10
    legacy 1–3, 13–14
    Minister of Health and Housing
        8, 176–9
    National Health Service 1, 2, 8,
        13–14
    political philosophy 9, 10, 11–12,
        13
    'Priorities' 10, 13, 128, 162,
        197–9
    resignation from government 8–9

review of the 'Communist Manifesto' (1921) 4
Shadow Foreign Secretary 9, 13
'The Coming Struggle for Power' (1932) 6
treasurer 117–22
'Tribune' 6–7, 9, 10–11, 13
'Why Not Trust the Tories?' (1944) 2
Bevan, David 3–4
Beveridge Report 86, 93
Bevin, Ernest 80, 224, 260, 275
Blair, Tony 1
Brailsford, Noel 6
British Broadcasting Corporation (BBC) 82, 259
Bulganin, Nikolai 239
Burma 267, 307
Butler, Rab 73, 229

C
Canada 132, 223, 237, 268, 294, 299
capitalism 4, 9, 12, 13, 19–22, 27–8, 32, 39–42, 43, 49, 52–8, 62–7, 68–71, 77, 114, 141–2, 154, 163, 174, 182–3, 184–7, 196–8, 210, 222, 226, 231, 234, 251–4, 266, 297, 302–5
Cecil, Robert 137
Central Europe 139, 181
Central Labour College (CLC) 4
Chamberlain, Neville 35, 40, 49, 132–3, 142, 206, 214, 263
Cherwell, Lord 240–1
China 13, 115, 163–6, 174, 182, 196, 223, 235, 276–7, 284, 295–7
Churchill, Winston 1, 5, 8, 39–42, 49, 81, 84, 88–91, 96, 103, 259–60, 262
Citrine, Walter 52, 81
Civil service 27, 93, 148

class
 capitalist class 4
 class conflict 5, 10–11, 12, 19–22, 23–6, 27–30, 31–4, 57, 103, 113, 129, 134, 135–7, 142, 149, 167
 middle class 119, 256
 ruling class 31–2, 40, 50, 57, 103, 107, 134, 136–7, 148, 149, 210, 226
 working class 4, 5, 12, 24–5, 33, 48, 57, 77, 136, 153, 181, 205, 208, 210, 211, 228, 256, 276
Cocks, Seymour 207–8
Cold War 9, 268, 279–81, 288
colonialism 33, 115, 118, 233–4, 261, 277–8, 286–8, 306–8
Common Wealth Party 86, 93–6, 99, 102
Commonwealth, the 294–7
Communism 9, 13, 82, 123, 174–5, 182–3, 184, 188–91, 192–5, 196–7, 209, 230, 233–5, 244, 252, 267, 277–8, 279–81, 284, 297, 304
 Communist International (Comintern) 96, 180–2
 Communist Manifesto 4
 Communist Party (Britain) 82, 86, 92–7, 99, 102, 108–9, 123
 Communist Party (Russia) 181–2
Conservative Party 1, 19–22, 23–6, 27, 37, 38, 39–42, 49–50, 61, 68–71, 72–4, 76, 81, 83–5, 86–91, 94–6, 103–4, 107–10, 111, 113–15, 117–18, 120–1, 123–5, 126, 128, 131, 134–6, 147–51, 154–5, 169, 170, 172, 186, 206–7, 214, 220–1, 229, 261–2, 272–4, 290–1, 298

Constitution 19, 27–8, 30, 43–5, 62–3, 136, 145–6, 159, 164, 243, 307
Conway, Walter 3
Cooper, Duff 259
Corbyn, Jeremy 1
cost of living 151, 170, 184
Cripps, Stafford 6, 22, 134, 150
Cyprus 234
Czechoslovakia 33, 132, 194–5, 207, 210, 257–8

D
Daladier, Édouard 142
Darlan, François 88, 227
Davies, S. O. 5
de Gaulle, Charles 220
democracy 1, 8, 9, 12, 13, 19–22, 31–4, 35–8, 45–7, 48–50, 57, 60, 82–5, 87, 94, 104–6, 108–10, 111, 120, 123, 139, 141–4, 147, 154–5, 158, 162, 164, 196–8, 207–8, 211, 213, 224, 257, 263, 287, 287–9, 296–7, 302–5, 306–9
Democratic Socialism *see* Socialism
Denmark 127, 138, 210, 257
direct action 5, 21, 77–8, 86, 94, 103, 113, 120, 170–1, 206
Djilas, Milovan 306
Dulles, John Foster 193–4, 233, 276

E
Eastern Europe 141, 159, 180
Economic planning 37–8, 43–7, 66, 128, 143–4, 160, 162, 185–6, 196, 283, 297, 300–1
Eden, Anthony 113, 115, 125, 137, 169, 171–2, 223, 229, 264–5
education 3–4, 8, 46, 146, 159, 177, 191, 227

Egypt 243, 272–3, 282–5, 286, 288–9, 290–3, 306
Eisenhower, Dwight 227, 229, 245, 247
empire 7, 9, 13, 33, 41, 207, 223, 260–1, 272–4
England 24–5, 76, 131, 134, 142, 145–6, 222
equality 50, 129, 153–5, 157, 166, 294
European Defence Community (EDC) 230
European Economic Community (EEC) 298–301

F
Fabian Society 95, 98
fascism 7, 10–11, 13, 20, 27, 33, 37, 38, 40, 43, 48, 55–7, 60, 81, 84–5, 94, 108, 135–7, 138–40, 202, 209–10, 221, 226, 230, 256, 258
Federation of British Industries (FBI) 54, 104
France 33, 47, 49, 126, 133–4, 138, 140–2, 180–1, 192, 201–2, 207, 209–10, 221, 225, 227, 237, 239, 257, 265, 267, 272, 276–7, 286
Franco, General Francisco 133–4, 204–5, 206–8
freedom 43, 48–9, 138–40, 149–50, 163, 167, 189, 197, 207–8, 210, 219–20, 224–6, 237, 257–8
Freemantle, Sir Francis 25

G
Gaitskell, Hugh 8, 9, 125
Gandhi, Mahatma 308
Garro-Jones, George 90
General Strike (1926) 5, 21
Geneva 175, 276–7, 279

Germany 33, 38, 50, 57, 85, 94, 115, 136, 138, 141–2, 158, 171, 181, 193, 205, 210–11, 218–22, 223, 225–6, 229–32, 255, 257–8, 268–9, 275
   German Labour Front 94
   reunification 171, 229–32, 237
   Social Democrats 231
   West German rearmament 115, 175, 270, 276
Ghana 294, 307
Giraud, Henri 220
Gramsci, Antonio 11
Greece 256
Greenwood, Arthur 89, 150
Grenfell, David 133, 216
Guatemala 233, 244
Guyana (formerly British Guiana) 115, 233, 244

H
Halifax, Lord 40
Health 31, 33, 36, 43, 154
Hess, Rudolf 142
Hitler, Adolf 8, 38, 40, 138, 141–3, 159, 209–10, 218–19, 224, 230–1, 257–8, 266
Holland 138, 210, 257, 262
House of Commons 5–6, 10, 19, 23, 27–9, 35, 39–41, 46, 56, 62, 70, 73–4, 76, 82–5, 88, 123, 134, 135, 207, 214, 237, 241, 263
House of Lords 27–30, 46, 62–3
housing 8, 23–6, 31, 83, 154, 216, 220
Hungary 194

I
imperialism 14, 33, 164, 226, 245, 272–4, 279, 282, 286, 288, 291

Independent Labour Party (ILP) 95–6, 102
India 220, 229, 271, 273, 294–7, 302–5, 307–8
Indochina 276–7
industrial democracy 46, 53, 61, 158, 162
Industrial Revolution 64, 66, 139, 161–2, 295–7, 300
industry and industrialisation 21, 31, 37, 43–6, 50, 52–7, 60–1, 64–6, 69, 76–7, 88, 95, 98–100, 105, 110, 145, 154, 157–62, 165, 184–6, 195, 197, 215–16, 224, 251–3, 260–2, 274, 282–3, 287–8, 295–7, 298, 300, 302–5, 308
   agriculture 145, 149, 160, 174
   coal 4, 5–6, 21–2, 29, 52, 71, 88, 95, 105, 145–6, 153, 160–1, 186, 211, 215–16, 220, 221, 261, 284
   electricity 71, 153, 161, 186, 216
   gas 153
   shipbuilding 49, 54, 160
   steel and iron 49, 53, 60–1, 65, 71, 110, 125, 145–6, 153, 161, 186, 261, 284
   textiles 54, 161
   transport 44, 49, 53–4, 61, 71, 95, 110, 153–4, 161, 216, 221, 261
inflation 69, 77, 125, 155, 184–7, 253, 302–3
insurance 59, 105, 150, 176, 186
   National Insurance 154–5
international law 194, 290–3
internationalism 166, 180–3, 228, 229–32, 244, 247–50, 259–62, 268–71, 275–8, 282–5, 290, 297

INDEX

Iran 264, 281
Iraq 281, 306
Israel 283, 291–3
Italy 10, 38, 126, 133–4, 135, 181, 202, 205, 211, 218, 219–20, 226, 232, 256–7, 260, 267

J
Japan 151, 223
Johnson, Tom 24
Jones, Sidney 3
Jordan 243, 245
judiciary 46, 63, 196, 248
    courts 20, 25–6, 27, 62–3, 135
    international courts 290–1

K
Khama, Seretse 115
Khruschev, Nikita 173, 182–3, 188, 190, 192–3
Kimche, John 7
King Farouk 282–3
Korea 229
    Korean War 9, 237, 267, 276

L
Labour Party 1–4, 6–9, 12–14, 25–6, 31–4, 35, 39, 50, 59–61, 75–8, 82–5, 136, 163, 169–70, 202–3, 206, 224, 226–7, 231, 276, 290
    1945 General Election 9, 59
    1950 General Election 109, 157
    1951 General Election 59, 109
    1955 General Election 113–16, 117, 122, 169–72
    1959 General Election 126–7
    as a federation 94–5, 102
    Coalition Government 42, 79–81, 84, 86–91, 92–7, 99–100, 140, 147, 150–1, 214, 216, 222
    Conference 3, 6, 9, 81, 86–91, 92–7, 98, 107, 115, 119, 151, 229
    Co-operative Party 120, 126, 156
    Executive 86–7, 90, 93–4, 102, 120–1
    Foreign Policy 32–3, 60, 115, 118, 226–7
    ideology 109–10, 111–12, 113–16, 117–22, 123–5, 126–9, 154
    in government 27–8, 60–1, 74, 108, 114, 155–6, 161, 177, 230, 275–6, 284
    intra-party disputes 8, 9, 12–13, 86–91, 92–7, 102, 107–10, 111–12, 117–22, 123–5, 126–9
    Left coalition 92–7, 102
    local parties 79, 86, 92, 94–6, 98–101, 119–20
    Party-union link 12, 31, 52, 75–8, 79–81, 92–7, 98–102, 103–6, 117–22, 123, 126
Laski, Harold 6
Lassalle, Ferdinand 50
League of Nations 141
Liberal Party 5, 27, 31, 39–40, 42, 79, 84–5, 95–6, 102, 109, 117–18, 128, 214
liberal values 37, 129, 136, 143, 162, 168, 288
    liberty 8, 38, 49–50, 71, 84, 87, 136, 139–40, 143–4, 149, 158–9, 162, 189–90, 207–8, 219, 225, 257, 305, 306–9
Lloyd George, David 5–6, 42, 133
local government 22, 76, 184, 210
London 4, 25, 92, 221, 261, 297

London, Jack 265
London Passenger Transport Board 44, 54

M
Macleod, Iain 69
Macmillan, Harold 238
Malaya 271
Malenkov, Georgy 183
Mander, Geoffrey 132
Marshall, George C. 230
    Marshall Aid 267, 276
Marxism 3, 4, 70, 153–4, 196, 284
Mellor, W. 6
Metro-Vickers 133–4
Mexico 133
Middle East 181, 237, 243–6, 281
Miners' Federation of Great Britain (MFGB) 5
Molotov, Vyacheslav 173
Monmouthshire County Council 5
Morgan, Frederick E. 241–2
Morrison, Herbert 8, 82, 216
Mussolini, Benito 134, 138, 219, 256, 258

N
Naguib, Mohamed 282
Nasser, Gamal Abdel 282–5, 286, 288
National Council of Labour 33–4
National Government 6, 21, 32, 60, 206
National Health Service (NHS) 1, 2, 8, 13–14, 71, 110, 153–6, 176–9
    National Health Act (1946) 154
national independence 164, 257–8, 261, 264, 277, 285, 286–8, 294–6, 306–9
National Service 32, 115
national unity 60, 84, 91, 103, 263

nationalisation *see* public ownership
nationalism 139, 231–2, 243, 273–4, 282–5, 292, 306–9
Nazi Party 43, 50, 79, 84, 89, 142–3, 158, 209–11, 213–14, 217, 218–19, 222, 225–6, 231, 255, 258–60, 264, 275
Nehru, Jawaharlal 297, 304–5, 308
neoliberalism 14
New Zealand 48, 223, 294, 299
Nigeria 294
Noel-Baker, Philip 133
North Africa 88, 218, 221
North Atlantic Treaty Organization (NATO) 11, 193, 247, 249–50
Norway 127, 138, 210, 257
Nutting, Anthony 237

O
oil 64–5, 133, 243, 262, 282
Oman 243
Orwell, George 247

P
Pakistan 271, 306–7
Parliament 5–7, 10, 12, 14, 19–22, 23–6, 27–30, 31–4, 39–40, 43–7, 53–6, 62–3, 68, 72–4, 75, 77–8, 81, 82–5, 93–5, 101, 103–6, 107–8, 111, 113–14, 120, 123, 131, 135, 137, 145–6, 147–51, 164, 171, 202–3, 206–7, 210, 214, 227, 229, 232, 249, 299–301, 308
    parliamentary democracy 22, 84, 106, 111, 123
Pella, Giuseppe 232
pensions 31, 33, 88, 154, 185
Plebs' League 3, 4
Poland 231, 257
police 27, 34, 46, 248, 292

Poor Law 88
Popular Front 100
Portugal 233
poverty 12, 36, 220
　global poverty 9, 232, 243, 271, 281, 283–4, 300, 307
power politics 9, 11, 14, 173–5, 188–91, 192–5, 223–8, 229–32, 233–5, 240, 243–6, 247–8, 267, 272–3, 279–81
Press, the 23, 42, 46, 72–3, 82, 93, 103, 107, 109, 117, 120, 124–5, 131–2, 137, 148–9, 169, 210, 219, 227, 229, 238, 259
　Daily Express 209
　Daily Herald 90
　Daily Mail 241
　Daily Worker 82
　Evening Standard 256
　Financial Times 186
　News Chronicle 41
　The Daily Telegraph 70, 233–4
　The Economist 297
　The Guardian 233
　The Observer 124–5
　The Times 193, 209, 244
Price, Sir David 73
private enterprise 4, 19, 41, 44–5, 49–50, 52, 54–8, 61, 65–6, 68–70, 125, 128–9, 153, 160–1, 170, 185–6, 190–1, 196–9, 214, 216, 243, 261, 268, 286–7, 296, 303
property (public and private) 4, 9, 19–22, 23–6, 27, 29, 31–4, 35–8, 43–7, 56, 59–61, 65, 70, 85, 87, 105, 128, 135, 140, 149, 153, 155, 196, 214, 221, 261–2, 283–4, 286
public ownership 7, 9, 35–8, 43–7, 52–8, 59–61, 62–7, 70–1, 87–8, 110, 113, 125, 128–9, 153, 160–1, 190–1, 196–9, 215–16, 221, 230, 261

R

religion 142, 243, 306–7
revisionists 9, 61
Reynold's News 103
Roosevelt, Theodore 264
Royal Arsenal Co-operative Society 98
Russia *see* Soviet Union
Russian Revolution 163, 190, 206, 222, 256

S

Salter, Sir Arthur 19–22
Sandys, Duncan 28, 75, 137
Scandinavia 127
science 49, 64, 68–9, 165, 176, 188–91, 197, 233–5, 240–1, 252, 267, 288
Scotland 24–5, 145–6
Shinwell, Manny 151
Sinclair, Archibald 132
Smith, Dai 1
Socialism 1–2, 7–9, 12–13, 19–20, 27–30, 35–8, 43–7, 48–50, 52–3, 60–1, 62–3, 64–7, 70, 87–91, 92–7, 101–2, 109–12, 117–22, 124, 127, 139–40, 151, 153–6, 157–62, 163–4, 167–8, 176, 180–3, 187, 196, 198–9, 209–10, 221, 231, 256, 275, 284, 286, 297, 299–301
Socialist International 180–3
South Africa 233, 294
South Wales Miners' Federation 3
Southeast Asia Treaty Organization (SEATO) 115
sovereignty 11, 87, 161, 248–50, 261, 264, 269, 284, 287, 291, 299–300

Soviet Union 13, 33, 123, 133–4, 141–4, 158–9, 171–2, 173–5, 180, 182, 188–91, 192–5, 196–7, 218, 223–6, 229–32, 233–5, 236–9, 240, 242, 244–6, 247, 251–2, 256, 260, 264–6, 268–70, 273, 277, 279–81, 284, 295–7, 304
space race 188–91, 196–9
Spain 159, 233, 249, 272, 307
    Spanish Civil War 7, 10–11, 33, 100, 131–4, 136–7, 201–5, 206–8, 209
Sri Lanka (formerly Ceylon) 294, 306–7
Stalin, Joseph 142, 173, 181, 192, 209
Stassen, Harold 236–8
State, the 12, 14, 21, 24, 27–30, 38, 43–7, 54, 56–8, 61, 66, 85, 133, 136, 143, 145, 149, 191, 211, 215–16, 248, 283, 295, 297, 307
    Corporative State 56, 58, 104
Strachey, John 6
The Coming Struggle for Power (1932) 6
Strauss, George 6
Sudan 306
Suez Canal 73–4, 272, 282–4, 286, 289, 292–3, 294
Supreme Economic Council 46–7
Sweden 127
Syria 243–4, 306

T
taxation 28, 113, 115
Taylor, A. J. P. 194
Tito, Josip Broz 306
totalitarianism 30, 38, 43, 45, 158, 194
trade 59–60, 69, 77, 253–4, 268, 284, 298–300, 302–4

Trade Disputes Act 93, 99, 103–4
Trade Unions 4, 12, 31, 46, 52–8, 75–8, 79–81, 92–7, 98–102, 103–6, 119–21, 123, 126, 153, 156, 170, 206, 210, 222, 228
Trades Union Congress (TUC) 52–8, 77–8, 93–4, 103–6, 110
Transport and General Workers Union (TGWU) 104
Tredegar 1–5
    Tredegar Urban District Council 5
Tribune 2–3, 8–11, 25, 39, 43, 82, 84, 102, 103–4, 117, 121, 209, 259
    founding 6–7, 13
Trinidad 133

U
unemployment 4–5, 7, 31, 36, 66, 69, 75–8, 114, 139, 160, 225, 251, 253–4, 302–3
Union Jack 103, 134, 135–6
United Front 100
United Nations (UN) 9, 115, 193, 235, 237, 245, 277, 286–9, 290–3
United States of America (USA) 48, 57, 66, 69, 109, 115, 132, 141–4, 154, 171–3, 176–7, 188, 198, 221, 223–8, 229, 230–1, 236–9, 240, 243–5, 247, 249, 251–4, 257, 265, 267–8, 270–1, 273, 275–8, 286, 289, 297, 299–300, 302, 304–5
    American Civil War 36

V
Vansittart, Sir Robert 257

W
Wales 3–4, 22, 25, 76, 145–6
Wallace, Henry 228

war 13, 31–4, 40, 79–81, 85, 88–91, 94, 165, 231–2, 237, 242, 244, 267–71, 277–8, 300
 and democracy 207–8, 211, 213, 224, 257
 First World War 42, 80, 163, 262
 post-war 43–7, 50–1, 52–8, 86–91, 97, 147–52, 211, 218–22, 223–8, 257, 261
 Second World War 7, 35–8, 39–42, 43, 48–51, 79–81, 85, 88–91, 94, 98, 138–40, 141–4, 147–52, 170, 209–12, 213–17, 231–2, 255–8, 259–62, 263–6
Wartime Coalition 42, 79–81, 84, 86–91, 93–4, 99–100, 103, 150–1, 222
 Electoral Truce 86, 89–91, 93, 99
welfare 28, 55, 57, 160, 212, 257, 309
Wells, H. G. 158
Western Europe 129, 198, 243
Westminster 10, 107
Wilkinson, Ellen 6
Williams, Tom 202–3
Wilson, Harold 271
Wood, Sir Kingsley 25, 40
Workmen's Compensation Act 88, 103–6
world development 9, 267–71, 286–9, 294–7, 302–5
 and democracy 287–9, 296–7, 302–5, 306–9
 World Mutual Aid 267–8

Y

Yemen 243
Yugoslavia 232, 260